This book describes personal experiences and information gleaned from others. Some names and identifying details of individuals mentioned in the book have been changed to protect their privacy.

Clearer representations of the photos in this book can be seen on Frank Spragg's web page www.frankspragg.com

Two Moments of Glory
© 2015 Frank Spragg

Printed in the United States of America

Cover Design:

Luminare Press
467 W 17th Ave
Eugene, OR 97401
www.luminarepress.com

LCCN: 2015931340

ISBN: 978-1-937303-45-7

Thanks Anita

TWO MOMENTS OF GLORY

FRANK SPRAGG

LUMINARE PRESS
EUGENE, OREGON

Contents

Forward vii

Preface 1

Two to Get Ready 5

A Little Town on the Hi-Line 25

Closed by Any Other Name 46

In and Out of Prison 62

The Beginning of the Rise 84

Up in Smoke, Up from the Ashes 95

The Catholic Arm of Bozeman 124

The Kid from Chicago 143

Enter McCloskey 163

Down to the End – Part 1 175

The Father, the Coach, and the Player 215

The Savior from the East 232

Archrival 253

Archrival – Reprise 283

Adversaries at the Helm 301

Down to the End – Part 2 317

Aftermath 349

Notes 363

Acknowledgements 366

Forward

The mission of the MHSA is to assure that the membership is provided with leadership and support in advancing equitable MHSA interscholastic activities for the growth and educational experience for students.

—The Montana High School Association (MHSA)
Mission Statement

WE ALL KNOW THE INCENTIVES AND THE POSITIVE OPPORTUNITIES that high school activities present. For most sports team participants, the high school experience was the beginning and the end of any athletic endeavor, but we often hear during interviews with accomplished athletes, successful businessmen and hopeful politicians that their team participation in high school not only molded their character and contributed to future achievements, but that their high school years were the best times of their lives. Those times are still the most pure of our country's obsession with athletics.

With that in mind I can tell you how interested I was in Frank Spragg's undertaking. The results of his exhaustive research got me hooked from the first "sit down." I finished the manuscript in the second "sit down." I thoroughly enjoyed the reading experience.

When picking up a book about a specific local team and tournament, one might think only those communities' residents would be interested in following the tale. Not so. Stories that occurred in Montana's smaller communities during sports' seasons are some of my favorites, because we can all relate to them, whether we viewed them personally or heard about them. Spragg's interviews with athletes, coaches and other involved in the game lend credence to the claim that the high school athletics are important in our lives. As the former athletes recall their experience, the reader recognizes that high school occupies a special memory in their lives. Through these interviews, Spragg tells how not just the athletes, but their communities orbited around the basketball season and how the MHSA tournaments were the culmination of this obsession.

These local stories are mirrored every year in some small town in this huge state with a sparse population. Basketball becomes the town and the town becomes basketball each year, somewhere. Montana has about 100 "small" schools, "C" in the list of MHSA's classifications. Some have never been to a state tournament, let alone won one. But regardless, the game is the social highlight of the week, the social event which defines what the those schools are about. There are Class C games, where all attendees are invited to eat together at the host school before the trek home. Frank Spragg's book illustrates why we should never forget how clean, how innocent, how good and how important the high school years and the associated sports activities are for young people.

I knew and know many of the people in this book. Many of you will too. That magnifies the fun in reading to the end. But a lot more behind-the-scenes information adds to this story. I love Montana high school sports' trivia. Now I know a lot more...

Jim Haugen
Former Executive Director
MHSA

For my wife Judith

who is always there for me.

Preface

IT HAD BEGUN WITH MY MEMOIRS, A QUIET MANUSCRIPT TO BE shared among family and friends. Particulary quiet when it came to basketball, because frankly, in my youth I wasn't much of a player. But I loved to watch, had to watch. During the winters in our town, basketball was the only consistent form of entertainment. And our school, Belgrade High, kept winning games and tournaments, not for one season, not for two seasons, but for the entire time I was growing up. I had to watch.

In 1956, when Belgrade may have been at its very best, it faced a formidable opponent, Wibaux, in the semi-final of the Montana State Class C tournament. The two teams were the best in the tournament, the semi-final the de facto championship. The ensuing battle became a legend, the star for Wibaux magnificent, a young man who would become central to a continuing story. Because in 1961 that same young man, Jim Owens returned to coach Holy Rosary High School against Belgrade, for another State Class C championship. This player-turned-coach himself developed into a legend. At least for me he did.

I finished my memoirs, tucked them away, but continued to wonder—whatever happened to Jim Owens? I made a few phone calls, which led me to Rosary player Joe Cahill, who shed a great deal of light on Owens, and promised to send me an article from the *Bozeman Daily Chronicle*.

When I received the article, I soon learned it was not about the 1961 Rosary team at all, but the 1960 Rosary team, which also participated in the state championship under a different coach, Neal Christensen, and a largely different player lineup. Nearly all of the writing focused on Rosary, but deep into the article was a short blurb about the other team in that championship—the Gildford Broncs from northern Montana. The Broncs won the title that year despite having their gym burn down. I stared at the print, wondered if a book had been written on the subject, figured it probably had, and placed the article aside for the moment.

But *had* a book been written? I made more phone calls, was directed this time to Don Miller, one of the Gildford players, who told me not only did the gym burn down but for a time Gildford was without accreditation, brought on by an adversary named Mary Condon. And no, a book had never been written. I was hooked. On the birthday of my granddaughter, Courtney Spragg, I determined that I would write this book. But I couldn't forget Belgrade and Jim Owens. I then made the decision to have the book cover both the 1960 *and* the 1961 State Class C tournaments with all that led to both of them.

The book has much more than teams and tournaments—it has towns, cultures, gyms, rules, politics—and more than anything— personalities. But without tournaments there would not be this book. So it is with tournaments that I will begin.

Frank Spragg

PART ONE

Two to Get Ready

MARCH, IN MY 1950S REMEMBRANCE, WAS A DEAD MONTH IN Montana. It was neither winter nor spring, a buffer month revealing nature's tapestry the folks at the State Office of Tourism did not want you to see. The landscape was sepia-tan, with leafless trees, dormant grass, dormant everything. And all encased in relentless mud, frozen at dawn, softened and ready to suck you under by mid-morning. The mud made dirt roads hopeless, fields bottomless. Farmers dare not work the ground or, if they could (which I once did), then something in the climate was dangerously off-kilter. Drought, we feared, would rule for the next three precious growing months. Not all was dreary: when the sun was out, the mountains—if you were lucky enough to live near them—still glistened with snow, a stark contrast to the dun on the valley floor. And snow could come to the floor also, sometimes profusely, but usually wet and often mixed with rain. More likely the snow on the ground had fallen some time ago, was receding, rained-on, trodden and dirty. If residents were truly fortunate, the crocus might be out by late March, those tiny flashes of white, purple, or yellow, but they were lonely forerunners of spring in a giant sea of drab. Given this scene, people had to love each other even more because there wasn't much outside to love. Folks kibitzed in stores, discoursed at pot lucks, dances, or committee meetings, and above all watched young men compete. Because this was the time for tournament basketball and in small town Montana if your team was winning then March was no longer ugly but quintessential beauty, the loveliest time of the year.

No other month could bring such rush, such euphoria, such despair as March could, all leading to the seminal moment of the season: the state championship. If my team, Belgrade High, wasn't involved, then watching the title game was merely great entertainment. But if the Panthers were out there, then seeing the boys warm up, hearing the bands playing, the din of the crowd, was not unlike being free on bail; I could still walk the streets and experience the pleasures of life, but that old trial was coming and I just couldn't enjoy myself. Because soon the buzzer would sound, the warm-ups would end, the players would confer with their coaches, after which they would gather around the center circle for the opening tipoff, and then the worst part of all: the playing of the national anthem. "The Star-Spangled Banner" was actually much better in those days, sung or played with dignity, the notes coming in straight tones as lyricist Francis Scott Key and tunesmith John Stafford had intended. But the playing of the anthem was also a stay of execution. The death sentence was upon us and now we had to stand silently for two eternal minutes before the sword would fall. I half hoped this messy case would be thrown out of court or *me* out of court so I could take the more sheltered approach of reading the results in the newspapers.

When I was very young, Belgrade was in a nail-biter against Helena Cathedral for the District 8 championship. As the contest drew to a close, I couldn't stand the tension anymore. I fled to the concession area where I paced back and forth until the drone of the final buzzer. As I returned to the playing area, I saw the Belgrade team members sitting in a circle on the floor silent and destroyed. For a child it had to be the most traumatic scene in the history of sports. I didn't understand in my tender years that my voice, along with the rest of the spectators', was not entirely helpless, that together we could give birth to momentum, could change the psychology of a game, and that, regardless of the outcome, when my parents tapped on my bedroom door the next morning, I still had the strength to get out of bed.

I had watched Belgrade against other small schools in those years, but after I completed the fourth grade, my world would change: my older sister, Sheila, elected to attend high school not in Belgrade but in nearby Bozeman. Gallatin County High School in Bozeman was not a small school, was instead a member of Class A, in short time to be included among ten high schools in Montana to form Class AA. Now our family watched games in Class C *and* Class AA, the micro and the macro if you will, including the wildly ranging experiences of post-season tournaments. Because anyone familiar with the scene at the time will tell you that big-school and small-school tournaments could not have been more different.

Class AA represented the largest schools; some enrollments exceeded 2,000 students. With this mass of humanity to draw from, these schools in theory provided the tallest and most talented players competing against each other. In reality there were weak sisters among the AA ranks, but for the best Class C school to beat the best in Class AA was like winning the national lottery. It would take a gnat-brain to bet against AA.

That said, if there were ten schools in Class AA there were *only* ten schools and eight got into the state tournament, so getting there was just a sniff of a challenge; for the better teams, no challenge at all. These teams didn't have to suffer through the one and only playoff game. And basketball was hardly the only activity in school during those long winter months. Students had skiing, wrestling, choir, orchestra, band, theatre, forensics, science projects, academic and vocational pursuits, service clubs, DeMolay and Job's Daughters and the parade goes on. Basketball became one more notation on the agenda, and if the team wasn't very good, far down the list. Many students from a Class AA school had casual attitudes about going to the state tournament. Oh sure, the arena was packed, the volume intense, but if your team didn't make it to the finals, well, there was always next year. And for many, when the tournament was over, thoughts of basketball were left immediately behind.

Particularly if their team wasn't very good, students just might go to the tournament with motives other than watching basketball. They could arrive in packs unsupervised and, once settled, decide not go to any games at all. They might stay in the motel and get drunk, do something "creative" like letting all the cattle out of the city stockyards, or get into a fight. Not with Butte kids, of course. Hoo boy! You didn't mess with the kids from Butte, those Irish/Balkan miners' kids. All a boy had to do was *say* he was from Butte and he was given wide berth.

I once went to a Class AA tournament in Butte with my parents, staying at the old Hotel Acoma, which should be given the purple ribbon for giving me the single worst night I would ever spend in a public accommodation. Everything in the room—the bad plumbing, the peeling, rusty linoleum, the general filth—needed a little TLB (tender loving bulldozing), but it wasn't just the state of the room that caused anguish for me that evening. Kids were running up and down the halls, jumping up and jamming their arms through the transom over our door. I was terrified; I thought it was the Butte boys come to punch us into fruit leather. Of course these froth-heads were from out of town; the Butte boys were home being safely tucked into bed by their mild-mannered, delicately featured fathers. Ha! And it wasn't just the kids. One summer day I was with my cousins in uptown Butte where giant blackened headframes[1] could be seen in the middle of an intersection, where you could pick up prize copper or manganese ore fallen from trucks, and we were going door to door selling stuff kids usually sell and we reach this porch where this old hag comes out raging telling us to scram NOW! Butte was a different place. And I'm off course.

Class C tournaments were, by contrast, happily, almost breathtakingly innocent. Class C had 122 schools throughout fifteen districts, each school with approximately 150 students or less—often much less—and of those 122 teams, a mere 32 made it through their districts to four divisional tournaments. Just getting to that level was

Frank Spragg

enough for bragging rights, and I want to say something here: the state tournament might have been a gaga experience for teams that could make it that far, but for the fan, the divisional tournaments were more fun—at least they were for a hanger-on like me. These tournaments were always held in a relatively small town far enough away from many schools that it was necessary to stay over in one of the few motels available. And so everyone was close together, and it became in essence an extended family reunion. We would pile into cars for our destination in the morning, head over the landscape in a caravan, stopping and descending like SWAT teams on a lonely café for lunch. Our landing place during the 1950s had always been Red Lodge, a scenic little village at the foot of the Beartooth Mountains. Red Lodge is a trendy draw these days, but in 1960, it was in transition, still a town much like the others in Montana. If it was no longer dependent on coal mining, as it had once been, neither was it yet a full-blown tourist town. The folks in Red Lodge looked forward to the tournament and put out the welcome mat. A luncheon at the gym, for example, was provided for the cheerleaders of all the schools; girls far and wide got to know each other.

Upon arriving in Red Lodge, my parents and one other family always stayed in rooms over a mortuary, which, with their hissing radiators, were delightfully old-fashioned. I say "delightfully" because Lucy made sure each room was white-glove, lick-off-the-floor clean. As nice as these rooms were, we were only there for sleep. The rest of the time we were out and about, attending all the games. At one of these I saw a young man in the crowd standing out like a beacon in his Navy uniform. That next summer, I would by chance be in the same elevator with him—still dressed in his Navy uniform—as we headed to the top of the Empire State Building in New York City.

If we weren't at the games, we gravitated south to the Bunkhouse Motel, which most of the Belgrade fans called home. Or everyone—and I mean *everyone* at the tournament—would flock to Natali's for dinner or after-game fun. There was no place in Montana more celebratory than Natali's after the 1955 championship when Belgrade defeated Lodge Grass on a last-second shot from mid-court.

Being where it was, Red Lodge had a climate of its own, so on any given year there could be a snowstorm of Biblical magnitude isolating everything, adding to the communal womb environment. During these storms, no one could go anywhere, certainly not leave town. Kids were holed up in their motel rooms; just going next door took planning. Members from different teams, if they were staying in the same motel, might get together and play poker. It was said that the streetwise Colstrip boys cleaned out their new friends from Holy Rosary who, with their sheltered upbringing, had little experience with cards. The snow was so confining that girls could be found in their rooms playing—*checkers!* High school girls playing checkers. You had to know they had few options.

The state tournament was usually held in one of Montana's cities, but not always. For three years in the early 1950s, it was in Conrad, sixty miles north of Great Falls. There simply wasn't enough motel room space in this town of 2,000 people for everyone who wanted to sleep there. Many, out of necessity, stayed in homes or were forced to lodge in Great Falls and make the long daily pilgrimage.

If the divisional tournament was a gas, the state tournament was the only conclusion that really mattered. A mere eight teams participated in the tournament; through the years, teams from some small towns would never ever have the chance to be there. If a town participated for the first time, for players and fans alike it was a sur-real *Alice in Wonderland* experience. You arrived wide-eyed, green as grass, just excited to be in town. You hoped your little team could win a game or two.

But maybe your little team would win more than a game or two and actually take the championship. WHOA! Now you are talking about a whole new brand of ecstasy…no, no, ecstasy would not be the right word to describe this buzzer moment. Shock would be a better word. In shock because your team from your little school, maybe one-fifth the size of the other schools at the tournament, had run the tables and taken it all. And then immediately, the euphoria sets in and you and your fellow fans will have the party that never wants to end. The next day there will be the caravan home, speeches, interviews with the press, more parties, banquets through the week, school classes blurred with vacation spirit, and then the most poignant part: the beginning of memories. The memories will be important over the years because your little school may not go to the state tournament again for a very long time, in fact much longer than a very long time because *your* little school may *never* go again—closed down or merged out of existence. It will be a death as wrenching as if a loved one had died. Granted it was a very slow decline, and you were expecting it to happen, but you suffer all the same.

AND SO IT WAS ON MARCH 18, 1960, TWO TEAMS WERE, ONCE AGAIN, closing in on each other for the Class C championship in Helena. Helena is the capital city of Montana, steeped in tumultuous history. It had begun as a mining camp in a ravine known as Last Chance Gulch, named so because the four men who were there had produced little of worth in every other mining venture they attempted; digging in the Gulch was supposedly their last hope. After the boom and bust, the camp should have died like many others in Montana Territory, but there were men in Helena of exceptional persistence and ability who kept the town going through flood and fire, through the financial panic of 1873, who would win two epic battles to make Helena first the capital of the territory and the capital again twenty-five years later when Montana achieved statehood. Helena became at one time the largest city in the state spreading away from the Gulch to the large valley north and east known as Helena Valley.

Helena had been home to the wealthy and powerful who had let their light shine in business and politics; the capital has more old mansions than any other city in Montana. One entrepreneur turned philanthropist was behind building St. Helena Catholic Cathedral, which stands today as one of the most imposing centers of worship in the Mountain West. Uptown in Last Chance Gulch were fine brick or stone buildings housing the businesses of old Helena. Today Helena is attractive, restored mansions on tree-lined streets, the upper Gulch made into a pedestrian mall. But many of the old buildings in the Gulch are missing, demolished by the "enlightened" fathers of the 1970s carrying out their design for urban renewal.

In 1960 there was no pedestrian mall and nearly all of the old buildings were still there, which should have made the Gulch more charming. But it wasn't. Many of the buildings were in disrepair; one can understand (if not agree) why the city leaders in the '70s wanted to tear them down. Most of Helena—the newer Helena out in the valley—was like any other town, generally very safe. When Belgrade was at the tournament in 1957, we went to the games, the restaurants, the bowling alley nearby, and thought nothing of it. But I understood, if my classmates did not, that I was not to walk up Last Chance Gulch.

My parents must have said something, I don't know when or where. I knew at the far end of the Gulch was the red light district, but even if I shunned such temptations, the Gulch in my understanding, was a dangerous place. There were shadowy folks up there, lowlifes who might permanently halt my return. I was happy to stay at the bowling alley. Or go to the games.

FOR THE GILDFORD BRONCS IN 1960, THERE WAS NO TIME TO CON-sider Last Chance Gulch. The Broncs from northern Montana were back in Helena for the championship after a disappointment the year before. In 1959 they were in the semi-finals, lost in a fluke and settled for third place. On this afternoon before the big game, team members were holed up at Jorgenson's Motel on 11th Avenue, a marked improvement over the motel they stayed in the previous year. They were doing nothing memorable—going from room to room chatting, patiently waiting for dinner to come after which they would head over to the Helena High School gym, watch perhaps the first half of the consolation game, then troop to the locker-room and dress for their own match to follow.

On that 1959 trip, because Gildford had never before been to the state tournament, the local administration came up with the well-intentioned idea that in order to make up for missed days at school, the team and other students would take a tour of Helena; they would see the capitol building, shake hands with Governor Hugo Aronson, go through the Charlie Russell Museum, look at the $50,000 gold display at the Union Bank, visit some industries, and tour the "controversial" brand new governor's mansion—controversial because six years before, the legislature had appropriated $125,000 for building the mansion and although it was exquisitely built and decorated, it was ten times the size of the average home and ended up costing $300,000, bringing howls from Republicans and Democrats alike. For three days during that tournament, when there were no games, the kids pounded the pavement; some said the wearing out of the feet cost them the championship. Whether the walking had anything to do with the outcome, no one could prove, but in 1960, the team was not about to take any tour.

And now it was time for dinner. The team members quietly walked to the adjoining Jorgenson's restaurant, settled in, and were ready to order. These pre-game dinners could be the stuff of lore. Just two weeks before, in Lewistown, prior to the Northern Division championship, the Gildford boys were eating dinner with only a curtain separating them from their Chester High School opponents. Chester was in the same District 11 as Gildford, the kids from both schools all knew each other, and tensions were understandably high. The Gildford boys were feasting on prime rib when suddenly a Chester mother burst through the curtain to make the rounds, giving each player from Gildford the chance to hear her special brand of denigration. Perhaps any of the players or Coach Tom McCloskey could have shut her up, but it was left to freshman Wes Whitaker to provide the perfect squelch. As team manager, Wes was on the low end of the pecking order, was given the least desirable piece of meat consisting largely of gristle. As the mother stood before him giving her spiel, he stabbed a piece of gristle with his fork, held it up to her nose, and said, "Here, lady, chew on *this* for a while!!" To a chorus of laughter, the mother retreated back to behind the curtain.

In short time the game would begin, and though the high school gym was arguably within walking distance, Coach McCloskey chose to transport the team by car. Helena High was the oldest high school in Montana, having opened in 1876, but the team was hardly traveling to the original high school. By 1960 the school was housed under its fourth roof, the current complex, including the gym, having been built in 1954. (The third school building was severely damaged by an earthquake in 1935; for a year the students had to meet in a cluster of passenger train cars until the building could be restored.)

The people in Helena were proud of their new school, not least the gym, which had a capacity for over 3,200 fans. With this facility, the school bid for and hosted the Divisional AA tournament in 1956. That tournament was such a success, giving a spike to the local economy, that when the state Class C tournament came up for bid the next year, it only made sense for the locals to place their Helena hat into the ring.

When a city bid for a tournament, several factors were considered before the bid could be granted. These included not only how high the bid, but also the city's geographical location, and how well the town could handle the crowds. Was the parking area large enough? Were there enough restaurants? Accommodations for people to stay? And most important of all, was the gym large enough to seat all the fans? Nothing was worse than a tournament where everyone who very much wanted to see a game could not get in. In 1979, Peerless played Flaxville for the championship, a particularly dramatic game for both because the two teams were from the same District 1C, in extreme northeastern Montana. At 6:30 p.m., just prior to the game, the director of the Montana High School Association, Jim Haugen, received notification that a man outside the gym was furious: he had driven 500 miles from Flaxville to see his team and now he couldn't get in because the game was sold out.

But Helena was in a good position to keep the tournament in 1960. It had the facilities and was relatively central to the entire state. Also, to make sure the gym was full, local merchants would buy up blocks of tickets and resell them. In 1957 the board of the MHSA had considered bids by the cities of Whitefish, Helena, and Red Lodge. Whitefish and Red Lodge were considerably smaller than Helena and less central geographically. Helena was awarded the Class C tournament and continued to host for twenty-two more years. Eventually, because of growing popularity, the venue was moved to the larger gym at nearby Carroll College, but in 1960 it was still at Helena High.

By 1960, it seemed as if Class C had been around forever, when in fact it had been introduced to Montana only ten years before. Before 1950 there were Class A and Class B; before 1934 there was only one class, and before 1911 there was no organized structure for high school basketball at all, certainly none for post-season tournaments. No irrefutable record exists as to who participated in the first high school boys' basketball game, or when it was held, but a good bet would be to cast eyes toward Billings. Girls' basketball had already been established there in 1903; in my sister's home is a photo of the 1905 Billings girls' high school basketball team, winner of the state title that year. The girls' program drew big crowds, but basketball was an inside sport, considered "sissy" by many Montana males who watched it, which is odd when you consider basketball was invented in 1891 to keep a group of young college *men* in Massachusetts occupied during the winter season. By 1905, the sport was sweeping the nation.

In the fall of that year, two brothers from Chicago, Dick and Tom Logan, swept into Billings with a "brand new idea" for the area. They had played YMCA ball in Chicago, had spent time previously in Billings, were coming to stay and thought basketball would be a great sport for Montana. They organized a Montana National Guard team which commenced its inaugural season on February 5, 1906 in the old Clark building, defeating Red Lodge 25-16. After that, the guardsmen vanquished four other teams including a win over the "celebrated, unbeaten champions" from Glendive—a curious assessment, when research indicates the Glendive team was also in its first season. The Billings men concluded with a win over Sheridan, Wyoming, thereby declaring themselves the champions of both Montana *and* Wyoming. This notoriety could not escape the notice of Billings High School, which in the following year organized a team of its own. Alas, the boys played but one game that season against Sheridan High losing by the baseball-like score of 6-1. It is not known if Sheridan then claimed to be the champion of anything.

By 1911, many high schools in Montana had some kind of boys' basketball program but if any team claimed to be champions it was not by the vehicle of any tournament. Then, one afternoon in early January 1911, James H. Hamilton, president of Montana Agricultural College (now Montana State University) in Bozeman, was sitting in the Old Drill Hall having an informal chat with John McIntosh, coach of all sports at the college, experienced news writer, and sports fan.

According to the story, Hamilton asked, "Why couldn't we bring six or eight of those high school basketball teams together to settle their basketball championship claims in a sort of elimination series?"

"That would be a natural," replied McIntosh. "Why haven't we thought of that before?"

That was the definitive question: why had no one thought of that before? When McIntosh brought up the idea to members of his basketball team, the response was "almost explosive." It was as if the idea for a high school tournament was hanging in plain sight, screaming for someone like Hamilton to put it into words. In addition, the idea was completely original with Hamilton—at least in Montana. There were tournaments for tennis and other sports involving individuals, but no one had heard of tournaments for teams. They agreed a tournament would be beneficial for "(1) inter-school relations, (2) broadening the college's public relations, and (3) would be welcomed by the people of Montana." It was a win-win deal; the only things left to discuss were the details.

Like "wildfire," President Hamilton's suggestion spread to the student body, the faculty, and through downtown ranks of athletic fans and supporters of college activities. It was welcomed and supported by the press of the state. Everywhere there was "prompt approval." Faculty and student committees were set up, and downtown organizations offered support. Invitations were sent out to all the high schools. Initially any school, which accepted the invitation was invited to the tournament.

Then the reality of logistics. Could all these teams afford to travel to Bozeman? If they could, where would they stay? How would they be fed? The goal then became to invite eight teams, upped to twelve, and finally sixteen. Eight teams immediately accepted the invitation, four more a few days later and finally three more after that bringing the total to fifteen.

Everyone seemed uncomfortable with the odd number. The plan was for single elimination; which teams would get the byes? Would they draw lots? Was it fair that some teams had to play more games than others? The problem was mostly solved when Big Timber (officially Sweetgrass County High School) finally accepted the invitation and became the sixteenth school in the tournament.

Bozeman was not ready to house 150 or more players and coaches in public accommodations. The challenge was so complex that the person handpicked to shoulder the responsibility was Professor W. D. Tallman of the mathematics department. The challenge required not only math but diplomacy. For example, how do you give all teams the same quality of housing? This problem was not solved to everyone's satisfaction at this inaugural tournament. Also, some hosts and innkeepers were displeased that "silverware, glassware, numbers on room doors and other items came up missing, that street signs suddenly appeared in lobbies and that these youthful guests had a habit of staying up all hours of the night."

Then a college professor, William F. Brewer felt that "the intellectual side" of this momentous event should not be "ignored" (as if basketball strategy required nothing more than physical prowess). He proposed that an extemporaneous speaking contest be held in conjunction with athletic events. All sixteen schools agreed to send a speaker.

The expense of the first tournament was supplied by a variety of benefactors: merchants, individuals, and the institutions of Bozeman. But there were other concerns: a suitable hardwood floor was installed, but the Drill Hall was meant for military drill, not a gymnasium. It had a capacity for 500 spectators, but organizers were wondering if enough people would show up. Also, the seats themselves were ridiculous. Some said rather than paying for the seats, fans should be paid to sit on them, they were so uncomfortable.

But the organizers needn't have worried.

The details were worked out. The big day, March 2, finally came. The teams and coaches all arrived by train. Shortly after noon, a parade began downtown on icy streets and ended in front of the Drill Hall. All seats were taken in the Hall by the time the parade disbanded. When the games began, the hall was filled to overflowing, the walls were "bulging" and not a few disappointed fans were still left outside. Because of unseasonably warm weather, the committee heads predicted that attendance at subsequent games would be smaller. They were wrong. Appetites were whetted for the next rounds, and the tournament craze was born. It was only fitting that the first winner would be Billings, the town where high school basketball in Montana had originated.

That first tournament was considered the "biggest publicity feature and drawing card ever attempted in Montana." It had such success in securing the good will of the high schools that, when the time drew near for the second tournament in 1912, the college committee in Bozeman determined that "no pain would be spared in making the second tournament eclipse the first tournament in every respect". All 32 accredited high schools were invited although it was assumed some of the smaller schools could not afford to come. In that second tourney, 25 teams participated with 22 games played. In the third tournament 26 teams appeared and in 1914 the number rose to 32.

It was becoming glaringly apparent that neither the college nor Bozeman was in a position to host a tournament for 32 teams. Not only were there too many teams and too many games: half of the games were one-sided because some of the teams had never practiced. The city could not house that many visitors and only a small percentage of people who wanted to see a game could get inside the Drill Hall. Another system had to be developed. In 1915 it was decreed that Montana would have eight districts, with names distinctive to the area of the state where the district was located. There was the Mining District, the Yellowstone District, the Flathead District, and so forth. Each district would have its own tournament, with the first and second-place teams of each district advancing to the state tournament in Bozeman. The extemporaneous speaking contest continued to be held.

In 1915, the state tournament was back to a more-manageable 16 teams although the Drill Hall was still too small for all the adoring fans. This system stood for another few years, but there were problems other than the size of the hall. In 1918 scarlet fever broke out, forcing the college to transfer the tournament to Livingston. In 1919, because of influenza, there was no tournament at all. That year, Gallatin County High School (in Bozeman) was declared the winner apparently because it showed "the best quality of play." There was one other change: the speaking contest was replaced by an essay contest. No doubt speakers could not get out of their sickbeds and take the train to Bozeman.

There was one more difficulty: some districts were stronger than others. Some teams, which made it to the tournament were dead on arrival. Others, which were worthy of being at the tournament and might even have won, were no-shows because they ended in third place in their district. So the college went back to the invitation system, really a hybrid affair in which all district winners won the right to be in Bozeman but some districts were allowed one representative, others three. This system would stay in place for as long as Montana State administered the tournament.

In 1923, Montana State finished building its new gym and named it Romney Gym after Ott Romney, director of physical education at the college. Now nearly everyone who wanted to see a game could get inside. This was huge for the advancement of the sport in Montana. As the years went by, popularity for the Big Event continued to grow: each year the newspapers predicted the number of visitors to be the best ever. By 1927 the tournament had become so important that Bozeman looked forward to "the hosts of athletes, speakers, writers, and spectators arriving in trains from the west, north and east, from the representative sixteen schools and from around the state." The Chamber of Commerce determined to make the downtown window displays "the very best in the history of the tournament"; each team represented by a business. Much was made, for example, of J.R. Poor & Son's display for Roundup, using "coal, a coal train and a boxing ring surrounded by a set of flappers [1920s women in bold dress] all set in a background of maroon and white, Roundup's colors." The best display was in the spacious windows of Montana Power which showed "on the left a giant scoreboard showing the result of each game by quarters. On the right were the various trophies going to the winners of basketball, speaking and writing."

Then the Great Depression blew in, casting a pall every year on tournament planning. The low point came in 1933, when not only the state tournament but divisional tournaments were cancelled because of the extended Bank holiday. Even if there had been a tournament, many of the 16 teams qualifying, could not have afforded the expense of attending.

Also, in most years the smaller schools invited to the tournament generally couldn't compete favorably with the larger schools. After a referendum, the high schools of Montana agreed to adopt a plan under which basketball—including the tournaments—would be administered by the Montana High School Association. Under this system, there would now be two classifications of schools: the 16 schools with the largest enrollments grouped into Class A, and the rest into 16 districts making up Class B. The eight Class A teams and the best eight Class B teams in the north would have a 16-team tournament. The same would happen in the south. The best A and B winners of each division would meet in a four-team round-robin tournament to determine the Class A and Class B winners. The setup was somewhat confusing to me until a book came out describing how one tournament actually worked. In each final round-robin, a Class B team (or less likely a Class A team) might not be the overall winner, but if it gained *the highest place for its class,* it would be declared the winner of that class. It was a strange system, perhaps, but put in place to save money.

Money continued to be an issue throughout the Great Depression, on into World War II. My cousin, Alfred "Shorty" Wise told me, when Belgrade lost the district championship in 1936, the coach was relieved, because the school couldn't afford to send the team to the divisional tournament. In fact, the handbooks of the era describe how a tournament would be run "if a tournament is held," or rules for a team advancing to a tournament "if the team decides to go." Financial conditions managed to improve during the war years to the point that the two classes of schools were kept separate through the divisional tournaments, even through the state tournament until the final game, in which the best of each class would meet in the final match to determine the overall winner. Whichever team lost would still be the winner of its class. By 1947, the same system stayed in place except the classes of teams were kept separate to the very end.

Through the years the smaller schools continued—as you would expect—to have difficulty competing against larger schools. For this reason the smaller schools in Class B had been separate from the 16 larger schools until the post season tournaments. By 1949 the director and board of the MHSA had observed long enough that even within Class B, the smallest schools could not compete. In the fall of that year, a major change was made, introducing Class C for the hundred-plus smallest schools in Montana. Class B would be reduced to 45 midsized schools with the 16 largest schools remaining in Class A.

Class C replicated the original Class B arrangement in 1934: there would be 16 numerically named districts, with the winners of every district playing eight playoff games to determine the eight-team slate in the state tournament. In that first spring, 1950, the tournament was held where tournaments in Montana had all started: at Montana State College in Bozeman. The winner of that tournament was Nashua; the second year 1951, it would be Poplar, both teams in or near the Fort Peck Indian Reservation in northeastern Montana.

In 1953, the system was altered to have two winners from each district play in four divisional tournaments, eight teams each, and from those four tournaments, two from each division would advance to an eight-team state tournament. In each district and division there would be a *challenge* game in which the 2nd and 3rd place teams would play (if the two teams had not previously met in the tournament) to determine which would advance to the next tournament. Beginning in the autumn of 1951, the Belfry Bats from south-central Montana assembled an unusual number of talented players and took the Class C honors in 1952, 1953, and 1954. Later in the decade Belgrade would win two additional times (insuring that half the winners from the decade would have names starting with B-e-l). The same 1953 system was as in place when the tournament was held in 1960, except that the number of districts had been reduced from 16 to 15.

IF GILDFORD WAS TRAVELING TO HELENA FOR THE SECOND YEAR IN

a row, it would be the debut for its opponent Holy Rosary High School in Bozeman. Until 1960, Rosary had not even won a district tournament for sixteen years, but now was in Helena with the team members a bit starry-eyed upon arrival. Yet, if the team was new to the tournament, it was not new to Helena or for that matter, to the ways of the larger city—if you could call any city in Montana large. Bozeman was approximately the same size as Helena, and only a hundred miles away on the old highway. Rosary regularly scheduled games with its parochial counterpart Helena Cathedral. And, games aside, many players and other students made occasional trips to Helena with parents. In that sense, Rosary might have had something of an advantage; in fact, in the minds of many, Rosary was in a superior position, had won in a more-challenging league. For the country boys of Gildford, Rosary was highly regarded. One member of the Broncs had a relative near Bozeman, who told him Gildford could not run with Bulldogs.

Still for what it was worth, the Rosary team was largely made up of country boys also. Upon arrival and for the three days they were in Helena, the boys would go from motel to restaurant to gym and back to motel, highly regimented, closely monitored. Not that it was necessary. These kids were arguably the most earnest, respectful, well-behaved, and likely intelligent group of kids in the state of Montana. Whether monitored or not, they came with confidence and with every intention to not just compete for, but to win the championship.

In their march to this very night, the Rosary lads had not had it easy. On a nonexistent budget, at the mercy of donations, they were staying in the same dreary motel the Gildford team had occupied the year before. They had battled and finally broken a long tradition of tournament mediocrity and non-advancement. In prior years they had suffered (depending on who you ask) coaches who were verbally abusive, destroying their spirit. They had lost teammates who moved away, who could have helped them greatly, especially in the post position. But compared with their adversary for the evening—compared with what Gildford had had to face and overcome over the previous eight years— Rosary's problems amounted to a seismic grain-elevator-sized pile of nothing.

Frank Spragg

A Little Town on the Hi-Line

THE WIND IS BLOWING AS I'M DRIVING WEST ON US HIGHWAY 2, through wheat country so vast, words can hardly give description. Distant mountains can be seen punctuating the horizon but rather than subtracting from the immensity, they add to it because they demonstrate how far away landmarks really can be. To the southeast are the Bears Paw Mountains which seem close enough but are in fact over forty miles away. To the west-northwest are the Sweetgrass Hills—sixty miles. Far to the south, barely discernible in good weather, the Highwood Mountains—eighty miles. To the north and northeast, however, there are no mountains. In these directions the only obstacle to my vision is the curvature of the earth. For all I know, this agriplain could roll headlong into Canada uncontrolled for miles after hundreds of miles until finally blocked by the boreal forests of the sub-Arctic. I have the same blank view to the west and southwest. The Rocky Mountain Front is out there somewhere, but from where I'm sitting, it might as well be in Australia. And yet if the land is huge it also includes the ultra-diminutive, for I am slowing down, ready to slap on my right-turn signal. I am about to enter Gildford, Montana.

Nervousness grabs me as I cross the bridge over Sage Creek, for I have an upcoming interview with three people I have never met, three members of the 1960 Gildford team: Don Miller, Gene Cady, and Chris Pappas. I am also anxious to see Gildford itself, for it has been the center of my mental focus for the better part of three months. Gildford is home to 185 people and, it seems, almost as many granaries, which cluster here and there around the perimeter, even infiltrating the town. The farmers here for generations have preferred to live in this little village and as much as possible like to bring their granaries and outbuildings with them. Some cattle ranching goes on around Gildford, but the granaries you see aren't for decoration. The Hi-Line is overwhelmingly tied to dry land farming, mostly winter wheat, but also spring wheat, Durham wheat (for pasta), barley, garbanzo beans, and peas. Not your table-variety peas but the kind for feeding stock, the legume family's answer to field corn.

Farming along the Hi-Line (named because the railroad running through here appears as the "highest line" on a map of the United States) continues to become ever more efficient. Lowell Miller (the brother of Don) invited me, on a later visit to Gildford, to see his farm and ride on a 100-foot-wide self-propelled weed sprayer, which looks like a tractor with wings. The spray comes out in a pulsating motion, which makes it easier to hit the target in this generally windy country. Inside the cab, the driver can program his computer, press a button, and the sprayer will travel absolutely straight along its intended path. Included in the computer is a GPS unit that gives the exact location at all times so there is never overlap of spray or strips of ground unsprayed. If the driver needs to veer off-track to reload chemical, he can, with his GPS, return precisely to where he was before.

Spraying for weeds is increasingly important because over the past twenty years, the farmers have skipped the step of cultivation. No more plowing, harrowing, or generally working the soil. Not having to cultivate is a great leap in progress because the soil can retain moisture and nutrients for a greater length of time; the outcome is a bumper improvement in crop yields. Farmers can go directly to seeding the ground with air drills up to eighty feet wide, appearing like platoons of giant fish hooks known as shanks with clear plastic tubes attached to the back of each shank for the transportation of seed. As each of these shanks, pressed down with 550 pounds of spring pressure, makes a micro-furrow in the hard dirt, seeds are blown through the tubes into the furrow from a tank in front of the drill.

Frank Spragg

The machine that has gone through change as much as any is the grand dame of dry land farming: the mighty combine. This thresher of crops is a monster; I had to climb a short ladder just to get to the driver's seat and thought it unwise at my age to jump back down to the concrete below. The combine I climbed was in a shop with the outer panels off; I could see a network of hydraulic channels running the length of the combine. Everything is propelled by hydraulics these days; only the transmission still runs on gears. The header, which includes the reel and cutter bar, is up to forty-five feet wide, meaning the combine can cut a forty-five foot swath of grain, three times the width of what could be cut fifty years ago. Headers are so big and expensive, they are often sold separately by a different company and can be attached to any brand of combine. The new combines have sensors that govern the machine to slow down when stands of grain are dense and speed up when the stand lightens up. The headers automatically speed up and slow down with the velocity of the combine.

One of the most remarkable features on the combine is the computer readout. The farmer can retrieve just about any data he needs from the computer: yield, moisture content, gallons per hour, bushels per hour—all data which, if converted, will reveal gallons per bushel, or job-cost efficiency. The day is fast approaching when the readout will even reveal protein content. This is important because protein content governs price of the grain, and so the farmer can determine the mix of grain hauled for a better price at the elevator. The computer can produce what looks like topographical maps of yield and moisture variation throughout the field. It has, like other machines, a GPS guidance system telling the driver where he is at all times, and if there is any breakdown, the computer will reveal the source of the problem and what part needs to be replaced.

Combines no longer dump grain directly into trucks anymore. Instead the grain is deposited into grain carts with a capacity for up to 1,500 bushels, carts pulled by tractors that can follow three to six combines at once. The grain is then transferred from the cart to eighteen-wheel semis, which take the grain down the highway to a distribution point. This transfer system makes it possible for the combine operator to never, in an entire day, throttle into neutral.

These machines don't come cheap and need lots of acres to make them viable. *Lots* of acres. Try five thousand acres in cultivation with an equal number in summer fallow. And yet this operation can be adequately managed by a mere two people. So over the years as farms have become relentlessly larger, more people, declared unnecessary, keep moving away. With fewer people trading in town, businesses in a small town like Gildford are forced to close. This process ramped up in the 1980s when the government offered a program called Conservation Reserve Program (CRP) that paid farmers for a minimum of ten years not to use their land for agricultural purposes. More than a few people were happy to take the money and permanently leave.

Today Gildford has an auto and farm machinery repair shop, an outlet for filter sales and cleaning, a roofing contractor, a grain elevator used at times by farmers for storage (all proprietors who have offices in their homes), a credit-card gasoline pump that needs no attendant, and exactly one retail outlet, Gildford Mercantile, the only real grocery store between Havre and Chester. The store is a wonderful little place that includes a delicatessen where owners Ted and Laura Hauser are happy to make a sandwich over which the average human mouth cannot possibly stretch. But if widened successfully, the intake is as tasty as you will find anywhere. The Hausers do no advertising, but the word is out for the armies of summer cyclists who include Highway 2 on their circuit. The store is also popular with workers who descend on the area during harvest season. Gildford Mercantile is more than a retail outlet: for years it has been a gathering place for people to play cards and socialize. It also provides a venue for activities associated with the local Baptist Church.

The little store is the pride of Gildford and looks much the same on the outside as when it was built in 1915. But the store exists because Ted Hauser, a refugee from Southern California, has brought his real business with him, which he runs in a garage out back—machining parts for the aerospace industry, some prototype parts, but mostly battery covers for reconnaissance drones throughout the world. Hauser explained the role of drones as an absolutely unprecedented aspect of warfare. People in Nevada go into control booths every day, decide where they will bomb (and kill), and then go home and eat with their families. Many of them seek counseling. Hauser told me the store pays for rent (the family lives upstairs), utilities, and *some* food. "But if the family wants clothes….." or just about anything else, then it must rely on his business out back.

This economic conundrum has had a domino effect on the residential makeup of Gildford. With houses up for sale at a very reasonable price, new people have moved in, people who are not a part of the old Gildford blend—residents who have known each other forever. They tend to be commuters—to Havre, to Chester. Some are railroad people, one man drives a Coca-Cola truck, a few are up to no good. Even though these people have moved in, several houses are still vacant, a sign of the long, slow population decline.

I should mention there is one other player in this mix that has been a major force in decimating the population along the Hi-Line. If you travel from Shelby to Havre you will notice that nearly all the little towns are on the north side of the highway. This is no accident. These pockets of population were founded on a transportation line much older than Highway 2: this is the path of the Burlington Northern Railway whose leaders in the 1970s decided that slowing down for every two-cent town was too inefficient. The company began building "unit trains," an engine and group of cars not meant normally to be taken apart and too long for the capacity of the traditional railroad siding which could take only five or six cars. At first there were 26 cars in a unit train, then 52, and finally 110. Just a few years ago, BN had only twelve stops in all of Montana although the number has gone up slightly with the ending of CRP contracts.

Still, this phasing-out of stops has rendered nearly all of the old grain elevators you see in small towns useless. Because these elevators were built so well, with long steel spikes pounded randomly through several layers of cribbed two-by-sixes, it is not cost effective to tear them down. So they just stand there slowly rotting away. Gildford has three such structures, one purchased by a farmer and used as his own personal mega-granary. But the other two have been empty for many years. These old abandoned elevators are the most visible signs of the four-decade legacy Burlington Northern has left in northern Montana and throughout much of the nation. It is interesting that a railway which has influenced the decline of nearly every small town is the same railway, then known as Great Northern, which was the lifeblood of the area for over a half century, indeed made it possible for Gildford and other towns to exist.

IN THE BEGINNING, BEFORE THERE WAS A GILDFORD, BEFORE THERE were any signs of modern civilization, there was the land, an endless sea of native grasses sprinkled with sage brush over which the Indians had hunted for centuries. The prairie attracted trappers in the 1850s and might have been the domain of cattlemen but it would remain pristine—for it was part of the Blackfeet Indian Reservation.

The beginning of change took place in 1888 when a vast area north of the Marias River was withdrawn as Indian reservation territory and ranchers began to move in along the plush land bordering Sage Creek. They chose a site for the creek crossing, which attracted a settlement known as Dayton, supporting a general store and a post office.

Meanwhile the Great Northern, led by chief partner James J Hill, pushed across northern Montana from east to west, frantically competing with the Northern Pacific Railway to build the first line from the Midwest to the Pacific. As the line came through, the Sage Creek crossing became an important link in the development of the railroad in northern Montana. A water tower was built on the creek from which water was diverted into a reservoir used for construction of the railroad up to the Continental Divide. The rail line was completed to Seattle in 1893, and then progress around Sage Creek for the most part stopped; there was little need for further development. The ranchers kept on ranching and needed all those acres anyway and nothing changed much for seventeen years. But it would soon change dramatically because if these acres were no longer part of the reservation, they were still on government land, and the government would make it possible for a large number of people to live here.

The impetus to settle the West had been due in part to the politics of the Civil War. When the South seceded from the Union, the United States government raced to build a railroad to the Pacific and develop the West before the Southerners could do the same. After the Union Railroad was completed through Utah in 1869, miners, stockmen and other settlers far removed from the railroad demanded one of their own. The government also did something else to settle the West: in 1862, it passed the Homestead Act.

These two developments helped to populate parts of the West quickly, but not initially most of Montana. Some areas in the new territory were beginning to be farmed as early as 1864 to help supply nearby mining camps. But the land near Sage Creek was not near any mining camp. Nor was it near any transportation system for easy transfer of people and goods, of getting products to market. It was subject to the Homestead Act but even so, it was part of the upper Missouri Basin, which everyone including school children knew as the "Great American Desert." Why go there when you could go to California or Oregon? The Sage Creek area seemed destined to be ranching country sparsely populated with people, even with the advent of the railroad.

By the beginning of the twentieth century, however, Montana's fortunes in crop growing began to change. There had already been great improvements in farming equipment and methods. Farmers now had steel moldboard plows, grain drills, twine binders, discs, harrows, steam-powered threshers, and other increasingly effective machinery. Farmers also learned the concept of "dry land farming" which, as historian Mary Wilma M. Hargreaves states, "is defined as agriculture without irrigation in regions of scanty precipitation." Farmers learned how to work the land while preserving moisture and agricultural experiment stations developed drought-resistant plants along with combining crop growing with livestock production.

In the Hi-Line region, if farming were to take place at all it would be the dry land variety. But 160 acres under the Homestead Act was hardly enough along the Hi-Line for a family farm. In 1909 Congress passed the Enlarged Homestead Act, which offered 320 acres free to settlers in Montana and other western states. If a settler "proved up" the land, plowing it up and making improvements to the land in five years, he could have legal title to the land. (In 1912 another amendment passed shortening the prove-up period to three years.)

The Great Northern Railroad saw a bonanza coming. The company promoted the land, telling people how wonderful it was, and that it could be theirs for free! Millions were spent in promotion that reached not only citizens of the eastern United States, but many parts of Europe. Jim Hill and others "used every conceivable method to publicize the fertility of the northern Great Plains and to lure farmers there. They offered prizes for crops and livestock, sponsored farm exhibits, ran agricultural display trains around the country, and spread advertising leaflets and brochures throughout the United States and Europe. They encouraged Europeans, especially Germans and Scandinavians, to migrate and offered them easy trans-Atlantic rates. Most importantly they offered the home-seekers cheap rail fares to their new homes either in boxcars or in the more comfortable 'Zulu' cars that provided sleeping facilities. For as little as $22.50, a homesteader could buy space in a freight car to bring his family, all his belongings, even seed grains and livestock from St. Paul to eastern Montana."

The land rush was on. In the first quarter of 1910, the Great Northern moved over 1,000 emigrant cars into northern Montana.

On one spring evening, the cars disembarked 250 people to Havre alone. The roads were frightfully primitive: as people came in, it was necessary to build towns only eight to ten miles apart, because that was as far as people could drive their buggies for supplies in a day's time. One location, thirty miles west of Havre and next to the reservoir on Sage Creek, was chosen as the new marketing center for the immediate area. Named after a city in southern England with a slightly different spelling, it would be called Gildford. Here is where the hammers would fly and the buildings go up. The little outpost of Dayton, one mile to the west, was left to die.

These homesteaders prospered in the early years. Not only could a homesteader have 320 acres of ground—if he married, he and his wife could each be considered individual settlers, each receive 320 acres and the young couple could start off with a section of land. And the climate cooperated. Not only did it rain in abundance, it rained at the right times, in the spring and early summer. With the onset of World War I, the need for grain sent prices upward. Life was good and with all the prosperity, Gildford was growing.

At the end of 1910, Gildford already had over twenty businesses, including seven lumberyards, two hotels, three saloons, a bank, a hardware store, and four livery stables. The year 1912 saw the construction of the first elevator and a newspaper, the *Gildford Tribune*. By 1915 there were over thirty businesses. In that year ninety-two cars of grain were shipped out of the little town. A second bank was opened after the first had been established the year before. "Gildford is a town that can do nothing but grow and prosper," wrote Joe Casey of the *Gildford Tribune*, "for it lies in the middle of over 800,000 acres of highly productive soil which has no limitations."

But there was no forgetting that farmers struggled with a hard-scrabble life in this harsh land. The summers were bone-hot, the winters brutally cold, offering sub-zero temperatures for weeks at a time, cold accompanied by relentless wind that knocked the wind chill far into the minus zone. The wind was a constant presence throughout the year; on one particularly drafty day, a would-be settler jumped off the train in Gildford and asked the agent if the wind always blew like this. "Of course not," laughed the agent, "sometimes it blows from a different direction."

The extreme weather was matched by troublesome soil; plowing virgin sod is a challenge under the best of circumstances, but here, especially to the north of the railroad, the land had been a glacial moraine during the Ice Age. The soil was unremittingly filled with rocks, all-consuming, it seemed. No amount of rock picking through the years has gotten rid of them. As cultivators became more advanced, they would dig deeper into the ground, digging up more rocks. These stones could be the size of a small pebble, a fist, a large shoe box. Or they could be bigger than that, much bigger. One day Don Miller was working the ground when he hooked onto a rock so large, a trench had to be dug next to it so it could be rolled over onto a flat bed and hauled away. Now sitting like a huge loaf of bread in his son's front yard, the rock is calculated to weigh 49,760 pounds or nearly twenty-five tons.

Despite the challenges of nature, when moisture was abundant and timely, prosperity grew along the Hi-Line. Then in 1917 a drought came that lasted for seven years. The drought was accompanied by grasshoppers, which could completely denude a field. And then there were the cutworms, the wire worms, the grassfires. People should have known the weather was cyclical but they turned a blind eye to it; either that or the Great Northern promotional campaign deluded them into thinking the land was utopia. All the homesteader had to do was show up for work and the rest would take care of itself.

They had security to some extent: the area already had connections to insurance. During the 1917 drought, for example, when there weren't any crops to pay debts on, 117 farmers around Gildford had insurance policies. If they had a net income of one dollar per acre, the insurance would kick in. In this case, 112 farmers were able to settle. But for five of the claims, the company refused to pay. One adjustor, seeing a mob of farmers coming after him, crept down the back stairwell of the hotel where he was staying and hid the reports in a ladies' outhouse. When they caught him he "fessed up" to where the paperwork was hidden.

Despite the drought, during World War I, the prices had been kept high to "unprecedented levels" because of the need for grain in Europe. But once the war was over, the prices plummeted. While much of the nation enjoyed prosperity during the 1920s, the farmers in Montana faced an early form of depression. Some 60,000 people left the state during that decade. Ranches were abandoned, the last bank in Gildford closed down in 1922, and the *Gildford Tribune* put out its last issue on April 23, 1925.

Yet some were tenacious and would not leave. I had the honor of sitting across the dining room table of a descendant of one of these people on a farm fifteen miles north of Rudyard. The visit with Mary Lois and Jerry Hybner was noteworthy—not only for discussion about their ancestors—but Mary Lois was the fourth-grade teacher of many of the Gildford team members featured in this book. As I looked at the students in the yearbook, I had either interviewed in person or on the phone at least half of them.

Earlier, on the phone, Mary Lois invited me to stay for lunch which I reluctantly accepted. I didn't want her to be overburdened by some interloper drifting along the highway. What I got was an experience I had not had since I was a teenager on our own farm, a practice I thought ceased to exist sometime in the 1970s. Everything was made from scratch: the vegetable beef soup, the bread, the chocolate chip cookies, along with home canned pears. This was not dinner but *lunch*, in a *home*, a *daily occurrence*. Mary Lois apologized for not having something more substantial, saying that earlier in the morning she had had pressing needs. As we were talking, Jerry was excited to have found a compatriot who had also driven the old John Deere "D." It wasn't until I returned to Oregon that I sheepishly remembered I actually had the wheel of the more modern John Deere "R."

But there was a reason I could visit with the Hybners where we were sitting now. Jerry's father Frank Jr. grew up in Czechoslovakia, had moved with his extended family to Texas and eventually to California because there were relatives in both states. One day Uncle John read about free land in Montana. The family arrived in 1912, with Frank taking out a homestead when he was only twenty-one years old. On the way up to Montana, Jerry's grandfather, Frank Sr. had a stroke that turned him into an invalid and a burden. It was tough going for the rest of the family. They all lived for a time in a small shack one-half mile from where we were sitting, and though the remainder of the family members took out homesteads and helped each other, it still wasn't enough. After the drought in 1917, Frank Jr. went to Oregon in the winters, worked on a farm, dug ditches for a plumber, worked in a sawmill—anything he could do. He did this for several years until he could make a go of it year-around on the Hi-Line.

A homesteader could be tenacious, even driven, but if he did not have help, support, associations with friends and loved ones, people who cared about *him,* then life on the Hi-Line could be hopeless. He needed for one thing commitment from his wife; if she were lonely and depressed back in that tar-paper shack with no one to talk to, if she wanted to go back to where they came from, then the whole settlement game was probably over. It only made sense that people were more likely to succeed if they came in large groups. Don Miller's grandfather, Henry Miller, and his wife, Lydia Beecher Miller, moved in from North Dakota, each with several brothers who came with them; there were numerous cousins, especially on the Beecher side, all who settled in the same area and hung out together. On Miller's maternal grandfather's side, the Penniwells, the association wasn't so much with true relatives, although there were some of those, but with friends, a huge clan that came out of Kansas. Working together, living together, and the general togetherness gave incredible strength and endurance.

Even so, at least one of the settlers made a go of it coming alone.

Frank Spragg

His name was Harry Cady, grandfather of 1960 basketball player Gene Cady, who came from Nebraska in 1911 at the age of twenty-six, homesteading east of Gildford, "as close to Havre and the railroad as possible because if I had to get out of there, I could." He would marry six years later, have six children, and then say he couldn't leave because "I had to figure out how to feed those six kids." In fact most of the members of the 1960 team came from pioneer stock. Dave Welsh's grandfather settled south of Hingham, and the Welsh family later moved to Gildford because Dave's father married a Gildford girl. Chris Pappas' situation was somewhat different: his father was born in Greece, came to the United States when he was nineteen years old, married a woman from Greece twenty-four years younger than he in an arranged marriage, then homesteaded ten miles south of Gildford. His father was sixty years old when Chris was born, and died in 1949, so Chris essentially grew up with a widowed mother. In a still different circumstance, Ken Whitaker's father landed in the Gildford area because he was finally able to purchase a farm thirty-five miles north of town. At age three, he had been delivered from a cattle drive passing through the area, was adopted by a family north of Rudyard (changing his last name from Baker to Whitaker) and did a variety of jobs before he was able to save enough money to purchase the farm.

If the settlers received strength in numbers, help came in another way also. G. Fred Mundy arrived in Gildford in 1911 and filed a homestead in the Chocolate Loam Basin north of town. By 1914 he knew the basin had a great future as a wheat empire. He had seen his first crop, a twenty bushel-per-acre output in a country of little rain. In 1915 he drew up plans for a flour mill, and construction began as soon as the ground thawed the next spring. Construction continued through the summer and the enterprise, known as Golden Grain Flour, was ready when the harvest began after Labor Day. During the Great Depression, a forty-bushel load of wheat brought in only fifteen dollars; it wasn't worth hauling to town. But the farmer could take it to Mundy's Golden Grain Flour and turn it into flour to last seven months. It brought feed to hundreds of cattle and hogs and provided breakfast cereal for the family. The "Golden Grain," milled from some of the highest-protein wheat in the world, became the top-selling flour in grocery stores back and forth along the Hi-Line. The flour was also shipped out of state to large wholesalers for retail distribution. As new methods were developed, the mill continued to expand and improve its products. Along with breakfast cereal, the mill made money with feed grinding, grain cleaning and treating. Going at a forty barrel-a-day capacity, the flour mill operated for thirty years until Mundy retired in 1951.

WITH THE CONTINUING ECONOMIC HARDSHIP OVER THE DECADES, Gildford's fate by the 1950s was to be another small town between Shelby and Havre, to have fewer businesses than before, to be in imperceptible decline. The stockyards had shut down in the early 1940s. The one remaining lumberyard closed its doors in 1953. A man by the name of Burt Twedt owned a hardware store, but it burned to the ground. He opened a new hardware store on the old highway (which ran just north of the present Highway 2), sold it to a man named Carl Vogt, and that store burned down also. Vogt tried to open a third hardware store, but that venture hardly got off the ground and closed shortly thereafter. Ted Crawford owned a grocery store, but in 1956 that store burned, taking an entire block of buildings with it. That left two bars, two cafes, an auto body/repair shop, and the venerable Gildford Mercantile, which in those days was called Campbell's Store.

For many years, the store had been owned by Francis Wilson. But he retired and as the result of a land deal the store went to Louie and Irene Miller (Lowell's and Don's parents) who were farmers and had no interest in running a store. They were going to close it down but instead sold the store to Monta Campbell, who if she were going to run a store wanted her son John to go into partnership with her. John was just getting out of the service and with no other career in mind, decided to take her up on it. They would run the store for over thirty-five years, finally selling it in 1986.

The Campbells restored the store to its former prominence, and it became vital to the economy of Gildford. The store was a pre-modern template of a Walmart: it had a complete line of groceries, a meat locker/butcher shop, clothing for adults and children, hardware, small appliances, garden supplies and tools, glass for windows, and galvanized and copper pipe. Plus, the store had a service for cutting glass for windows and cutting pipe to length. John and Monta were a team, striving to always provide top-flight service. Over the years they had a loyal customer base.

Yet, even in the 1950s, with improved roads, folks were starting to make the trip into Havre, the county seat of Hill County, for cheaper prices in chain stores. Some goods or services could no longer be purchased in a town like Gildford at any price. If there were a dental appointment or a child taking piano lessons, the family would make another trip to Havre. These trips had to be thought out carefully, because Havre was thirty miles away. Still, Havre, the only small city for miles in every direction, was becoming the destination for Big Shopping.

Living in a very small town was an adjustment for someone not used to being there. When Carla Nelson Clevenger moved in as a high school freshman from Missoula, she was in for culture shock. There was no movie theatre; everyone would travel twelve miles west, to Rudyard, for a movie on Saturdays and then drag the streets of *that* tiny town. There was no place to shop for fashionable clothes; she had to go to Havre to buy clothes. The next year, when Gildford went to the state tournament, Carla and a few other girls were asked to speak and answer questions before a class of senior students at Helena High School. Helena students asked them, "You have one store, no theatre, what do you do?" They just couldn't believe it, couldn't believe the lifestyle.

In this part of the world, people could view one, *maybe* two TV channels if the signals deigned to cooperate. They were fortunate if they could get access to something American, a program out of Great Falls. Mostly they had to be satisfied with a Canadian channel that featured hockey and bowling. Either way, Canadian or American, the reception was snowy, the choices limited, everything over by 10:00 p.m. Locals would never have the opportunity see American youth trends via "American Bandstand." It was better in those times to listen to KMON radio from Great Falls for rock-and-roll music. There were few other forms of entertainment: one night the Inkspots performed in Rudyard; it was a really big deal. Other groups would travel around, perform at local high schools.

Gildford, however, still very much had its own social identity. There was tremendous unity in the 1950s: most people had relatives in the area; at weddings and funerals, everyone turned out. There was so much food brought into a home, no one could eat it all. People would have their own socials, the churches were involved to a degree, but it was the school—a very small school by this time—that really drew the town together. Lynn Fried Hayden, one of the cheerleaders for the 1960 team, told me she had never dreamed of going to a larger school. The school was the extended family. When Lynn graduated from high school, she and her fellow students could expect gifts from many people in town. As all the kids were walking in a (very short) line, many of people in the building were crying.

One of the biggest events at the school was the prom. When I think of 1950s proms, I see a gym floor packed with teenagers in suits and formals; the only adults were a few scattered chaperones. But in a tiny town like Gildford as in all the small towns along the Hi-Line, the prom was an all-ages affair. There were as many or more adults than there were teenagers, all freely intermixing. And the children were all there, venturing out on the floor, but more likely behind the tables serving food and drinks. Anyone from the area could attend a prom, and many kids from other towns did, either as a date or because they tended to attend any dance in the region. But the class

Frank Spragg

spent months planning the prom, had been in the gym for hours decorating, and the townspeople weren't about to allow the prom to become the backdrop for disorder.

The weekend dances were a different matter altogether. They could be held in any town along the Hi-Line, but were mostly held at the community hall in Rudyard. These dances were well-attended; if it was a big night like New Year's Eve, everyone in the region would come. It was chance to meet new people, dance to a live band; the hall was packed and with drinking going on outside the event could turn rowdy. Some of the most raucous dances were in the summer at tiny outposts, near ghost towns, at a ranch near the mountains, at a country school, or at a pavilion, all with plenty of space for parking on the grass. Fisticuffs outside these dancehalls were frequent. Usually they were the result of sheer drunkenness, but the spark could be community rivalry. Relationships could be edgy, and all it took was some lubrication to set off the spark.

Kids tried to do what they could during the off hours, go to a dance, go to a movie in Rudyard, or if they didn't have enough to do, get into trouble. Jack Fried, who graduated from Gildford in 1959, told me there were two groups of kids in Gildford: the good kids—"goody two shoes"—and the bad kids, and with few exceptions outside of school, the two groups did not mix.

The class of 1959 had a total of four students, all boys. Fried and another boy, David Saller were bright but "lazy as sin." They never did any homework, matched tests, and came out with C averages. Mediocre as these results were, they were the best in the class. When it came time for class graduation, Fried and Saller flipped a coin to see who would be valedictorian. Fried lost the flip, so he was designated honoree for the evening, something he wasn't particularly looking forward to, considering his effort for the year. But the ceremony was even worse than he expected. Myron Loe, the school superintendent, was so upset that when it came time for him to congratulate the class and hand out pins, he instead made a diatribe of it. He lashed out at the class of four for refusing to study and do any work after having so much potential. He singled Fried out and refused to give him his pin. Loe gave the pin to Jack's parents who in turn gave it to him later, but everyone was in agreement—including Jack himself—that he didn't deserve it.

Fried was a hellion in those days. He was so crazy that when he came into the movie theatre in Rudyard, because he "was likely to say something stupid", his sister Lynn and her friends would duck down in their seats so Jack wouldn't know they were there. One early morning about 3:00 a.m. after a dance, after they had been drinking, Jack and Noel Preeshl loaded fishing gear into a truck, went to the Tibor Reservoir southwest of Chester, got all stinky and dirty and then attended the Catholic Church that morning in the neighboring town of Hingham. Needless to say, their parents were "mortified."

And then there was the evening with Allen Tew. By this time Fried was out of high school but came back to Gildford in the summer to run the farm for his father, who had broken his leg and couldn't get around. The farm did not stop Fried and his friends from going to Havre to pick fights and chase girls. One night at the Buttrey's Grocery parking lot, where all the kids hung out, Fried was with Tew when he got into a fight with a Havre boy and, as he put it, "got whipped as usual." At this point one of the Havre kids pulled out a bullwhip and started snapping it, which made a frightening racket. Tew walked back to Fried's car and pulled out a .22 pistol that Fried kept under the front seat for shooting gophers. He pointed the pistol and started shooting into the air. Even as drunk as he was, Fried knew this was a "no-no." You just didn't pull a stunt like that in downtown Havre, the county seat of Hill County.

Fried told Tew to get into the car, and they roared away through the nearest alley. He then told Tew to unload the pistol and get it into the trunk before they got into serious trouble. When Tew pulled out the pistol it went off, lodging a bullet into his little toe. Fried then went "screaming" down to the Deaconess Hospital where Tew could be treated. While they were in the waiting room, the police arrived and asked them if they knew they were being chased through Havre on the way to the hospital. Fried ended up in the county jail overnight before his father came down to bail him out. He had his license taken away and was also charged with contributing to the delinquency of a minor which, at age sixteen Tew certainly was. (After a number of years Jack Fried turned his life around and has become, as he puts it, a model citizen.)

During the summers, many of the kids were busy working on farms; during the busy season the girls could work until midnight washing dishes and preparing for the next day. But they still had a chance to hang out with friends. They would go over to Fresno Lake every day, down to the old abandoned stockyards where all the kids met. There could be drinking parties at the cemetery. They did silly things, like go down to old Highway 2 where there was a bridge and pretend like they were fighting each other to get cars to stop, and then they would hide. They all thought this was very funny until one car stopped and a man jumped out and started shooting at them. Lynn Hayden said that was the closest she has ever been to death.

There were no police in Gildford or any of the neighboring towns (except for the possible exception of Rudyard). Members of the Hill County Sheriff's Department might come through, but very infrequently. Thieves would have had a field day when Gildford went to the state tournament because *everyone* left town. Carla Clevenger said several of the kids in Gildford would have had rap sheets had there been police but there were none, so pranks were committed with impunity— especially at Halloween. On this night, a cow was guided into a Kremlin (another neighboring town) bar and once in, displayed gratitude by defecating all over the floor. The kids would all get together, unhook a railroad car, and then push the car across a road, blocking it so regular cars couldn't get through. In one incident a car was unhooked and, because it was on a gentle slope, got away from the kids who were pushing it. It would have rolled onto the main track were it not for a "debar" rail, a diagonal piece of track that slowed the car to a halt.

Through the long cold winters, there would have been nothing for kids to do—nothing much for anyone to do—if it weren't for one activity that became the most unifying force of all, that would bring people fiercely together. Every year, the good citizens of Gildford and little towns around the nation should take time out and bow in reverence toward the great state of Massachusetts. Because in 1891, in that Bay State, James Naismith gave Gildford and other towns an invention that would change everything: he gave them basketball.

During the winters there was no indoor soccer in Gildford, no volleyball, no womens' sports of any kind. Girls in the 1950s never believed they could play sports, didn't even think about it. Because Gildford was in flat country, there was no skiing. Sometimes kids would shovel snow off the reservoir and play a little hockey, but hockey had no tradition in this decidedly south-of-the-Canadian-border culture. There were no hockey teams; no one really knew how to play. During this long dark season, there was rudimentary television after 5:00 p.m., no video games, no Internet. At one time Gildford had a football team but by the latter 1950s, that program had long since passed away; there weren't enough kids to form a team. In the spring there was a track program but it was primitive, lasting a few weeks. Basketball became everything. On winter nights the kids had something to do and the townspeople had something to watch. More than anything, basketball gave people in Gildford an identity.

For years Gildford was in a local basketball league, with towns along the Hi-Line playing each other. The dominant teams in this league were the larger towns: Chester, thirty miles on Highway 2 to the west, and Big Sandy, sixty-two miles (by paved highway) to the south. By the early 1950s, however Gildford would find that its most formidable opponent would not be Chester, Big Sandy, or any other team of five talented boys who could chuck a round-shaped object through a hoop. Instead, that opponent would be a group of people

Frank Spragg

in Helena wearing not basketball uniforms but the office-wear of a bureaucrat. The folks in Gildford soon discovered that if they could not defeat these bureaucrats, they might not have any meaningful basketball at all.

Closed by Any Other Name

FEW TRIFLES OF MONTANA HISTORY HAVE BEEN MORE FORGOTTEN than the accreditation controversy along the Hi-Line. Local historians have ignored it. People, who lived where it took place, unless they were in the middle of the fray, are hard pressed to know much about it. The dispute has become so consigned to oblivion that when I brought it up to the Hill County Superintendent of Public Instruction, who had been in her position for many years, she knew nothing of it. "Whatever you find out," she implored, "please let me know."

The main players in the fight are all dead, so it has been nearly impossible to string together a day-by-day, blow-by-blow synopsis. I came heartbreakingly close in tracking down one man, Ray Peck, who a friend of his said "would have told me the whole story." But by the time I discovered where Peck was, he too had passed away. At any rate, his physical health was in rapid decline; he might not have been in a position to speak. Longtime Gildford residents Lloyd Curfman and Irene "Shorty" Stuart were marvelous in giving me their best; they knew all the local participants well and could give the general picture, the motives behind decisions. But Curfman did not join the Gildford School Board until 1958, one year after Gildford, Hingham, and Inverness were restored to full accreditation. Stuart was more of an onlooker, never directly involved. But both knew the hammer-blow to a town when accreditation was taken away.

WHEN A HIGH SCHOOL LOST ACCREDITATION IN THE 1950S, IT WAS like being sent to prison. Not only was state aid withheld but, as with

Gildford and other Hi-Line schools, levy tax dollars as well, forcing locals to pony out of their pockets to keep the schools going. Students' grades were not recognized by many institutions of higher learning; the student in some cases had to take additional exams to prove he or she was fit for college. This non-recognition could force a downward spiral: schools were being penalized because they were too small, and now parents were transferring sons and daughters out of these schools to one that was accredited, making the school even smaller. Being dropped made it hard to attract teachers; the pay was abysmal leading to revolving-door turnover. Some subjects, essential to meeting state standards, were not taught because no teacher could be found. But the kick in the groin that hurt the most was that sports, including basketball, were rendered impotent. The team couldn't compete in the usual post tournaments anymore; in fact the school was subject to the so-called "snob" order, meaning it couldn't compete against another accredited school. If it did, the latter school could also lose post season tournament privileges.

The consequences of not having accreditation were severe enough that the decree was seldom implemented. Indeed, there were safeguards in the state constitution to prevent this from suddenly happening. The school had to go through a series of warnings over a period of years, each new warning more serious than the last. The first and most lenient warning was called "Accreditation with Advice," meaning the school had not met one or more standards. Then if nothing was done or conditions worsened, it was on to "Accreditation with Warning" "Probation" "Final Probation," and finally the dreaded "Dropped"— the accreditation taken away.

These penalties could be for any type of violation, such as not teaching all required subjects, a teacher not certified for the subject being taught, a building inadequate or unsafe, or required materials and teaching tools not available. A school could also be cited for not having enough students. The measuring stick for this was called Average Number Belonging, or ANB, and would prove to be Gildford's downfall.

No one familiar with the Hi-Line in those days would have confused Gildford School District #20 with elite education. There was no orchestra training, no choir, no foreign languages, no tennis or golf teams, no advanced placement classes—indeed, few frills. The effort had been born from settlers trying to have their children taught the very rudiments in semi-frontier circumstances. The first school was shelved in the second story of an abandoned saloon, but soon enough in 1912, the townspeople had a one-story school built with a second story added two years later to house the growing enrollment. In 1917 the district was large enough that it added a high school, a modest two grades perhaps, but it was a start. Seven years later the high school was enlarged to four grades with the building upgraded as well, first in 1923 and again in 1925. School District #20 was becoming the little district that could.

In 1937, Work Progress Administration money became available and the Gildford people, along with folks in a host of other communities, had a nice new school built, a school the town could never have afforded otherwise in the depths of the Great Depression. In these confines, the kids were taught the basics, but they were good basics, dispensed by caring teachers. At graduation, the kids knew enough to seek higher education, take on future challenges and, in many cases, become remarkable individuals.

Still the school had deficiencies and was under the watchful eye of the superintendent of public instruction and Board of Education. As early as 1923, Gildford was put on "probation" for reasons unspecified. Then for the next twelve years the school was given a clean bill of health. Suddenly in 1935, the state issued a stern warning that if Gildford didn't increase space for learning, it would lose accreditation. The district fixed that problem and just as abruptly was on good footing again for another eleven years.

Three state entities were responsible for overseeing a school, making sure it ran properly. Two of these were the governor and legislature; by law, the governor was to send a budget to the legislature, in theory with a fair share for education. The legislature would then do what folks in public instruction hoped it would do: pass the budget, with a portion for education known as the State Equalization Fund vital for the running of a school.[2] If necessary, the legislature would pass bills to advance education in Montana.

The third body was the Board of Education, consisting of eleven members: eight from around the state who were able volunteers, who kept their own professions, met at least quarterly, and were appointed by the governor. Also on the board were the attorney general and the governor himself. The board members had no staff, were not administrators in their realm on the board, but were to assimilate the information and recommendations they were given, and then vote on policy. Rarely did volunteers on the board have direct influence with the legislative branch of the government.

There was one last member of the Board of Education who was central to everything involving education in Montana, who rightly should know more than anyone else because of a first-rate background in the field, who had staff members that went out and visited the schools, and who, with this information, was in a position to advise the board properly. This individual set the agenda for the board and the board by law was to act on her recommendations which were almost never voted down. She was the person who advised the governor and she (or a member of her staff) testified before the legislature in an effort to stretch education's fair share within the budget. All added up, she was in a position to have enormous influence on the governor, legislature and the board. That person was another elected official, the superintendent of public instruction (SPI). In the mid-1940s, that superintendent was Elizabeth Ireland.

Miss Ireland was first elected in 1929 and served in total sixteen years. She was a woman of no small ability, working her way through the University of Montana, Columbia University, and continuing on for her doctorate as she rose through the ranks of education in Montana. She had begun teaching in Tacoma, Washington, then moved to Montana, where she taught in a country school near Chester, eventually becoming the superintendent of Havre Public Schools. While in Havre, she had been "instrumental" in the establishment of Northern Montana College. As state SPI, she had dealt with education through the Great Depression when no one had any money, and the war years when there was an acute shortage of personnel. By the time she ran for reelection as state SPI in 1948, she was listed in *Who's Who in American Education.*

Because Ireland had lived in Chester or Havre for many years, there is a sense that, had she had remained SPI into the 1950s, the Hi-Line accreditation story might have been very different. Because when she looked to the towns west of Havre, she saw not just people but *her* people, many of whom, it seems, she had known forever. This background was reflected in a statement she made during her 1948 campaign for SPI: "None of Montana's schools should be abandoned or consolidated *even though they have a low enrollment.* The education of Montana youth is centered around these schools........the schools form community centers and are necessary to the population of these communities" (italics added).

But when she ran for reelection in 1948, Elizabeth Ireland was sixty-seven years old and no match for her opponent in charisma. One reporter in a backhanded way said as much: "Mary Condon.......the pretty and spunky teacher, *something new in Montana politics* stole the show at the Democratic State Platform Convention in Billings with some pungent and pert oratory" (italics added).

Mary Margaret Condon. Stole the show. At that convention, gubernatorial candidate John Bonner and attorney general candidate Arnold Olsen had won "rousing applause" for advocating programs to help veterans. Then it was Condon's turn to speak. She rose to the podium and said, "I can't agree with giving veterans everything." She paused. The audience "gasped" and Condon turned to Bonner who "looked like he had ice water thrown at him." She turned back toward the audience and completed her thought, "They've *earned* it." The audience "roared its approval".

Condon didn't have to say anything to turn heads. She had heard plenty of "wolf whistles" when she was a Red Cross worker in the India-Burma-China theatre during World War II. According to those who were around her in Montana, she could still get them as SPI, when she stepped outside her office or elsewhere when she appeared in public. "Good looks, poise, figure"—that was an apt description of Condon. She would not marry until she was forty-five, but apparently had the opportunity whenever she wanted. In moments of frustration she was known to say she would "get married and go back to Iowa" where she had originally come from.

Her good looks were matched by charm and her skill as a first rate raconteur. Much later in her life, when she was a fixture on Capitol Hill in Washington, D.C., she delighted in telling a story about a vote against a filibuster in the Senate. "This little nun, not quite five feet tall, came up to the two of us and told us a certain senator was with us. We looked at one another and my partner responded, 'Sister, when Senator Jones votes to end the filibuster bill, Mary and I will throw our arms around each other and leap over the balcony to the Senate floor.' The vote proceeded. Senator Jones voted against the filibuster. There was gentle little tap on my shoulder and the little nun said, 'Jump, lady, jump!'"

Again, after Condon had been in our nation's capital for a time, she came back to Helena and stopped in the office of the current SPI, Ed Argenbright. She commented on the rugs covering his office floor and then said, "When I was the superintendent, I had these new bright red rugs. A certain legislator came into the office one day, noticed the rugs, and said, 'Wow Mary, these rugs sure are bright! They look like they could come out of a bordello.' I responded, 'Well, you would probably know.'" That was Mary Condon, great for a sound bite. Just after retiring, when asked about her plans, she said, "I have been working for fifty-three years. Why do I have to do anything?"

And she was just as often feisty. "Listen, Buster, if they don't get more money, they'll quit; and I'll go with them—-and I won't go quietly, either." She was the newly elected SPI lashing out against an "economy-minded" legislator, fighting for higher pay for her staff. She had come by straight talk naturally: at her first job in a small rural high school, after already being assigned to teach five classes as well as directing school plays, training the marching band, and advising the student council, she was given two additional classes in history, all on an annual salary of $932. At the end of the year, the superintendent gave her a thirty-dollar check for teaching the two history classes. She took the check to the chairman of the school board, tore it up, and told him, "I remember another bargain made for thirty pieces of silver and that one stunk too." She then quit.

Condon didn't get to where she was by merely being colorful. She was whip-smart, worked hard, and cared deeply about education. It was well known in Washington, after she became a lobbyist, that if you hit a snag over education, the next move was to go see Mary. She was well connected and knew which levers to pull. And to a degree, she was altruistic. She was happy being SPI even though the salary was only $7,500 a year. She would have continued on had she won the election in 1956. She then became a lobbyist in the nation's capital (one of the first who was a woman) because she was offered the job by the National Education Association.

She was born October 10, 1916, one of three children to David Joseph and Sarah Rose Stack Condon. She showed grit early, setting the record for the junior boys' high jump in her school at age eleven. After going through high school in Cedar Rapids, she graduated with highest honors at Mount Mary Junior College and then obtained a B.A. degree from the University of Iowa. In addition to school, she worked as a hostess in a restaurant, a cashier at a men's clothing store, and a graduate assistant grading history papers. She was making $120 a month going through college, sending some of the money home.

In her efforts, Condon ran headlong into prejudice. After graduating from Iowa during the Great Depression, she could not find a job, partly because openings were few in number, and of those few, several would not consider Condon because she was Catholic. She then sought a loan from the school to complete her master's degree, but was turned down because the man on the scholarship committee opposed scholarships for women. It took several faculty members to lobby successfully for her loan.

Condon graduated with an M.A. and, with all her education, landed that infamous rural Iowa teaching job with its pitiful salary. Then her luck began to change. She became a Red Cross recreational program director in Asia during the war, was "top gal" at a B-29 command base—a combat rest camp and replacement depot—planning activities for fighting men, capturing their fighting spirit. She sang with dance bands and won a jitterbug competition. For the rest of her life she would consider winning that dance competition one of her proudest moments.

After the war, the Red Cross sent her to Montana and the Dakotas to be an educational field consultant. Soon she was hired on as assistant professor of history as well as the dean of students (one newspaper sniffed, "That's right— Dean over Men") at Eastern Montana College in Billings. It was in Billings that Condon, "on a dare," tossed her hat into the ring for state SPI on the Democratic ticket. It happened to be on June 9, the last day a candidate could file before the deadline, but also the last day that candidate could withdraw from the ticket. The very next day, Condon got cold feet and tried to back out, but it was too late. Her name would be on the ballot, and because she had been unopposed for the Democratic primary, would now be facing her formidable opponent Elizabeth Ireland for the general election. Condon had no choice but to campaign vigorously and won in a shocking upset. Condon would always say, "I didn't win the election; my predecessor was defeated." At the tender age of thirty-two she was the new superintendent of public instruction.

Condon may have campaigned hard, but she won partly because

she was swept in on a Democratic landslide. This meant that in office, she was politically in good company with newly elected folks like Governor Bonner and Attorney General Olsen. Bonner commended her for acquiring more money for Indian schools, for making progress in the school lunch program, and in general streamlining her department. The SPI can be on contentious footing with members of the Board of Education because the SPI is elected while the board members are all appointed by the governor. But here too, Condon seemed to have plenty of allies. This would prove important when it came to decisions on accreditation, because it was only a matter of time before Mary Condon began to turn her attention to the Hi-Line schools west of Havre.

Gildford District #20 ran afoul with the state again during the late 1940s for offenses such as incomplete reporting or a science teacher lacking necessary credentials. The district not only solved these shortcomings, but added a myriad of physical upgrades to the building,[3] all on recommendations from William King, the new state high school advisor. These changes were important, perhaps imperative, but they would become back issues behind the major concern creeping up on Gildford: the number of students attending the school.

The farms on the Hi-Line after the end of the war were increasingly large, all requiring fewer families with the family size itself decreasing. School numbers were bound to drop: in 1936, for example the student enrollment in Gildford had been forty; by 1950 it would be down to twenty-four. Neighboring towns Hingham and Kremlin experienced similar downturns. Inverness, on the west end of these troubled schools, was so small that the people there considered closing it down. This was bad news because to remain in the good graces of the state, a school needed to have an ANB of twenty-five students. It looked as if Gildford, Hingham, Kremlin, and Inverness would never again be able to meet that standard.

Mary Condon, along with a host of others, looked at these statistics and became more than a little concerned. She began to think the best solution might be a form of consolidation, but was not yet set on that position. In magazine articles she was quoted as saying that in some cases schools might have to consolidate but that decision *"always rested with the local school board"* (italics added). In another statement she said, "Montana does not have a planned program of school district consolidation as do many states in the United States today. School district consolidation and reorganization *is a matter left to local communities"* (italics added). That was her stand for now: the state superintendent and Board of Education were not to push local jurisdictions to either close or consolidate.

But as she conferred with members of her staff and members of the Board of Education, increasingly it made sense for this string of villages along Highway 2 to form one school. After all, they weren't that far from each other; they weren't *isolated.* If it were a school like Jordan out in Garfield County, or Ekalaka down in Carter County—towns that were truly isolated—if attendance numbers in those towns fell below the standard, then the state would have to live with it; the kids had nowhere else to go. But in Hill County, beginning with Kremlin, it was ten miles west to Gildford, another six to Hingham, six again to Rudyard, and finally another six miles to Inverness. From Kremlin to Inverness was twenty-eight miles. Maybe one school wasn't enough for the area; maybe there should be two schools, but Condon and the board were moving to the sentiment that they could no longer live with the situation as it presently stood.

It came down to cost. A recent study compared cost per pupil in the five Hi-Line schools separately with four other Montana schools, each with roughly the same number of students as the five Hi-Line schools combined. By consolidating, the new school would cut costs by over half. On teacher salaries alone, the savings would be $200 per pupil. These were numbers that confirmed what Condon and others were already thinking. Of course a new school would have to be built. And the new district would have to purchase a bus; Kremlin and Gildford presently had no buses. But these additions were just hallmarks of progress and would pay for themselves over a relatively short period of time. The parents and everyone in the area should appreciate the kids having a much better education.

The school leaders among the five schools seemed to lean in that direction before the study was made. In the early spring of 1950, a series of community conferences over the "solution of the high school situation" were held in Hingham. In the final meeting, the planning committee members agreed that the biggest problems were "steadily decreasing enrollment and increasing cost of education." The State Board looked on the proceedings with rapt approval and promised any help if needed. Condon followed with her own encouragement: in a letter dated February 2, 1950, to the Hill County Commissioners, she expressed appreciation for the "independent study" of the school crisis and encouraged "adjustments" to "increase efficiency" in secondary schools. But again she repeated that "the matter is entirely up to the people of Hill County." She went on to suggest experts in education who would lend a valuable hand in the study.

On February 16, the school boards for Hingham, Gildford, and Kremlin presented a resolution. They agreed that "something of a constructive nature must be done. Be it further resolved: It is the consensus of this group that the *said communities consolidate into one high school,* the exact place to be determined later" (italics added).

Everyone in 1950, if not happily, seemed to be on the same page. The state was "heartily in sympathy" with the Hi-Line taking time to find the best solution for consolidation. But the relationship between the two sides had now changed. No longer did the state consider consolidation a thoughtful option. It had become the *only* option and the leaders of the three schools had a year to come up with a final plan. The locals had to ask the state to allow them to operate as they were for the coming year—a petition which was granted.

By the end of 1951, however, the five schools had still not come up with a consolidation plan, so Condon and the board turned up the heat. On March 6, 1952, Hingham and Gildford were placed on "terminal probation"; in other words by the following year, both schools would be dropped from accreditation (Inverness was already without accreditation). But there was one from Hingham who would not allow this to happen. He would stand up, do the state's bidding, and oil the road for consolidation. His name was George Spicher.

Spicher (pronounced *Spiker*) was the mayor of Hingham and one, many would say later, who was ahead of his time. For example, he had city water in Hingham long before neighboring towns did. As Lloyd Curfman would say, "If he didn't have a dollar today, he would take action and worry about money later. That is the way he lived, the way he ran his business and he was successful." He loved to debate, could see both sides of an issue, and he was not shy about his opinions. Some in other towns considered him to be a problem maker, but he could make his point without being contentious. In truth, he was likable; in Hingham, with his brother Rodney alongside, he was the leader, the town spokesman, and became squarely behind consolidation. He had good reason to feel this way; the enrollment numbers for the schools continued to decline. Kremlin had twenty-one students, Gildford nineteen, Hingham twenty-three, Rudyard forty-seven, and Inverness a hopeless eight. Spicher told the press on March 14, "There is nothing else that can be done. We must consolidate our schools, or face the unalterable fact that our children will have no high schools to attend next fall."

On March 20, in Hingham, a mass meeting was held, and every local who could get in was there. Even Condon attended with her administrative assistant, C.R. Anderson in tow. Two plans came out of the meeting: one would have Hingham and Gildford merging with the school in Gildford. The other plan promoted by Spicher and the Hingham people would combine all five schools into a single institution. In fact Spicher knew the perfect place for the school, about half way between Gildford and Hingham on old Highway 2. At the conclusion, as Mary Condon said goodbye and walked out the door; she must have felt encouraged. Even if the single-school plan wasn't adopted, the merger of Hingham and Gildford was enough. Rudyard had enough students, and Kremlin, on the east end, was considered "isolated." It looked like real progress was being made.

But in Gildford, reality set in; for many it had never gone away. They were thinking, "We are gaining the whole world but we are going to lose our soul. And what is that soul? It is our school. We don't have much but we have our little school and we have our basketball team. That's right! We are the Gildford Broncs, who have been battling all these many years the Hingham Rangers, the Kremlin Foxes, the Rudyard Panthers, the Chester Coyotes, and all the rest, and we have a young crop of kids coming up, the best we've ever seen, and we have a chance to beat these Kremlins, these Hinghams, these Rudyards, and not only that, we can for the first time win District 11 and move on to the next level,……but then…..but then……. we were going play them but now, WE ARE GOING BE *THEM!!* There will be a new school with a faceless, generic name, new colors, a stupid new mascot nobody wants; now you tell me, is this right? *IS IT??* The roads around here are poor, don't have good drainage, and it is tough enough for some kids to get to school as it is, and we don't have buses so the parents will have to drive the kids even farther to school. Or if we buy a new bus, some kids will be on that bus for hours. We won't have our school anymore so maybe people will want to shop near the new school and our businesses will dry up. What will become of us? *What will happen to Gildford?*"

The controversy became more mired as the months went by. Rudyard had shown some interest in consolidation, but the new school would have to be in Rudyard. After all, the school was more than twice as large as any of the others; if Rudyard wanted to stand on its own, it didn't have to worry about losing accreditation. Hingham wanted to have one combined school, a school near Hingham of course. Gildford showed more signs of not wanting to consolidate with anyone, while Kremlin and Inverness couldn't be thrilled about a new school far away from them.

Meanwhile Condon continued to harden in her position. For her it was consolidation or nothing. When talk turned to physical upgrades in buildings, she had said, "While improvements to buildings are good, a building alone does not a school make." The emotional changes, the identities through sports, the very identity of the town, the ability to improve the school in all the other areas; none of this meant anything to Condon. She said she was willing to close schools, if necessary to force kids to go to another school. A new bigger school would give the kids a better education; it was so obvious to her; why couldn't the people understand?

Meanwhile, George Spicher aside, leaders along the Hi-Line were hardening in *their* stance; the Hill County Planning Committee held several meetings and by June 20, voted on five plans: a single school, five schools remaining separate, and various configurations in between. Of the 300 people who attended, 296 wanted to keep the five schools.

On July 14, a forty person delegation led by Fred Mundy of Gildford, the man of flour-mill renown and former state senator, came to Helena to see Mary Condon and members of the board. These people had come from the June 20 meeting and made clear they wanted to keep their schools; they felt they had a right to keep their schools. Several people talked about how bad the roads were; rancher Fred Schmidt from Box Elder said a new irrigation project on the Marias River covering 127,000 acres would bring additional families to the area, and Mundy said "All we want is fair deal and have our schools accredited."

Condon responded that this was "just an attempt to use political pressure in an election year" (Condon was running for re-election against Elizabeth Ireland, and once again would claim victory in a close race). The spirited delegation defense swayed several members of the board who would have placed Hingham and Gildford on probation for another year. But Condon would have none of it. She insisted that Hingham and Gildford would not be opened the following fall, and that there would be space for the students in Rudyard and Kremlin. Her parting shot was, "It is up to the people what you want to do."

The members of the Board of Education were hardly monolithic in outlook. Two members, G.A. Bosley of Great Falls, and Genevieve Chambers from Cut Bank, who lived closer to the Hi-Line, tended to be more sympathetic to the schools' cause. In addition, with the 1952 elections, Montana now had a new governor, Hugo Aronson, a Republican from Shelby, and a man who would generally find himself crossing swords with Condon. In that July 14 meeting, the board had voted 7-2 to give Hingham and Gildford one more year of terminal probation ending in the spring of 1953. Condon was one of the two no votes.

But Mary Condon had arrows in her quiver the others did not: her staff members had visited the schools and presented Condon with knowledge and opinions the board members were not yet privy to. And traditionally in Montana, board members usually followed the recommendations of the superintendent of public instruction. As the months rolled into 1953 it was clear the Hi-Line was not going to bow to consolidation. So the board would have to take the next step and Condon would have her way.

On March 23, 1953, at 9:30 a.m. the board met in special session in the Governor's Reception Room in Helena with the meeting called to order by Governor Hugo Aronson. The secretary called roll with the following board members present: Emmett Riley, Merritt Warden, Clarence Popham, Genevieve Petro, G.A. Bosley, George Lund, Genevieve Chambers, Horace Dwyer, Attorney General Olsen, Governor Aronson, and Condon. The minutes of the previous meeting were amended and approved as amended. The chair appointed the following committee to review requisitions for capital items and authority for out-of-state travel. At 10:00 a.m., the chairman requested the secretary to open sealed bids for general and sub construction of the new Men's Residence Hall at Montana State College. At 11:15 there was a fifteen-minute recess. When the board reassembled, Governor

Aaronson advised that Lieutenant Governor Gosman would preside at the afternoon session in his place, as he was leaving the state. From then on, before and after lunch and on through the afternoon, the board waded through a series of issues: a report on the Miles City Industrial School; the resignation of a member of the Board of Examiners and his replacement; dues for membership of the Association of Governing Boards; and a host of other topics.

And finally the last subject of the day: the continuing problem with the schools on the Hi-Line. After discussion, "On motion of Mr. Popham and seconded by Mr. Lund and carried, the board approved the removal of Hingham, Kremlin, Rudyard, and Gildford from the accredited list." Only Bosley voted no. Then Lund moved "that the districts of Inverness, Rudyard, Hingham, Gildford, and Kremlin be informed that the Board of Education will give consideration to accreditation of a consolidated program for a high school district embracing the above-named districts on or before the June 1953 meeting of this board." Again Bosley voted no. The date for the next board meeting was April 13, the motions duly made, seconded, and carried and the board adjourned at 5:30 p.m.

The deed was done.

In and Out of Prison

THE BOARD HAD BLATANTLY OVERREACHED. HIGH SCHOOL SUPER-visor, Bill King, the man who actually inspected the schools, had advised that only Gildford lose accreditation and now four schools were taken out. The most egregious action was against Rudyard. When the people in Rudyard sought reasons from the State Board why it was dropped, no one would give them an answer. Rudyard had nearly fifty students, was in fine shape according to King, and had never been put on any preliminary level of warning.

The Hill County Planning Board held a meeting in Gildford on April 7, with the school boards and other interested parties from the five schools in attendance. The participants were up in arms that the state was being arbitrary, and that the lack of accreditation, the with-holding of state and county funds, was in effect closing the schools. The state people were forcing the Hi-Line to do their bidding rather than trying to work out a compromise with consideration for the needs and wants of the people in the communities. Hill County requested a meeting with the state in the next couple of weeks to try to work toward some kind of dialogue.

That meeting was held in Havre on April 28. "At the suggestion of Mary Condon," the Board of Education stressed that the SPI and board "have no intention of granting accreditation......If some plan of consolidation is not submitted to the State Department of Public Instruction by May 15." If the plan was submitted, the state would review it by May 27. Otherwise, the state would not come to Hill County "merely to listen to pleas of residents of the districts."

The state had clarified its position, now the Hill County Planning Board decided to clarify the wishes of the people in the five districts. A special poll was to be taken among the people in each of the five districts with three questions:

- Do you favor one consolidated school?
- Do you prefer two high schools even if you might have to give up your own?
- Do you favor a high school in each town?

The ballots also contained this statement: "You should understand that as far as the State Department of Public Instruction and the State Board of Education are concerned, if there is no consolidation, there will be no accreditation for the schools involved and subsequently no state or county funds authorized for the operation of the high schools."

The vote was taken and these were the results:

- Inverness: For one high school 15, for two high schools 45, for five high schools 87.
- Rudyard: For one high school 2, for two high schools 77, for five high schools 80.
- Hingham: For one high school 124, for two high schools 11, for five high schools 60.
- Gildford: For one high school 4, for two high schools 18, for five high schools 155.
- Kremlin: For one high school 13, for two high schools 16, for five high schools 151.

The people on the Hi-Line had spoken. Hingham, with Spicher and others behind him, continued to push for one school with the school close to them since they were the centerpiece in the string of towns. Many in Rudyard were happy with a school in their town that included Inverness. But except for Hingham, all the towns overwhelmingly wanted the schools just as they always had been. The lines had been drawn.

A carefully crafted letter by Rudyard merchant Morris Ewald, displayed in various newspapers on April 13, was sent to Governor Aronson. The letter listed fourteen reasons why the state should not go through with consolidation. Among the reasons was the destruction of the family, turning neighbor against neighbor, but also because the Tibor Dam was being built, and this would bring in a significant number of families. The letter must have worked: the governor sent out an announcement that the SPI, the State Board of Education and the Hill County Planning Commission that included the five high schools would meet again on June 15 at the Havre High School auditorium. At that meeting the governor made the point that he had to be gone from the afternoon portion of the March 23 meeting. Had he been there, he likely would have gone along with Bosley in voting against taking away accreditation. Some good came from the Havre meeting: following a "heated discussion," Rudyard and Kremlin were re-accredited largely on the personal survey of High School Advisor King. The two schools had "improved their school administration and in general qualified for a higher state rating." One suspects this was a cover. There was no way Rudyard should have had its accreditation removed. As for Kremlin, all along it had been considered isolated, at the eastern end of the string. The other three schools continued to be refused accreditation, with Inverness "shelved entirely."

WERE THE CONDITIONS AT KREMLIN HIGH REALLY THAT MUCH DIF-ferent than those in Gildford? Possibly, but there is strong evidence that the battle between the state and Gildford, was as much personal as political. One person told me Condon grabbed one Gildford board member, Murvin Hanson, by the tie to get her point across. This seems unlikely considering the nature of the man, but for Condon and the board, the members of the school board in Gildford were a thorn in the posterior.

Gildford always had three members on its school board at any one time. When the school was without accreditation, the total number of people who served on the board over four years was four. In the beginning, the members were Thomas (Bud) Toner, Leonard Grimes, and Ruth Tew. Later on Toner was replaced on the board by Murvin Hanson. There is general agreement that no one person dominated the board, and yet some people seem to think the members varied in their being up to the task. In fact, under normal circumstances, they might not have worked particularly well together. But now, under crisis, they were forced into common purpose. This is commendable because they came from significantly different backgrounds.

Bud Toner was on the school board for a total of twelve years, leaving in the mid-1950s and coming back to serve again into the 1960s. Like many who lived in and around Gildford, he did not have an easy life. His father died from cancer when he was a boy; at age seventeen, he moved out from Minnesota to live with his uncle. He farmed north of Gildford, married a woman with three children and then together they nurtured five more of their own. He was well-liked in Gildford and active in the community. John Campbell, who knew Toner well, said he and Toner were in the volunteer fire department together; many times, the two of them were the only ones out on a call. Because of circumstances, Toner never made it past the eighth grade, but his daughter, Lynn Hayden, said he was constantly educating himself. As she said, "He was a font of information; you could ask him any question and he could tell you the answer or fool you into thinking he knew the answer. He would have remembered everything no matter how old it got." She went on to say that he never talked about people. He might get mad at someone but was not one to talk about it. He tried to be above the fray.

Toner remained on the school board for two more years and when his term was up gave way to Murvin Hanson. Any discussion of Hanson must begin with an unusual family arrangement he became part of as a young man. His older brother Orville had gone off to Spokane for barber school and while there, met a young woman from Idaho whom he subsequently married. Murvin traveled to Spokane to visit his brother, met the new wife's sister and married her. And *then* the brothers' younger sister Lillian made the trip to Spokane, met the wives' brother and married *him*. So if you want to play loose with semantics, you could say the combined offspring are triple cousins.

Orville and Murvin came back to Gildford to live; Orville became a barber as he had intended, but managed at the same time to run the post office, help his dad on the farm, even to become co-owner of an insurance business. In that capacity, he would later on become critical to the school. Murvin had graduated from college at Northern Montana and for four years taught and coached at Gildford. But his father needed him on the farm, so for the remainder of the time he was in Gildford would help manage the property.

People disagree on his view of the accreditation issue and how it formed his feelings as to where he fit in with the community. His daughter said he was for consolidation and, because of his position, felt ostracized by the people in Gildford. It was the motivation for the family moving to Arizona. She went on to say that he ran for the legislature in the late fifties but lost because he was a staunch Republican. Curfman said no to all of this; Hanson fought valiantly to have Gildford's accreditation restored and to have the school remain independent. He and others say the reason the Hanson family moved to Arizona (after he lost the election) was that they had wintered there, his wife became involved in a business, and it made good sense for the family to move. Also they had a son, Levi, who was a near-genius, and they decided he needed the type of schooling Gildford could not possibly offer. And if he lost the election, it was for reasons other than his political stance. The Hi-Line had plenty of Republicans. More likely Hanson lost because beforehand he did not have enough political exposure.

The general consensus seems to be that people thought highly of Hanson; he was well regarded by former students who had him when he was a teacher and a coach. He was intelligent and capable; while he was in Gildford he was chair of the Hill County Soil Conservation Board, the Crop Improvement Association, and secretary-treasurer of the Gildford Farmers' Cooperation, as well as being active in his church. After he moved to Arizona, he became the president of the Tucson Chamber of Commerce. As we have seen, his son was brilliant, graduated years early from college, and became an engineer. His daughter became a successful businesswoman in Arizona. He was the man of reason who could bring minds together on the board. Which makes it more untenable that Condon would grab him by the tie and give it a healthy jerk. Some said he could lose his temper and it is possible that, in dealing with the state, he did not always keep his lid on, but generally he was the man who helped keep the board on an even keel.

Leonard Grimes served on the school board for eleven years beginning in 1952. He was married with four daughters and farmed south of Gildford on the way to Box Elder. I have a photo of him with other members of the school board; he appears as a rather large man with regal enough bearing. But he remains a mystery to me because opinions of him run all over the map. His daughter, Marilyn Wolery, said he was kind and others, concerning his daughters, would more than agree. To their consternation he was protective of his daughters to a fault; they might generate problems but in his eyes they could do no wrong. One said Grimes could be stubborn; another that he was easy going but would get himself into predicaments others could avoid, get into accidents because he didn't take necessary precautions.

Wolery agreed her father was easy going and normally enjoyed being on the school board. He had become good friends with Lloyd Curfman, who came on the Board in 1958. Curfman said Grimes was good to work with on the board; that he was fair. Campbell thought Grimes and Hanson would have had "equal leadership skills." But Wolery said the accreditation issue was a different experience for him. The pressure, the confrontations, and the trips to Helena put Grimes under stress. When he was dealing with accreditation he was a different man.

Which leaves the remaining member of the school board, a

woman, who I would say, far outflanks the others for sheer interest. Ruth Tew had a background nothing like any of her peers. She was born Ruth Moore in Brookfield, Illinois, a suburb of Chicago, in 1907, a child with two older brothers. Little is known of her father except that he was "a drinker." Her mother was hardnosed. When Ruth was in her thirties, married and ill, her mother came out to care for Ruth's kids. Lawrence, the only surviving child, remembers his grandmother "being mean" (but for some reason not to him) and "very strict." When Ruth was young, she was made to practice the piano; the house was kept cold so Ruth had to rub oil on her hands to keep them warm.

The structure in the home must have benefited Tew to a degree, because she sailed through the University of Chicago, eventually getting an M.A. at that institution in both English and math. After graduation, with little deliberation, Tew hopped a train to Montana. It might not be unusual, even in those times, for a bright young college graduate to run off on a travel venture. What is curious, almost unsettling, is that for no good reason she disembarked in Box Elder and once there lived as if she had never been anywhere else. She taught in Box Elder for six years and met a young cowpuncher, Kenneth Flatness, whom she would marry, who never even finished high school "because everyone was poor in the thirties." Flatness ran the family ranch and worked part-time in coal mines near the Bears Paw Mountains. He also got on the rodeo circuit, because that is what all his brothers did. On July 5, 1942, he was killed in a rodeo accident; the horse turned over on its back and crushed him.

He and Ruth had been married for eight years. She was widowed with four young children, struggling to cope. She accepted a job teaching in Geraldine, a small village a hundred miles south of Gildford. She had been there two years when Gildford rancher Melvin Tew arrived in Geraldine, stepped into her life, and the two would soon marry, a marriage of convenience. Melvin needed a wife, and Ruth was "starving to death." The Geraldine School District didn't have much money.

Life should have been easier; Melvin was a good businessman. He managed to stay afloat during the Great Depression when others couldn't. During that time he purchased approximately four thousand acres for fifty cents an acre; others couldn't pay their taxes so Melvin lapped up their farms, turning the additional land into a large sheep ranch. When the children were still young, the ranch was already paid off.

According to his step-son, Lawrence Flatness, Melvin "worked hard and was an honest man," but over time developed a problem with alcohol. He could go off and be gone for weeks. Sometimes, Lawrence remembered, he just sat in his pickup drinking whiskey. It was tough on Ruth with a husband drinking all the time. She worked on the ranch long hours until she was deadly tired. Melvin thought all food should come from the ranch so they kept a huge garden and during certain months canned all the food. The task was made infinitely more difficult in the early years because there was no electricity until Lawrence was six years old. Meanwhile Ruth was raising four young children from her first marriage plus another son with Melvin. After the birth of her fifth child, she came down with cervical cancer, another battle she was forced to win. It seemed Ruth Tew was living the exact opposite lifestyle one would have expected from a rising star out of the University of Chicago. All this time Tew might have taken a teaching job but in her grasp of priorities, the children came first; even when the first four kids were in high school, she taught only as a substitute.

It was proper that Tew concentrated on her children, but Gildford High was deprived of an exceptional teacher. When she finally did teach full-time after her first three children graduated, she became the favorite of many students. Tew could have a sense of humor if the situation called for it, but generally she was no-nonsense. If a student did or said something stupid, she would embarrass him. Lynn Hayden remembered that Ruth had a sarcasm about her, "Whooh! If you gave an answer that was not even close, she could make you feel like you were two cents." She was stern, Hayden said, "but she really taught you. I had a great respect for Ruth." When the kids left high school, they knew math; they could write essays. If the students got less than a great education elsewhere at Gildford High, in her classes, they had a first-rate preparation for college.

At home, Tew was more relaxed in the upbringing of her own children, but she had her ways and moments. She believed her children should be called by their formal names: Kenneth, David, and Lawrence. One day Lawrence informed his mother he had a chance to play football if he switched to Havre High School. Flatness was muscular, tough as nails. The Havre football coach, who was also the JV basketball coach, saw him at a JV game and after the game asked him,

"What are you doing down here?"

Flatness asked, "What do you mean?"

"You need to come to Havre and play football."

Flatness had really never played football, but he was ready to go. When he told his mother, Ruth "went through the roof." Her good friend's son had a serious injury; he had been a musician, and when he was hurt in football, he could never play his instrument again. Lawrence kept after her for two or three years to let him go; he even had someone lined up to stay with, but Tew would have none of her son playing football.

Tew was capable of public tongue lashings, as well. One target was John Campbell, co-owner of Campbell's Store. Books, comic books, and magazines were included in the many categories of merchandise Campbell sold in his store; when distributors brought the materials to the store, he and his mother would ferret through them to make sure no inappropriate literature reached the racks. But apparently they didn't weed hard enough. One day Tew came in angry; one of her sons purchased a book from the store she deemed off-color. Campbell said she "really gave him a talking to." But mostly, he said, "she was a wonderful person." She was likable, respected, even beloved by the people in Gildford.

Again, one description at the top of the list by those who knew her is that she was "exceptional." Flatness said she was the smartest person he had ever known. Tew may not have measured up to Mary Condon in subtleties, but she was probably just as smart. Of all the accolades Tew received over the years, the one that may have carried the most weight (although Tew was certainly never aware of it) came from none other than Mary Condon herself. In a letter to one of the board members, Genevieve Petro, Condon fumed, "Mrs. Tew has been without question the most difficult person to work with I have ever known." If Ruth Tew had not had time to be a full-time school teacher while her kids were in school, she made time to be on the school board and she came to make a difference.

Condon went on to say in that letter, "The Hingham board has been considerably more reasonable and cooperative." Of course, many of the people in Hingham wanted consolidation and those in Gildford did not, but regardless, Mary Condon and Ruth Tew were two bobcats in a burlap sack. Lawrence said his mother "told off Mary Condon; us kids were kind of proud of that." At that April 13 meeting, according to the newspapers, Tew "angrily" laid out seven ways the folks in Gildford had improved their school.

She and the other board members were angry because they were frustrated. Edmund G. Toomey, the attorney who represented the Hill County schools, had said, "No Montana state law compels us to consolidate or close down our schools. Consolidation is just a guinea-pig experiment against the Hi-Line districts." But Gildford could legally be without accreditation. On June 15 the Board of Education met in Havre, and this time on a motion made by Mrs. Chambers and seconded by G.A. Bosley, the board was asked to reconsider its action on March 23. The recorded vote on this motion "reveals that there were two 'Ayes' and eight 'noes'. The motion did not carry." On March 23, 1954, exactly one year from when the accreditation was first taken away, the three schools applied for accreditation and were again turned down. Condon wrote to the Gildford school board, saying, "No evidence was presented concerning improvement of conditions in the high school, to enable the board to make a decision. Your letter merely stated that you met all standards, for which no evidence or specific data were supplied." Condon went on to say that if Gildford wanted the High School Supervisor King to come inspect the school, King would need to visit with "specific information" from the school that he can verify. On May 20, the Gildford school board fired off a letter saying they were ready for the inspection. King completed the inspection but after his own diagnosis, on June 17, the board voted to leave the three schools non-accredited.

Such was life in a non-accredited school. Condon had told administrators at Hingham that the schools should consolidate because with the current education the kids were receiving, they would not do well in college. This scare caused one father to transfer his daughter to Rudyard so she would be accepted by the Northern Montana College of Nursing. In Gildford, Jack Fried remembered having to take extra exams to be accepted at Montana State College. In Missoula, the University of Montana traditionally awarded a scholarship to the graduate of every school in Montana with the highest grades, but Marcella Kocar, who achieved this distinction in Hingham, was not given this scholarship until her sophomore year. In fact, when she went to Missoula for her first year, she was put on probation for a quarter to prove she could handle higher education. These roadblocks did not stop students in these non-accredited schools from progressing. Of the seven graduates from Hingham in 1955, four (including Kocar) received advanced degrees in college. Kocar became a professor of teachers' education with several schools, including University of Central Michigan, where she retired. Of her fellow students, Darryl Patrick became a professor of fine arts, Carole Brennan received a master's degree and became an elementary teacher, and Bob Chvilichek had no trouble getting into Carroll College and eventually received his Ph.D. in education. These kids would prove that where there was a will, there were several ways.

Basketball was a different matter. On September 10, 1953, the Montana High School Association laid down the rule that accredited schools could no longer play non-accredited schools. Arden Vie, the superintendent of Chester High School was given "warning" that "the rules would be enforced." If Chester or some other accredited school failed to heed the rule, they "would no longer be able to participate in interscholastic sports." Gildford, Hingham, and Inverness were now reduced to playing each other or an oddball conglomeration of other teams. They would play Coutts, just over the border into Alberta; or Hogeland and Turner, two tiny schools northeast of Chinook and a good distance away. They would play the Great Falls DeMolay or the Havre High B squad, or really any team that would accept them as an opponent.

In late October, the MHSA held a meeting with representatives of the District 11 schools in good standing and modified their relationship to the three unaccredited schools "slightly." The eight surviving members could still play the non-accredited schools but they had to schedule each other first. In other words they had to schedule fourteen games before they could think about "outsiders." Same with the mid-season Hi-Line tournament, which had been around for thirty years and was the event people looked forward to all year more than just about anything. It took place before or after Christmas, and was a major social event; everyone got to run into people they hadn't seen all year. The MHSA said this about the Hi-Line Tourney: the member teams would reserve three nights first and the non-members essentially could pick up the scraps if there were any left at all. This ruling, even though modified, ruined the Hi-Line tournament. The next January 1954, only five teams entered; by the next year it was gone.

Of course the three beleaguered schools could still no longer participate in the District 11 tournament. Paul Preeshl, who had the bad fortune of spending his four years at Gildford High during the four years the school was unaccredited, was bitter about his experience. There were kids there who had talent, teams that were good, or good enough, but it didn't matter. At Gildford, Hingham, and Inverness, the kids were never going to have the chance to shine in an arena where the shine meant something.

If the three schools couldn't be in District 11, well, they would just have to form their own little event promoted as the Sage Creek Invitational Round Robin Tournament. Sponsored by the Hi-Line High School Confederacy, the inaugural event commenced on January 29, 1954, at the Hingham gym with four teams invited: Gildford, Hingham, Inverness, and the Havre Colts (Havre High School JVs). The Colts, for some reason, bowed out so in their place came the Christian Youth Organization from Shelby. Gildford easily won the Round Robin with Paul Preeshl, Kenneth Flatness, and most of all, Dick Crites, who was the overall top scorer with 66 points in three games. The tourney results and photos were splashed all over the front page of the *Liberty County Times*. It is unclear whether this outpouring was due to strong support or sympathy, because the coverage the following year, in 1955, was dramatically scaled back to a small article at the bottom of an inside page (Coutts from Alberta won that tournament).

This not allowing schools to be a part of normal sports was beginning to create untidy complications. In February 1955, Ray Peck, superintendent of Hingham High sued the MHSA to allow the Rangers to play in the district tournament. Quickly, District Judge E. B. Elwell from Havre issued a restraining order against the MHSA. Because of this, the district tournament was forced to be rescheduled a week later which in a domino effect threw back the Northern Division tournament a week as well. On the eve of the District 11 tourney, the restraining order was dissolved and Hingham was denied the right to play in the tournament.

Gildford decided not to follow Hingham into the courts specifically for sports but long before in the summer of 1954, all three schools had had it up to their chins with the state thumbing its nose at them. They would each head to court to restore their accreditation. On August 31, Case #10634 was filed with Gildford District #20 and school board members Leonard Grimes, Murvin Hanson, and Ruth Tew as the plaintiffs, being represented by attorneys Edmund J. Toomey and Michael J. Hughes. The defendants were Mary Condon as Superintendent of Public Instruction; all members of the State Board of Education (even the "good" ones); The Public School Equalization Board; Attorney General Arnold Olsen; State Auditor John J. Holmes; State Treasurer Edna Hinman; even Governor Hugo Aronson. For good measure, defendants included the Hill County SPI, the Hill County Treasurer, and the Hill County Commissioners. The three schools were not against everyone, rather the "latter officials being named so as to bring all the parties before the court." The case was to take place in Havre with District Judge E.B. Elwell again presiding on the bench. The state didn't feel comfortable with Elwell, thought him too sympathetic with the local folks and so had him disqualified. In November, the case was moved to Conrad, where it would be decided by the judge of the Ninth District Court, Judge R M Hattersley.

In the opening statement, Gildford included a fallback position: if the school couldn't get accreditation, it at least should get its levy money back; after all it was Gildford's money! As Rodney Spicher, President of the Hingham School Board, concurrently asking the same thing for Hingham maintained in a letter to the state, "We do not ask any money from the State; we are merely attempting to secure the money raised within the boundaries of our school district." The case would drag on for nearly five years, with the judgment, made on May 29, 1959, awarding Gildford its levy money.

But Gildford and the other schools didn't have to wait that long. On March 13, 1955, a bill permitting non-accredited schools to share in county levies was signed into law by Governor Aronson. The

Board of Education had opposed the bill, saying it would "take the teeth out of the entire school accrediting system." But the bill had wide, almost universal support; it passed the House 75-4 and cleared the Senate 53-0. The message was clear; sympathies around the state were swinging toward the three schools.

By the spring of 1955, Ruth Tew was president of the school board. No doubt encouraged by passage of the bill, which meant Gildford now had county levy money and, with a little more out of local pockets, could at least survive; the Gildford School Board decided once more to take on Mary Condon and apply for accreditation. In a letter dated May 16, Gildford petitioned to be reinstated beginning July 1. The school board maintained that the school had undergone a complete makeover both inside and out, adding critical equipment and instructional materials.

The district had pulled out all the stops; what more could it do? The school board was itching to get someone back over for talks and an inspection, so anxious in fact that when the Board of Education was planning a meeting in Miles City, Tew sent a telegram that the three schools were making available a light plane to have the members flown to Havre. Understanding that the Board of Education was receiving a lot of flak from the public for its rigid stance on the Hi-Line, one board member Genevieve Petro, sent a letter to Condon suggesting that the board should at least visit the schools. But Petro also claimed that Condon was getting a lot of "unfair criticism because it's repeatedly stated 'The Board hasn't even been here—they just do what Miss Condon says.'" Petro went on to say she had not changed her opinion on consolidation. Petro lived on a ranch in the southeast corner of the state and knew isolation; she had little sympathy for these schools she deemed close to each other. She thought the special plane trip would be too expensive (it is unclear who was paying for the trip).

On June 7, Condon replied to Petro. Hingham had made great improvements and was close to meeting the standard for Average Number Belonging. She suggested this: Rudyard form a district to include Inverness and other outlying areas. A new district could be centered in Hingham that would include Gildford, and Kremlin, while it has a low ANB is twenty miles from Havre and sixteen miles from Hingham; it is isolated and should remain an independent district. As for Gildford, she saw no reason for board members to waste their time visiting buildings; King and his assistant Mr. Tindall had already visited Gildford. "We have 175 high schools in Montana—if the Board of Education is going to do an on-the-spot of one, every other school in the state has the right to expect the same degree of attention." Although Gildford had made some educational improvements, it had fewer than twenty students with no prospect for increase. Gildford, she decided, should be linked up either with Hingham or Kremlin because she could see no basis for accrediting Gildford.

Condon added that the law[4] was very plain on accreditation: the state has educational standards and the schools must meet those standards. Condon dismissed giving the people on the Hi-Line a hearing: "These people have had innumerable hearings during the last six years, and that roughly 90 percent of the Board's time spent on accreditation has been devoted to the Hi-Line situation." Condon spoke of one man who was led to believe the people on the Hi-Line had been ignored. "This is typical of the type of unfair and dishonest campaign Mrs. Tew and company have been carrying on." It was in this letter that Condon spoke of Tew as the most difficult person to work with she had ever known.

Not surprisingly, on June 18 the Board of Education once again voted to refuse reaccreditation to Hingham and Gildford. *The Havre Daily News* had reported, "The chairman of the Gildford High School Board, Mrs. Ruth Tew, made a personal plea.….Mrs. Tew said Gildford's teachers are trained well. It had a model sports field under way and a shop building planned." But was the board, led by Mary Condon, going to listen to Ruth Tew? The situation for Gildford looked hopeless.

THERE WAS A DEVELOPMENT BREWING, HOWEVER, WHICH NO ONE could ignore: the campaigns leading to the 1956 statewide election. On the Democratic side, Condon faced a primary foe in Kathleen Ramey, a Helena teacher, who wasted no time trashing Condon on all-inclusive matters such as abusing the law, wasting money, neglect of teachers and students—egregious shortcomings that anyone would find difficult to pin on the conscientious superintendent. In her litany of complaints, Ramey said nothing about accreditation or consolidation.

The Republicans offered Jean Crockett who was unquestionably sympathetic to the plight of the Hi-Line schools. She hailed from Chinook, only thirty miles east of Havre, and for eighteen years had been a member of both the Chinook high school and elementary school faculty. She promised to work for a host of improvements in Montana schools, "*regardless of size* (italics added)." She "promised to *leave control of the schools, as often as possible, in the hands of people who support those schools with their taxes* (italics added)." No opinion of Mary Condon was ever recorded by Ruth Tew, at least not in the newspapers, but in this case, she promoted the actions of others to be her voice; she was named chairwoman of the "Crockett for Superintendent" committee for Hill County.

Crockett, however, was not alone in seeking the Republican nomination. There was another woman on the horizon who had far greater visibility and chances of winning than either Crockett or Ramey. Her name was Harriet Miller and on April 18, 1956, she would file to run for the $7,500 position of superintendent of public instruction.

Harriet Miller passed away a few years ago at the age of ninety. At age eighty-one, she was still the robust mayor of Santa Barbara, California, no small accomplishment for someone of that age. Both while she was Mayor and before she took that position, she had chaired more organizations than one could care to count. Public service had always been her bailiwick; like Condon, she was in Washington, D.C. for a time as director of the American Association of Retired Persons

(AARP). President Carter appointed her to serve on the Occupational Safety and Health Review Commission (OSHA) and other federal commissions.

Unlike Condon, Miller would never marry, but at the time she was running for SPI, she was at least as photogenic. Dolores Colburg, who worked closely with Miller as an assistant and who later became superintendent of public instruction herself in the 1970s, said, "Harriet Miller was a beautiful woman who carried herself well." The newspapers often referred to her as "pretty." The *Independent Record* once said of her, "Judged by Hollywood standards......Harriet Miller probably would rate with the best of them. Although her name has never been in lights on a theater marquee and she has never been on the Jack Paar Show, there is little doubt that if she applied the same tenacity of purpose to reaching movie stardom as she has to other tasks, she'd make the grade."

But Miller was never meant for Hollywood. She was born July 4, 1919, the first Fourth of July baby in the little town of Council, Idaho. Throughout her elementary and high school years she was in a unique position: both her parents, Colwell and Vera Miller, were her teachers. "Both my mother and father were dedicated teachers," Miller would say, "They instilled in me great respect for the profession. Although I entered other fields, I always harbored a desire to become an educator."

After graduating from Meridian High School in Idaho (her father was the principal), she enrolled at Whitman College in Walla Walla, Washington, graduating *magna cum laude* with a degree in chemistry. While at Whitman, Miller obtained the Phi Beta Kappa key and was listed in *"Who's Who in American Colleges."* She also served as president of the Alpha Chi Omega sorority.

After she left Whitman, she immediately took a job in lab work, first for the government, but eventually as a research chemist for four years with the Atlantic Refinery Company in Philadelphia, where she also obtained a master's degree at the University of Pennsylvania.

"My work in Philadelphia was most interesting," she explained, "but I had a great desire to live in the West."

She had that chance when Dr. Maurine Clow, who had been dean of women at Whitman—when Miller was a student—and now assistant Dean of Women at University of Montana, offered Miller a position on her staff. Miller remained in Missoula for three years before taking a year's leave of absence to try her hand at writing. She had a keen interest in education and "formulated a long-range program which I wanted to put into operation. That is why I entered the race for state superintendent of public instruction."

Miller was brute smart, a tenacious worker who could be tough with people but was usually not outspoken like Condon was, never one for the memorable sound bite—who could rouse the crowd and steal the spotlight as Condon so ably could. But if Miller was not a wowser, neither was she controversial; in certain ways she was more politically astute, would draw back and say the right things.

She indeed said the right things, and it resonated with people because she exuded sincerity. She certainly connected with people on the Hi-Line. At a meeting in the Hingham school gymnasium, she told a large crowd, "If a community is willing to finance its school and the children are getting an adequate education, then the school should be allowed to continue. The decision to consolidate or close a school should rest with the local people. I do not favor arbitrary consolidation. I realize the consolidation issue is very near and dear to the hearts of the people of the Hi-Line. The school is the heart of the community.....I have a soft spot in my heart for small schools because I had attended a two-room school in Idaho. Bigger schools aren't always better schools."

Miller cemented her ties with the people when she warned about federal aid for education. She said, "I believe in local control of schools and local control of government; if we turn to Washington, we are asking for trouble. I think we in Montana can finance our schools here."

Miller was indefatigable in her campaign. She went to all the towns, the fairs, the rodeos, and kept reminding people she was from a small town, and fairs and rodeos were part of people who were integral to education. When she came to Havre in July, she told everyone she enjoyed being there and planned on returning for the Hill County Fair and Rodeo. Before lighting in Havre, she had just been to the Marias Fair and Rodeo in Shelby. She had gone to countless similar events all over the state.

Miller had in her favor a frosty relationship between Condon and Governor Hugo Aronson. Condon opposed Aronson's recommendation to the legislature that the Montana School Foundation be dispensed with (she succeeded in having the recommendation defeated), and her continued support of federal aid to education, something Aronson (and Miller) opposed.

But Miller still might not have won if it were not for another ally, working for self-interest of course and not so much for her but against her opponent. This was the oil industry, formidable and deep-pocketed, willing to spend $300,000 during the campaign to keep Condon and Arnold Olsen, who was running for governor against Aronson, off the land board.

Montana held to the traditional formula that two out of every thirty-six sections of land over which the state had control would be set aside for the benefit of public education. In some areas of the state, these set asides had great potential for natural resources and, altogether leased out, could bring an immense amount of money into the state coffers. The land board made the decision on how and to whom the land was leased. It had four members: the governor, attorney general, secretary of state, and superintendent of public instruction. (Today the state auditor is also on the board.)

The contention over leases in 1956 had to do with how revenues from oil drilling were divvied up between the state and the oil company. Current law at the time gave to the state royalties of 12.5 percent plus signing bonuses (first year rents) and annual rentals. Oil backers in the legislature, mostly Republicans but one notable Democrat, said the oil industry was not able to realize money out of its investment at current rents and percentage for royalties; in fact the larger oil companies were paying 17.5 percent on thirty wells and 25 percent on two wells. Oil sympathizers said the percentage didn't have to go up anyway because beginning in 1951 there was an oil boom and the state was getting plenty of money from royalties.

Olsen and Condon saw it differently, that the oil industry was getting a windfall and should be paying more. When the legislature passed a "Forever Lease" bill in 1953 maintaining present lease agreements for an indeterminate amount of time, Attorney General Olsen took the new law to court, tying it up for two years until the US Supreme Court declared it constitutional. During the campaign, Aronson said the state lost $11 million while the law was tied up in court. The Democrats said no such thing, that the oil boom was over by 1953 and that, at the most, the state was out was one million dollars.

Even though Condon was on the lands board, most of the controversy did not affect her office. Friends and advisors urged her strongly to stay out of this fight; it was Olsen's battle so let him get bloodied up. But "Mary being Mary" could not stay out of the fray. Big Oil then turned its fangs on her. They spewed in the newspapers how her actions would "thrash" the industry. "It would be a terrible thing for Montana." The powers of oil not only worked out front but behind the scenes, doing "nasty, really nasty" stuff, generating innuendos, conducting whisper campaigns. Condon would say, "First they have me sleeping with every man in town. Then they say I'm a lesbian. I say, will you make up your mind!"

With help from the oil industry, and building her own "campaign drumfire" over the lease of state oil lands, Miller defeated Condon on November 6, 1956, for the general election (Olsen was also defeated for governor). The new superintendent of public instruction followed through on her promise: when her high school advisor, Bill King, inspected Gildford and Hingham high schools, he found that "conditions at the two schools in Hill County in general complied with accreditation requirements *except* for minimum enrollment." In other words even if the two schools were below ANB requirements and had little prospect for achieving them, each could still function as an accredited school. Accreditation for the schools had been favored by Miller. She indicated "that removal from accreditation.......roused communities into action, bringing about facility improvements and opportunities." On Monday June 17, 1956, the State Board of Education met and voted to reinstate Gildford and Hingham as accredited schools. (After ten years of outer darkness, Inverness was also reinstated as an accredited school.) The long fight was over.

By 1956, the Montana High School Association relaxed its snob rule to the point that Gildford and Hingham could schedule just about any team they wanted during the season. But now, with reinstatement, they could once again enter the District 11 tournament. By this time, Havre Central was elevated to Class B, and in its place would be Inverness. There were ten teams in District 11 on the eve of the 1957-58 season: Big Sandy, Box Elder, Kremlin, Gildford, Hingham, Rudyard, Inverness, Joplin, Chester, and Oilmont. It was time to play basketball. Real basketball.

The Beginning of the Rise

CLASS C COMPRISED THE SMALLEST SCHOOLS IN MONTANA, BUT it doesn't take a rocket scientist to know that even here—and maybe more so in Class C—the playing field was never level. It could never be: some schools were merely small, others tiny, microscopic, to go extinct by the 1950s. *Sports Illustrated* came out with a short piece mid-decade spotlighting Neihart, a high school in the Little Belt Mountains that enrolled only seven students, all boys. The cheerleaders came from the elementary. I thumbed through a 1959 District 12 tournament program that included Neihart: all the other teams in the district had at least ten players. Neihart had five. If one player fouled out or was injured, the team would make do with four.[5]

In the 1953 Southern Division tournament challenge game, held in Red Lodge, Belgrade battled Sumatra for the honor of advancing to the state tournament. In 1994 my wife Judith and I drove east through one of the loneliest stretches of eastern Montana hoping to see—expecting to see—Sumatra. But when we arrived at the intended location, all we could see was more prairie. In May 2012, I again traveled through the area, this time from the opposite direction, determined to spot something, *anything*, that could prove to me Sumatra existed. I first saw Vananda with its ghostly, abandoned schoolhouse; it was all beginning to look familiar. Then I passed the tiny hamlet of Ingomar. After that, nine miles farther, I noticed a singlewide mobile-home post office on the left side of the road. Just past it was a bright green house with a smattering of outbuildings, machinery, trucks, and bales of hay. I had seen Sumatra. Then it hit

Frank Spragg

me why Judith and I had not seen Sumatra in 1994; we were looking on the wrong side of the road! At one time Sumatra had as many as 1,200 people in town, a grocery store, a bank, a church; there were still several homes there in 1953, kids coming to school not only from the little town but from ranches far away, some of them staying in Sumatra for the school year. But one by one, the buildings were all torn down or burned. The school burned down in 1965, and everything, except for the few buildings I saw had gone back to the land. From this point as far as the eye could see—in some directions you can see a very long way; the terrain is gently rolling—there was nothing betraying human interference.

During that challenge game, people in the stands felt sorry for this little team with only six players, but these boys, stock-strong, had nearly won the game (Belgrade won by one point). As isolated as they lived, the kids developed into a subculture with its own refinements. Between games, two of the players drove to Natali's restaurant in a car bedecked with a longhorn hood ornament, pulled out of the car, walked into Natali's wearing Stetsons, sat down and, in full view of opposing players, coaches, and anyone else within eyeshot, unveiled roll-your-own cigarettes, lit up, and started puffing away. When their coach was asked about this, all he could say was, "What am I supposed to do, kick 'em off?"

These "schoolets" were hardly reserved for the emptier pockets of the state. In District 8, the area in and around Gallatin Valley where I grew up, Wilsall, Clyde Park, Gardiner, and Willow Creek were the smallest schools, the eternal doormats; you could count on it as with the inevitable onset of winter. They were never going to be out of the loser's bracket in the district tournament—not last year, not next year, not ever. The same held true for the Southern Division tournament: two teams came out of District 7, that vast sparsely populated area northwest to northeast of Billings and represented by such schools as Lavina, Ryegate, Musselshell, Melstone,—and Sumatra. But these teams coming were the best of the worst. No team from District 7 had a magpie's prayer of making it to the finals. These schools were miniscule, isolated; who would want to live out there? Who would want to coach there? Consequently, they were playing against schools with four or five times their enrollment. They couldn't drop down to Class D—there was no Class D—so year after year they had to play firewood for the big boys. It wasn't fair. In an oddball way these perennial also-rans, which had only basketball, were the real winners, because they had the courage to get up for one more sucker punch when they had suffered one just the night before.

This all may be, but it was possible for one of these teams some-where in the depths of Montana to break out of the mold. For a school that tiny to win the Class C championship required a huge element of pure dumb luck. You can talk about the desire to be competitive, the will to win, the will to prepare, but the school had not the resources to serve it. The coach was powerless to generate it. He was likely the shop teacher, the English teacher pressed into action because *someone* for goodness' sake had to be the coach. He probably didn't know squat about basketball, had never had much interest, and besides, coming to this burg was just a beginning before something better came along. Coaches in these small towns were notorious for moving on after a year or even in the middle of the year.

Merely having five talented players—if the coach was lucky to have five—was usually not enough. Where were the substitutes? An opponent with an enrollment of 125 students could afford to throw in fresh blood during a game, maybe not the best blood, but good enough to contain the enemy until the front dogs had time to catch some wind. But a school with thirty students, what did it have for a bench? It was lucky to have a bench; a bench occupied by one kid who would rather be working on Dad's old truck, another who was more comfortable tooting the saxophone, both who were fodder for the good guys during practice. Or you could have a boy who had future potential, but was still a 4'11" freshman, no good to the team. And now, heaven forbid, the star fouls out or worse sprains his ankle and this saxophone player who had been sitting on wood all season is now suddenly thrust into a big-game situation to which he cannot contribute. (During a game with Holy Rosary, a Belgrade player smacked into a wall knocking out two front teeth. Bleeding, he turned and gargled, "Now I can't play my trumpet!")

For a school with thirty students to win the championship required something from the ranks of the gods and in 1960 Gildford seemed to have it. Actually, theoretically, Gildford was a school of forty-four students because in 1960 it was blessed with twenty-two boys. But twenty-two was still only one third the number coming from perennial favorites in District 11, Chester or Big Sandy. Gildford had to have something more. That something was a group of young kids with exceptional native ability, who had known each other from the time they were toddlers, who played ball together before memory served them when it all started.

At first it was Don Miller, Gene Cady, Gary Cady, Dave Welsh; others would come later. They would meet at someone's hoop, perhaps Miller's, or maybe Cady's. But these baskets were in full brunt of the wind. The more attractive location was on the east and front side of Welsh's "barn." Really it was a storage shed sixteen feet high and ten feet wide. The shed is no longer there; in its place is a row of Russian olive trees. But it was here they would play before school, after school, all day on weekends, all through the fall because there was no football, often through the spring because there was little of baseball. They would play all summer until, at an early age, they were considered old enough to drive a truck or tractor. If they worked on the farm during the summers, after work they would congregate and play again until dark. They would even play in the dead of winter when they wore gloves or, disdaining gloves, would have fingers so chapped they would be cracked. In this bitter cold, the ball would deflate, making dribbling impossible—so they had to learn to pass. In fact at any time of the year, with the ground uneven, they had to pass and learned to pass with intuition and accuracy. Over time they were like brothers who had an emotional connection, who knew each other's thoughts, who could anticipate every move from their mates until by the time they reached high school had become a self-taught machine running on instinct. Any wise choice for a coach with these kids was to tweak here and there but generally get out of the way.

In truth, the kids did have coaching at a younger age. Their first official coach was George Sande (pronounced *Sandy*) who led the seventh-grade team. Not only was he their first coach, he may have been the best pre-college coach the kids would ever have. Everyone loved Sande, players and non-players alike. He was a local boy who went off to Germany in the military, stayed to teach, met his German bride and came back to Gildford. He taught the kids fundamentals, and with this, no matter what kind of coach the kids would have in high school, they could remember and draw on Sande's tutelage. This was important to the people in Gildford. They knew they had a special group of kids in the wings, a collection of talent that could take the school where it had never gone before.

Because in all the years Gildford had supported a boys' basketball program, there wasn't much to remember, a team mostly in the middle of the pack raising sights for a decent showing in the local Hi-Line tournament. In 1936 the Broncs won the Hi-Line but after that came a long dry spell. In 1950, with Lowell Miller at center, Gildford burned the competition during the regular season but fizzled in the district tournament. For the next three years the Broncs went nowhere and then beginning in the fall of 1953 came the depressing four years of non-accreditation.

With the team still under the thumb of the state, the preparation of Sande would do little good in the 1956-57 season, when Don Miller became a freshman. Gildford had good players: David Flatness, Lawrence Flatness, Paul Preeshl; the team would finish third place in the district during the regular season, but the school of course could still not play in the district tournament. The loss of accreditation was due to small enrollment, and because of that, any freshman, if he had talent at all, would likely make the first string. Miller was on the first string. The team had been coached by Hugh Neill; he would coach them again the following year and, by that time, the school would be out from under the ogre of non-accreditation.

I had the privilege of visiting with Mr. Neill, now up in years, at his home in Choteau. He and his twin brother Howard attended school all twelve years in tiny Windham, seven miles east of Stanford in Judith Basin County. As was customary in the rural 1930s, he had his own primitive means of getting to school, sometimes by wagon, sometimes by bobsled. Through high school, Neill played four years of football, four years of basketball and, like many players of his day, worked around a pot belly stove stuck out onto the floor, a far greater threat to well-being than any star from an opposing team. The gym happened to be next to a mercantile store, owned by a "Jew," Neill said; sometime after he graduated, the owner set fire to his store and, by accident, the gym along with it. So Windham got a new gym and said bye-bye to the pot belly stove.

For all his time on the basketball court, Neill had no plans to coach or, for that matter, to be in the teaching profession. He instead aspired to be in the medical field, had served as a medic in World War II, first in North Africa, then Italy, receiving a bronze star in 1944 for saving a soldier's life. After the war ended, he headed home, married his sweetheart and, with very little money, headed for college to pursue his dream.

His years in higher education would not add up to a charmed life. First Neill went to a Catholic college in Great Falls, but transferred to Rocky Mountain College in Billings because it had a better program. But when he arrived in Billings, the man in admissions didn't like Catholics and wouldn't accept his credits. So he ended up going to college for five years with 225 credits, mostly in science, and a 3.7 GPA. In Billings he would get out of class at 3:00 p.m., work at J.C. Penney until 5:30, then do janitorial work until 1:00 a.m. followed by a three-mile walk home. He no longer had time for sports.

By this time, Neill had his sights on being a doctor. He applied for medical school in Eugene, Oregon, sent a transcript, and had an interview with three doctors who told him that if he were accepted, his name would be posted on the bulletin board in the administration building. After the first week he did not see his name on the board. With a wife and two young children camped in Eugene, with precious money burning up fast, he and his wife agreed to stick it out one more week. After that second week, his name was posted. He was accepted to medical school. But the man back in Montana who said he would sponsor him and help him pay his way, backed out of the agreement. Neill had no choice but to go back home and get a job. For two years he taught in Montana.

After those two years Neill decided to take another swing at acceptance in medical school. This time he sent his transcript to Pacific University in Forest Grove, Oregon (Pacific still had a medical school at the time). The officials there wanted an interview, and Neill was again accepted. By this time his wife was seven months pregnant with their third child. The family drove out to Forest Grove, and this time Neill came with a job in hand and thought he had all his bases covered. But he arrived at 11:00 p.m. to find the manager had rented their apartment to a couple from Illinois. The Neill family was forced to rent a hotel room, eat on the floor, all the time becoming nervous because their furniture and household goods had not materialized. They never did. They were instead lost somewhere in Washington State. The dean at Pacific had told Neill the school could pay him a small stipend while he acquired his Ph.D.. It sounded interesting but the money wasn't enough, considering he would have to buy all new furniture and household goods. The Neill family upped and returned to Montana, where Neill would teach at one school or another for twenty-seven years.

He first got a job in Wibaux but didn't like it there. He then landed a job in Inverness where, in addition to teaching, he was pulled into coaching basketball. His career in coaching did not get off to an auspicious start. This was the era when Inverness had no accreditation and Neill found himself begging teams from other schools to play his team. But that wasn't the worst. On his team was a boy who collapsed during practice; it was discovered he had a brain tumor. All the boys had been examined—it was the law—but somehow his tumor had remained undetected. The doctor was concerned about his physical exertion but the boy pleaded with his parents to let him play and, reluctantly, they gave in. Not long after, during the first quarter of a game, he was bringing the ball down when *poof*, he was dead.

Neill stayed in Inverness one year also, then accepted the offer to teach down the road in Gildford, where he would coach for four years. His life in the military had made an impression on him which became evident in the way he handled himself in Gildford. He had learned boxing in the army, had been a part of what were known as "smokers": a system in which a soldier would participate in a match having no idea beforehand who his opponent would be. The men wore headgear and gloves that were huge in these bouts because the army wanted no one to get hurt—at least not in boxing. Neill would teach this sport to several of the kids in Gildford. Chris Pappas remembered Neill getting kids up on the stage, teaching everyone, and one day when everyone else was gone, Neill allowed Pappas to really go after him, which he did, and then BOOM, Neill hit Pappas right between the eyes giving him a nose bleed. "It was a natural reaction for him," Pappas said, and Neill immediately apologized (Pappas never said anything to his parents about the incident).

Neill carried his military bearing to basketball practice. He was like a drill sergeant involving the kids for lengthy periods in calisthenics. They would perform out on the court before a game; one player would be out front as "commander" for a few minutes, then turning the command role to another. Neill liked a methodical slow-down game, half-court on offense and a 2-1-2 or 1-2-2 zone defense, which he switched constantly from one to the other during a game to keep the opposition off guard. His players said he spent much time teaching defense but had little game plan on offense except to bring the ball down for half-court play. Neill himself said he frowned on his players dribbling one-on-one, preferring them to pass, to throw a set number of passes before a shot was taken.

Neill had it tough in Gildford because for three out of the four years he coached, Gildford was also without accreditation. But life began to get better for him. He had that 1957 team, which managed to gain third place during the regular season, not a bad accomplishment considering there were ten teams in the "district" (Gildford, Hingham, and Inverness were still not considered to be a part of it). And now in 1957-58 accreditation was restored and except for Paul Preeshl, all the other players were back. Only one boy on the first string was a senior—David Flatness who at 6'5" might have been college material but had polio as a young child which shortened one leg. It was skinny, over an inch shorter than the other and ended in a deformed foot. Flatness could only stand on the ball of that foot which limited his mobility. He could not jump but he was strong as a mule, got his share of rebounds, and though he ran with a limp, could get up and down the floor surprisingly well. Alongside was his brother Lawrence, a year younger, also a big husky kid although three inches shorter than his brother. Around school David and Lawrence were known as cowboys because they grew up on a ranch and could handle any animal, having taken after their father and uncles who had been on the rodeo circuit. Lawrence had much experience roping calves and bulldogging steers. He and his brother could also handle humans, who learned not to antagonize them—that is most humans: one day in school, Neill got mad at Lawrence Flatness and punched him in the face (Flatness said he deserved it). By now Don Miller was a sophomore on this team at his full height of 6'3". He was not as stocky as the Flatness brothers but very mobile; even as a sophomore he would usually be the high scorer on the team.

These three players made up a formidable front line on offense, but on defense, Neill played his team "backwards": the tall guys guarded out front with the shorter boys under the basket, the idea that, with the big guys waving their arms, there would be no room for the opposition to get the ball in down low. At guard, Gildford had young freshman Gene Cady who already was often second to Miller in scoring. Rounding out the squad were George Travor, who sometimes started, the Parker brothers, Bruce Brown, and another promising freshman, Dave Welsh. This was the team Neill had to work with, a bunch of youngsters who would only get better. But according to Lawrence Flatness, many of the people in Gildford didn't seem to notice. Here was a town with not much to do in the winter but Flatness said there were still plenty of empty seats during the games.

As in 1957, Gildford could harness most teams in District 11, but if the Broncs were really going to go anywhere and make it to the Northern Division tournament, they had to unseat the two traditional bullyboys, Chester and Big Sandy. Particularly Big Sandy had a tall team; even the guards were 6'2" or 6'3". During the season, Gildford won nine games; in a few of them, Neill didn't mind running up the score. In its only game against Box Elder, Gildford won 76-36. In two games against hapless Hingham, the routs were 79-28 and 85-16. But in the first game of the season against Chester, the Broncs lost 57-41. Later in the season Chester would again win 58-50. But Gildford continued to improve as the season went along. In the first game against Big Sandy, Gildford lost 55-50. In the last game of the regular season, the Broncs took the Pioneers to overtime before bowing 61-59. Its final record for the regular season was nine wins against five losses, the remaining loss to Joplin. It looked as if Gildford really might have a chance to place high in the District 11 tournament.

Every member of the Gildford team was thrilled to be in the district tournament held at Havre Central High School. In the first game, the Broncs easily polished off Oilmont 69-38 (Oilmont had given them tough competition during the season), but now came Chester for the semi-final, and this time Gildford won in overtime 60-55. In the championship against Big Sandy, Miller poured in 28 points with strong support from Cady and David Flatness, but it was not enough. Big Sandy won going away 64-56. It remained for Gildford to defeat Joplin 53-46 in the challenge game, and for the first time ever advance to the Northern Divisional tournament, which in 1958 happened to be in Choteau.

The tournament in Choteau was like being in a dream. Gildford was there and Chester was not. The Broncs had to pinch themselves to make sure they were in Choteau. Maybe they should have pinched harder.

Their first game was against Stanford, which had two outstanding stars on its squad, Dennis Kennedy and Larry Creekmore. Kennedy in particular was a young man of unusual athletic ability. I personally watched him tank a baseline scoop shot at least ten feet away from the basket. But according to Neill, the Gildford team members had more than Stanford to stop them. The night before the game, the manager of the team talked several players into what became an all-night poker session. Neill couldn't figure out why some of his boys seemed dead the next day when Stanford hammered Gildford 80-64. The following afternoon in the losers' bracket, after another apparent nocturnal exchange of cards, Gildford lost to St Leo's 73-64. When Neill found out what happened, he was furious. Even now, he says, he gets angry when he thinks about it. Of the players I talked to, none remembers any all-night poker parties and surely would have if they had taken place. They did acknowledge some players got into poker during road trips, but not at the divisional tournament. Neill continued to teach at Gildford for one more year, but after what happened in Choteau, he swore he would never coach again. And he never did. At the dawn of the 1958-59 season, with all this talent one year older, Gildford would find itself with a new coach fresh out college, a North Dakota boy named Roger A. Freih.

Frank Spragg

Up in Smoke, Up from the Ashes

MUCH GOOD CAN BE SAID ABOUT ROGER FREIH (PRONOUNCED *Free*). He came from a good Christian family in Edgely, North Dakota, the third in a family of five children. His parents, John and Eva Zink Freih, had always been active at the local Lutheran Church, a religious lifestyle that rubbed off on Roger who remained a Christian throughout his life, always striving to instill these values into his own children.

Like his parents, Freih was esteemed wherever he went. For many years he lived in Bowman, North Dakota, running a gas station with his son Terry and daughter Lee Ann, until he passed away at the age of fifty-three from a heart attack. One friend said the station was the largest in town; Freih loved running the place because he was always with Terry and Lee Ann and made lots of friends, people coming in for one service or another. The kids always had the coffee pot on and during the holidays, when everything else was closed, they would fix ham or something, take it down to the station for the customers, brew some coffee for them. He had been active in Bowman at the Lutheran Church, the American Legion, the VFW, always mixing with people, enjoying life, enjoying his family. He had loved teaching also, until just after moving to Bowman for one year, he got so sick he had to quit.

He had begun his life on May 19, 1932 in poverty, his father having difficulty making a go of it on their small farm near Edgely during the Great Depression. John had worked hard on the farm, growing wheat, corn, barley and oats, milking nineteen cows, but the income from the farm wasn't enough. So John moved into town and became a carpenter, moved up to being a contractor, and was reasonably successful. The parents would never declare themselves wealthy but over the years continued to prosper. They owned a nice home in Edgely which (remodeled) still stands.

Freih went to college, but his education was interrupted by a stint in the military, being deployed overseas during the Korean War. Freih liked the military because he could be around guns and ammunition. His father was a hunter; Freih and his brothers grew up with that, and Freih knew guns. One day, after some time in Korea, he was unloading large shells into a dugout when he accidentally dropped a shell on his foot. It went off, wounding him and killing several of the soldiers in his unit. He was flown to a hospital in Korea and soon after transported to Japan. He was awarded the Purple Heart because he had done everything he could to save the other men; the evidence of the award was shown on his discharge papers, but he never actually received the award. Like most in the military who had seen action and soldiers killed, he avoided talking about his life in Korea.

Freih seemed to have always wanted a career in education. It began as a peer-group thing: two of his army buddies were looking into teaching and Freih decided that might be good for him. He had another powerful incentive to attend college: the government would pay for it. Without government help, he wasn't going to go far; before going into the military he tried to put himself through college working at the local Red Owl Grocery Store but he couldn't pay expenses on the wages they paid him.

He went to Ellendale Normal College in Edgely, graduating in 1958. But when he sought a teaching position, he looked not within his own state, but west to Montana where teachers' salaries were significantly higher. Freih was offered a job in Gildford teaching history and science and, like those before him, was pressed into being the basketball coach.

Freih loved sports all the time he was growing up. He was on the football team during high school, playing the center position. After teaching in Montana, he moved back to St Thomas, North Dakota, because he had the chance to start a football program there. He also played baseball which was a family tradition; his father had coached a team for many years and it became a given that Freih and his brothers would be on the team.

He also played basketball in high school but did not like that sport much; in fact, he really didn't know basketball. It showed when he arrived in Gildford. Several on the team have said that Freih was a poor coach, but that assessment does not give the full picture of the man. Rather than being a poor coach, he was a non-coach. As Lawrence Flatness said, "He was just a cheerleader: 'Go kill 'em guys!' he would say. He was a sweetheart kind of a guy, didn't teach the kids one thing. 'Go kill 'em guys!'"

But if he didn't help the team, neither did he hurt it. And this was perfect for these kids in Gildford. Gene Cady said he didn't have any problem with Freih. "He was an easy, happy-going guy......like a kid.......He was fun, like riding to the ballgames, practices and things like that, he was an entertaining guy, could converse. He had that little mustache and a grin. He came from North Dakota and didn't have any idea about coaching. He didn't know any more about it than the man on the moon and here he was six months later down in Helena and the reporters were talking to him. He was a bit taken back and awed. He was just an ordinary guy." Don Miller said Freih tried to keep things organized "so the players wouldn't get mad or chew on one another. Mostly, he kind of let us go, we took care of business and it turned out pretty good. Freih tried to be positive, didn't do anything negative. The team was self-taught, there were no set plays and so other teams couldn't come up with a plan against us." That was the point. It was useless to scout Gildford because every night it came with a different game. In that odd way, Freih made the team better.

Miller, Cady, and Lawrence Flatness were all back, Miller now the center with Flatness and 6'0" Cady at forward, all who could score creating a dangerous front line for the opposition. Cady said this about Flatness: "He was a vital part of the team in 1959. He was bigger than Miller that year; he wasn't quite as tall but way heavier. He looked a lot like a football player." The starting five had two new guards: one Dave Welsh who had been in Gildford his entire life, and the other, a new kid in town, a boy who fit right in; as Miller said "We took him as our own."

His name was Ron Nelson and he would become a phenomenon because no one ever moved to Gildford and then to become invaluable to the team, the missing piece of the puzzle, well, in a minor way it was right out of Hollywood. Nelson had been born just over the border in Williston, North Dakota because there was no hospital in small town Brockton where he lived and where his father managed the local grain elevator. When he was in the third grade, his father had the opportunity to be part owner of a tavern in Frenchtown far away on the other side of Montana, fifteen miles west of Missoula. The family was in Frenchtown for over two years when his mother Audrey and father Ervin decided running a tavern wasn't the appropriate enterprise for people with their values. So the family hopped the short distance to Missoula where Ervin got a job with Presto Logs, and almost lost an arm in an accident. Audrey became convinced the lumber business was too dangerous. When a threat of a strike moved forward, Audrey and Ervin knew he had to find a new career; in truth, he was happy to get away from his present job. Ervin and Ron moved to Gildford when an opening came up to run the local GTA grain elevator; Audrey and daughter Carla followed a couple of months later, after the house was sold. Ervin managed the elevator, Audrey worked at a bank in Havre, Ron was a starter on the basketball team, Carla eventually became a cheerleader, and in a blink of an eye the Nelsons were part of the Gildford family.

Nelson has said moving to Gildford was the best thing that ever happened to him. He could always shoot, but he was a late bloomer, only 4'11" as a freshman in Missoula, and still a runty 5'3" as a sophomore. He was never going to make the team at this large Class AA school. Now because he had a chance to show his skills in Gildford, he was able to get a four-year basketball scholarship at Rocky Mountain College in Billings, and work his way up through the business world, eventually becoming vice president at Nike Corporation. Nelson continued to grow in high school; by the time he arrived in Gildford, he was 5'8" alongside Welsh who, as his counterpart, was the same height.

Freih's team also had a better-than-average bench for a school of Gildford's size, and this is where he fell down on the job. He had George Traver, David Saller, and Chris Pappas who would be on the starting five the next year. But Freih rarely chose to play the members of his bench. Traver, who sometimes had been a starter with Hugh Neill, got so frustrated with just sitting there that one night, he turned to Freih—perhaps trying to appeal to Freih's sense of values—and yelled to the delight of everyone within earshot, "Put me in Coach. I don't smoke and I don't drink!" This use of subs logic seemed to fly over the head of Freih. Fortunately his inaction was not a factor in the outcome of the season.

The main competitors for the season, as usual, were the Chester Coyotes and the Big Sandy Pioneers. They were the only schools in District 11 with over 100 students, the only ones large enough to supply a pep band at the games. In two years Big Sandy would be upgraded to Class B. Still the Broncs were off to a good start at the beginning of the season, dispatching Hingham 62-19 in the Rangers' own gym, enduring a slip losing to Chester by two points at home, then three easy games: Box Elder at home, and two away, against Kremlin and Joplin. Gildford should have savored the game against Box Elder: it would be the last game the Broncs would ever play in their cherished gym.

FROM THE VERY BEGINNING AND FOR MANY YEARS, GILDFORD HIGH School never had a gym, at least not a real one. The first basketball game was held in 1915 in the basement of the Episcopal church, but soon enough, the action moved to a community hall sandwiched between a saloon and Chinese laundry on one side and Young's Mercantile on the other, all in a row facing the railroad tracks. Dances, the viewing of silent movies, and any number of other activities were held at the hall, but on certain nights the room—and you can call it a room—was cleared for basketball. A few years ago, the structure was moved and incorporated into a larger building on Lowell Miller's farm to be used as a cattle pen. Lowell and I measured the little hall. It is 13.5 feet to the ceiling, 23 feet wide and 48 feet long. This was the space the kids had to work with, assuming there was no out of bounds, assuming there were no spectators, and when you think about it, assuming there were no baskets. With proper ceiling, walls, and floor, the community hall might have made an idiosyncratic hand ball court.

The town lived with this small space for twenty years. Then in 1937, the Works Progress Administration stepped in and provided money for Gildford to build a brand new gym and school which were an addition to (and separate from) the school built in 1923. This was manna from heaven; the town, mired in the Great Depression never could have afforded the gym otherwise. The school would make use of this gym for another twenty-two years, a gym still much better after two decades than many others around Montana.

The mid-to-late 1950s was the beginning of Class C schools building brand new gyms with full-sized courts and brand spanking locker rooms. There wasn't much seating in these gyms, and there shouldn't have been; it was the right number for the size of the town. But they were so *spacious*; I remember suiting up for games in Clyde Park and Willow Creek and marveling at how large the courts were, how bright the gym, how clean! And no wonder. Because up to this time most gyms in Class C had left much to be desired for proper basketball, some far more than others.

Old gyms in small towns were everywhere on the spectrum of

quality. Some I saw in Three Forks, Townsend, and Holy Rosary were cracker boxes, yet adequate. A player had plenty of room for a layup, to get out of bounds, to shoot a long shot and not worry about the ball hitting the ceiling. If the ball hit the rim or backboard, the rim and backboard were properly anchored. In other words, the facility might be cramped but it wasn't weird. I say this because not a few gyms around Montana could be given the latter description.

Often it was a matter of cracker box to the extreme. In many gyms, such as those in Superior or Big Fork, it was necessary to have two "ten second" lines, or "over and back" lines as many called them, the line a team, after taking the ball out, must cross in ten seconds to be in front court. On a standard-sized court, or one with decent length, the line intersects the center circle and is half way from one end of the court to the other. But in tight quarters such as these, it was necessary to set the line back, or there would be hardly enough space in the front court to play.

Some gyms had woefully low ceilings making it necessary to "flat line" a long shot, or a shot with little arc; a good example would be the old gym in Broadus. That gym was not as old as some, had been built with WPA money during the 1930s. But whoever designed it had never played basketball. Roger Quaring, who has lived in Broadus for many years and did janitorial work in that old building thought the ceiling likely had been sixteen feet high. In a gym like this, the home team had the advantage because the players had practiced and mastered shots under the low ceiling (which of course gave them a disadvantage when they were away, playing under a high ceiling). In some gyms the ceiling might be high enough but had dangling light bulbs just waiting to be hit by a ball, sending a shower of glass to the floor. In others, players in the corners, or in some cases off to the sides, were intimidated by overhanging balconies which would obstruct the normal arc of a shot.

It comes as no surprise that in many gyms there was precious little space between the edge of the court and a wall, or the crowd, or both!

The backboard could be tacked directly to the wall, making it impossible to drive for a layup with any speed. Very often, the end of the court nearly abutted the front of a stage; if the edge of the stage had a lip it created the new danger of being impaled. Here again, players from the home team learned to overcome such handicaps. In Jordan, hometown player Ernie Bozarth, "a fiery go-getter," would frantically run down the floor, scream in for a layup, land on the stage running, turn around, jump off, and be back in the action at the other end of floor within seconds.

If there was ever a gym in Montana that could lay claim to none of the amenities a gym *should* have, it would be the little Quonset hut in Reed Point; just the words "little" and "Quonset" say a good deal about this building. The ceiling, already low in the middle sloped roundly to the sides as all Quonset huts do, making most arced shots impossible. But there was more—or I should say *less*. The floor had no out-of-bounds on the sides or ends. Fans literally sat with their bodies inbounds; the only way the ball could go out of bounds was to hit one of the walls. When a player took the ball out to pass it in, he had to stand between fans. The baskets were tacked onto the walls on each end, extending out a miniscule two feet. This meant that a player drove in for a layup at his own endangerment. And the floor was ridiculously small, not much bigger than Lowell Miller's calf stall. There were two ten-second lines, which tangentially touched the center circle on each side as they crossed the width of the floor. In this little hut, the player took the ball out and traveled a mere ten feet before reaching front court. And to top it off, when players finished an exhausting session of playing in Reed Point, they hopped the bus for a mutually stinky ride home. The Reed Point facility had no showers.

Reed Point was considered the worst gym in District 6, the area west and south of Billings. But Fromburg's gym was nearly as small and had a sinister imperfection which was a threat to any ballplayer who ventured under it: the Fromburg gym was made largely of brick, not only the outside walls but several parts of the inside, including the fronts of the balconies. Each balcony was only four feet deep from front to back; there was just enough room for one row of folding chairs and a squeezy space for fans to get up and pass behind the chairs. People could pack in as you can imagine; one evening a fan pushed forward in his chair in an effort to let someone pass by, dislodging a brick no longer properly mortared, which fell down and landed on the head of an unsuspecting player below. The player, though sporting a hefty gash in his head, managed to finish out the game.

Some gyms were not only inadequate but crossed into the bizarre. The Rudyard gym in District 11 looked like a boarded-over skating rink. The actual playing area was cratered four feet below the landing around it, guarded on three sides by a two-inch pipe fence. On the fourth side were steps leading down to the floor, but it was too cumbersome for most participants to run to the end and down the stairs, so the players (and the cheerleaders when they went into action) simply swung under the fence and down onto the floor. Once on the floor, a player had a tiptoe inducing six inches of space out-of-bounds before touching the wall behind him.

Some of the strangest gyms might have been in my old home, District 8.

Everyone I talked to in District 8 remembers the Wilsall gym, the goofy one. In fact the Wilsall gym was very small; like other gyms with similar dimensions, it required two ten-second lines. Otherwise it wasn't a bad gym. The out-of-bounds area, though slim, was sufficient; the ceiling didn't restrict long shots, the floor was fine. The one basket in front of the stage had to be pulled up during theatrical performances, was not anchored well as it should have been and rattled backward when hit by a ball. OK, advantage one to the home team. But what set Wilsall apart was the structure itself: it was made of logs. And when you were in the gym there was a cavity of seating at the center on each side of the floor. These cavities were about a third of the length of the floor and looked as if they each might be taking up inner space, but this was not true. As you circled outside the old log edifice, it looked as if it were about to give birth to twins. Back inside, each cavity seated fifteen people in front on the floor level and narrowed as you moved toward the back until at the sixth row the bench was quite short. The gym was heated by hot-water pipes running through the back of each cavity, creating a sauna-like experience for those in the back row. Which meant if you were trying to survive a game, it was best done in a swimsuit. Some players remember a pot belly stove in the Wilsall gym but the stove—in fact, two stoves—were down the road at the gym in Clyde Park. What makes that gym memorable is that it is now intact as a hardware store. The room size is the same, some faded markings on the old floor still there; the only change is that the balcony area has been made into offices. Go visit sometime. Before buying your new wrench, examine the floor.

The old Manhattan gym (before the new one was built in 1956) didn't seem unusual at first blush; I watched a few games there and didn't remember anything out of the ordinary. But of course I was young and not very observant. The Manhattan gym had a stage at one end, not the usual stage setup in most gyms of the era, two or three feet away from the floor, a distinctly separate feature enclosed on three sides by walls. The Manhattan stage was part of the floor itself, raised when there was a theatrical production and lowered for basketball. It was an ingenious idea, it seemed, a two for-one-deal, the same objective accomplished with less space and money. Actually, when the gym was first built, the stage was in a permanently raised position. But the rest of the floor was so short that when a tournament was held at the gym in the 1920s, a player twice tipped for a basket on a center jump ball.

Then someone came up with the idea of having the stage mounted on eight screw jacks, which made it possible for hand-lowering it to the level of the floor. Once the stage was lowered it was perfectly flush and level with the rest of the floor—at least that is the way it was when the jacks under the stage were first built. But just six months later an earthquake created a tilt in the stage. From then on, for the next thirty years, the front of the stage was still the same level as the rest of the floor but the stage slanted downward so the back was three inches lower than the front. It must have been an eerie feeling heading for a layup downhill. As you might have already figured out, the basket support was directly over the back of the stage and came down with it. So if a player tried a shot from the front of the stage or the rest of the floor, he was shooting at a basket three inches shorter than the basket at the other end. The gym also had a swimming pool built directly underneath it: the steam from the pool wafted up and warped other parts of the floor. Some thought pillars holding up the ceiling were out on the floor itself but thankfully this was not true. However, they were very close to the edge of the floor.

In Harrison, the gym was unusual not for what it was but for its location. The school itself had a very small gym, used today for shop classes—which gives you an idea of its dimensions. There was also a gym six miles away in the tiny hamlet of Pony, and the gym there wasn't all that bad; in fact for one year games were held there, but the people in Harrison didn't want to travel to Pony so it was decided to have the games at a local community hall, really a dance hall next door to a bar. Which meant that during a timeout or halftime, or just about any time, fans could go next door, juice up and become more "convivial" or in a "fighting spirit" or whatever leverage-thru-beverage they wished to exact for the remainder of the game. Because this was a dance hall and not a gym, there was no need for a locker-room, right? So the visiting team dressed in a small room where the beer was stored, and of course these boys showered back home.

Many a small town fan would love to have had a new gym in those years, if there were only the money! In at least one case, a town was blessed with an unwanted mishap which forced its hand. Such was the situation with Willow Creek, which had a gym at the time, many said, the worst in District 8. According to longtime resident Leroy Miller, the building should have been condemned. I only saw the new gym, so I can't confirm, but apparently most of the length of the gym had space for out of bounds and seating except, incongruously, the last ten feet on one end leading to the stage, where the edge of the playing floor abutted directly against the wall. The gym was also heated unevenly, leaving one end toasty and the end next to the stage frigid. In the locker-rooms, the shower stalls did not drain properly; the players brought in pallets to stand on while taking a shower so their ankles wouldn't be submerged in water. These problems might have been material for comic opera, but did not tip the balance of decision for a new gym. What did was a balcony on one side which had seen better times. During a game, too many fans congregated on one part of the balcony causing it to sag, seizing the door underneath so the players could not open it and head to the locker-room. The folks in Willow Creek soon had a new gym.

The Gildford people would find themselves in a similar fate although they at the time didn't necessarily want a new gym. The gym in Gildford was not regulation size, but was considered adequate by all who went there, probably as good as most other gyms in District 11. Originally the gym had a stage on the south end with folding chairs along the east side and bleachers along the west side. In actuality there were seats for the players but no official seats for fans. But from the moment the gym was opened for business in 1937, the place was packed. It was the place to be on a Friday or Saturday night when the team was in town. In an effort to accommodate fans and to help gain back the school's accreditation, the gym was improved, with better bleachers on one side along with a sanded and resurfaced floor. The folks in Gildford had a gym they could be proud of.

On Thursday, March 28, 1958, the gym barely escaped a fire. At the south end of the gym a blaze started under the stage. The flames spread in the opposite direction from the gym to the old portion of the school and caused $50,000 worth of damage. The gym was spared.

On Tuesday evening, January 6, 1959, all was quiet in Gildford. The day had been overcast, temperatures in the teens with almost no

Frank Spragg

wind. Little was going on in town; high school students were practicing basketball in the gym but were heading home by 9:00 p.m. The team members and the coach made sure the building was secured; as they left, saw nothing amiss. That same evening, Ken Knutson, Jack Sweeney, and Mack Brownlee left their homes in Gildford to bowl at the K Lanes in Rudyard, something they did regularly in the winter. After they finished bowling, they stopped to get something to eat in Rudyard, as they customarily did, and then headed back to Gildford, arriving about midnight. As they drove by the school they noticed flames inside, and immediately turned in an alarm. Local fire fighters arrived about 12:30 a.m., entering from the new addition of the school, which had been added only two years before at a cost in excess of $150,000. They saw that the halls in the new addition were already ablaze. After putting out the fire in the halls, they entered the old building and began to fight the blaze there. Then the available water ran out and people were sent for more. In the meantime fighters were brought in from Hingham, Rudyard and the Hill County department in Havre. About thirty trained firemen battled the blazes, along with numerous individuals and farmers who used trucks of their own.

But there was no water system in Gildford, no systematic way of obtaining water locally and easily. Men fought valiantly, but it was too little too late. The blaze broke through the center of the building and a tower of fire burst forth. Making the situation exponentially more difficult, a wind began blowing briskly from the southwest and the firemen were beginning to give up all hope that the new addition could be saved. But with additional help and water, the new addition was preserved except for minor damage. It was preserved because the wall dividing the new building from the old was pushed in toward the still-burning old building by a combination of extension ladders and belt-holding hooks. Superintendent Myron Loe, along with some helpers, broke into the school office and removed the safe, all the records, and the office furniture. A temporary office was set up in Loe's home.

The fighters continued to battle the fire until 3:00 a.m., when the wind died down and the flames were under control. All left at 4:00 a.m. except for a skeleton crew staying behind to stifle embers. The only damage to the new addition was in the front halls and smoke damage. But the old portion of the school and the gym were destroyed, along with some equipment purchased that very year, such as eight new manual typewriters, thirty-six new assembly desks, new text books, and a new IBM electric typewriter. It was determined that the fire began in the boiler room between the gym and the new addition. The total damage cost was an estimated $300,000. Students would have to attend class temporarily in a nearby church and in classrooms in Rudyard and Hingham. As the fire still smoldered at 9:00 a.m. the next day, the scene at the Gildford School looked bleak.

But not for long. Orville Hanson went to work.

Hanson was co-owner of Hanson-Sande Insurance, a local agency. He had been the district's insurance agent and as a nearly lifelong resident, had an emotional interest in settling the claim. He had one thing going for him: prosperity was on the rise along the Hi-Line, the taxable value of buildings was going up, which made it easier to collect the total amount of money in the claim. But no one company would carry the entire liability for the school. So Hanson-Sande grouped together five different companies to cover the liability, "fought the insurance companies" after the fire, and "got every dime they were insured for, which was unheard-of at the time." But this still amounted to only $263,000 leaving $37,000 to come from a different source.

Plans for construction began almost immediately. Lloyd Curfman, Art Rambo, and Leonard Grimes drove over to Kalispell, met architect Gehris Weed, who had just designed the brand-new gym in Cut Bank (which ironically burned down later) and who would draw up plans for the new school and gym. In a matter of days, as soon as the fire marshal gave the go-ahead, new construction began. To save money, farmers at no cost brought in fill dirt; it was a community effort. As the new school and gym were nearing completion and the district began to run out of money, the general contractor, Chris Fuglevand, from Havre, furnished the floor of the gym on his own dime as a contribution to the community. The project was completed in the summer of 1960 and dedicated the next fall. Harriet Miller was invited to be the featured speaker. The Gildford District had a new gym and school, and when it was all over, didn't owe a penny.

The basketball team resumed almost as if nothing ever happened. The Broncs had to do something; they had a "home" game against Big Sandy on Friday and an away game in Rudyard on Saturday. Fortunately Hingham and Kremlin came to the rescue. After the local boys finished their practice after school, the Gildford team had the run of their gyms. It was two nights in Hingham, say Monday and Wednesday, and two nights in Kremlin, Tuesday and Thursday. This was a big-hearted move on the part of Hingham and Kremlin because they were allowing practice facilities for a team that was stomping the heck out of them. The schedule was rigid: at 6:30 p.m. sharp, the Gildford boys loaded into cars and headed ten miles east to Kremlin or six miles west to Hingham. Ron Nelson remembers having to miss the last ten minutes of "Leave it to Beaver" every night when he went to practice. The generosity did not end with Kremlin and Hingham: every time Gildford was in a District 11 game considered a home game for the Broncs, Gildford was awarded all gate receipts. It was nice to be among friends.

The team now developed a quiet fire of its own. It had to play all games on opposing courts, but that seemed to strengthen the team. And the kids were helped by the home fans who flocked to every game, no matter the town, and since all these gyms didn't have that much seating anyway, with the exception of Chester and Big Sandy, the Gildford fans took up half the space. The Gildford crowd was just as loud as the home fans, so psychologically every game was on neutral turf. There was no reserved seating, but generally the home fans would settle on one side of the gym and the Gildford folks on the other. It might not be too wise to sit next to someone you would like to punch in the nose.

In that very next game against Big Sandy on the Pioneer's home floor, Gildford lost by a single point. This was an emotional boost. Gildford chalked up three more victories before traveling to Chester and losing by only three points. After that, Gildford rattled off seven straight victories to finish out the regular season. The last win had been in Big Sandy by three points. Several of the players said something clicked within the mentality of the team after the win in Big Sandy. They knew they were playing on a higher level, and it revealed itself at the District 11 tournament in the gym at Havre Central. Gildford beat Joplin in the first game by 14 points, Chester in the semi-finals by 19, and Big Sandy in the championship by 18. Everyone in District 11 was in shock.

The Broncs were thrilled to be back at the Northern Division tournament, this time held in Cut Bank in that shiny new gym which seated 3,000 people. And this time they were not about to go down two and done. They were first paired against Moore, a team fifteen miles west of Lewistown in District 9. The Bulldogs had been in the state tournament in 1956 and would go again in 1961. Their coach, Ervin Holsinger, had been coaching in Moore for ten years, which was unusual for Class C, but he was from Moore and loved living there. He would coach there for another three years before moving on. Moore was always competitive under Holsinger, had some good tall kids moving up the ranks, but on this first night they would lose to Gildford by 19 points, 56-37.

Next up was Simms, a team from District 12, the area generally surrounding Great Falls. Every year there were teams in Class C that didn't make it to the state tournament but should have, were arguably some of the best teams in Montana but destined to have an off night or bad luck at the worst possible time. Simms could have legitimately made that claim in 1959. The coach at the school, Don Rose had been at Simms since the early 1950s and would coach there into the

1960s before moving within the district to Cascade High School just south of Great Falls. The team had done well in 1958 before losing in the semi-finals in the divisional. This year, they expected to advance much further; up to the game with Gildford, Simms had a 23-1 record, losing only their very first game to Brady (another District 12 team). Simms was not a tall team but the boys played well together, had good chemistry. The team had guards Bill Miller, an excellent shooter—he once made 50 out of 53 shots in practice—and Roy Allen working the ball around the perimeter, a form of "stall ball" until they could get the ball inside for a layup. The center was Charlie Matthews, with Fred Lefcico and Gary Baker at forwards rounding out the first string. On defense they played mostly man-to-man. In the first game of the tournament, Simms defeated Geyser 49-26 and was on a tear.

The Cardinals would hardly tear up Gildford. And the game would end with one of the strangest thirty seconds of any tournament game in Class C. Gildford had jumped out to a small lead and maintained it for most of the game. But Simms crept back and with forty-five seconds to go, tied the score at 47-47 and seemed to have the momentum. Then something just snapped with the Broncs; no one can explain it. They put on a wild display of scoring in just thirty seconds: five field goals and three free throws, never missing a shot while Simms got in one basket. The final score was 60-49.

For the championship, Gildford would meet the Power Pirates, one of the more underrated teams in the divisional tournament. Simms had beaten them five times, including the championship of District 12 by ten points. Throughout the 1950s Power had been in the middle of the pack in District 12 but at the beginning of the 1958-59 season, the Pirates had a new coach, Chris Small, a man bursting with enthusiasm, who kept telling the kids how good they were. And though many of them were skeptical, as the season went along, they began to believe him; if he told them they had potential, it was found to be true; they did have potential and would continue to get better. Small had the gift to be able to watch other teams, to decipher what he could do to take the advantage away from an opponent more talented than his team, whatever that opponent might be expected to do.

He changed the team offense from a methodical half-court, passing around the perimeter to an up-tempo game, frequent fast breaks, and if the team went into half-court, penetration was the byword, work it inside as fast as possible and keep it there. If the ball had to be passed back out, then get it back inside. No more passing around the perimeter. He was a big believer in the pick and roll. His players weren't unusually speedy but they could get up and down the floor well enough. Power had improved greatly under Small, and the future looked bright; Ron Dahlman was the only senior on the team. In Cut Bank, Power defeated St. Leo's in the first game and then upset talented Stanford, which still had Kennedy and Creekmore, in the semifinals. Stanford and Simms had been considered the two favorites in the tournament. But Power would not be a pushover for Gildford.

Gildford led throughout the contest, but only by a hairbreadth margin. The Broncs were ahead 13-12 after the first quarter, 23-21 after the first half. At the end of three quarters it was all tied up. The game was becoming very tense. In the fourth quarter, Gildford opened up something of a healthy lead then decided to stall. It was a mistake. Power roared back, but Gildford managed to stay above in the end, 47-46. It would be Gildford and Power at the state tournament in Helena.

Gildford at Helena. At the state tournament. The fans could hardly believe they were there. Lynn Hayden said, "We walked into the gym and when we made the first basket, oh my gosh, we made two points at the state tournament! Then we won a game and I couldn't believe it!"

The state Class C tournament in 1959 will be remembered for being awash in parity. The newspapers said as much: "No Solid Favorite in Eight Team Field in State Class C Tourney" said the *Havre Daily News*. Every representative of a losing team in that tournament I talked to thought his team should have won. Belgrade should have beaten Gildford, Gildford should have beaten Superior, State School should have beaten Superior, Townsend should have beaten everyone but went down in three games. Two of the most competitive teams in Class C—Simms and Bridger[6]—weren't even in Helena. To accurately predict the winner was a matter as easy as taking on a slot machine.

Another reason the tournament will be remembered is because of a single player, a player who was a prolific scorer, could shoot from anywhere, who stuck in people's minds to the point that when his team was again mentioned as part of the state tournament in 1960, most fans (and players) thought of him even though he was no longer involved. To begin with there was the name: George Yelloweyes. How can anyone forget a name like that? He had come from a completely dysfunctional family in the Northern Cheyenne Indian Reservation, both parents alcoholics, had been caught in burglary and theft as a teenager, and ended up at the State Industrial (correctional) School in Miles City. The rumor that he broke into the same candy store so he could return to State School every year was not true. What was true is that State School was in the state tournament in 1959 (as it had been in 1958) and Yelloweyes was the undisputed star. The team had other good players: Andy Tenas, power forward, and Charles Potter, center, both who had never played basketball before coming to State School but who turned out to be very good by the end of the season. Emmanuel Big Head played small forward and was a great outside shooter. Ray Wilson and Andy Ortiz were the guards, Ortiz very speedy and Wilson, although he had troubles controlling his temperament was very confident in big-game situations. The team also had good substitutes, as well they should have, because at State School, sixty to seventy kids tried out for basketball; it was the only thing they had, and when Coach Joe McDonald was forced to cut most kids from the team, many of them would turn away crying. And the boys who did make the team had to behave themselves because if they didn't they would be forced off the team, to stay in the dorms with sixty other boys on hand willing to take their place.

State School had the talent, but the other players were on the floor largely to serve Yelloweyes; they would set all sorts of picks for him so he could get away for a shot. Yelloweyes was known to shoot hook shots from mid-court, with either hand. I had the good fortune to watch him when he was in top form. In a Friday afternoon game between Belgrade and State School in the losers' bracket, Yelloweyes had 26 points, an already lofty number, at the end of the third quarter. But in the fourth quarter, he shifted into a new zone, throwing balls up from everywhere. No Belgrade player could stop him. Denny Langston of Belgrade remembered, "My brother Phil guarded him, then I guarded him, fouling out hanging all over him. He made a hook shot from center court; I will never forget it. What do you do? The guy was totally unconscious. The other players threw screens so he could shoot. That's how it was; he was hotter than a pistol. He was unbelievable. I will never forget it." Yelloweyes ended with 46 points and Belgrade was eliminated from the tournament. McDonald later looked at the shot chart; if the three-point rule had been in place in 1959, Yelloweyes would have scored 59 points.

Nevertheless, the reason State School fell to the losers' bracket is because the team lost its first game to Superior. Some would argue no excuse is good enough for a team to lose a game, but State School had one that approaches validity: on the previous Sunday, McDonald's father became very sick, so the coach traveled to St Ignatius to be with him. The plan was for the assistant coach to work with the players, drive them over to Helena on Wednesday—the day before the tournament began—and McDonald would drive over early on Thursday to join the team. But as he was driving, his car broke down outside of Missoula, was towed into town to be fixed, and by the time he arrived in Helena it was just before game time in the afternoon; both the coach and the players were unsettled. Still in the beginning of that game, Yelloweyes came down the floor, the Superior players

Frank Spragg

knowing nothing about him, had never seen him play and backed off him when he crossed mid-court; it didn't occur to them he would shoot from the 35 foot range. He made three straight shots from there, and just like that State School was up 6-0. Then the Bobcats settled down, overplayed Yelloweyes on his right and won the game by 18 points.

Yelloweyes deserves a side note. Not only was he a great player but throughout his life, to those who knew him, he was a gracious person. He would go through some hard times before he passed away, but ended reasonably well. After the 1959 season, he graduated from high school, but Coach McDonald talked him into coming back to State School, where he lived like an off-campus student, free to come and go as he wished, to attend Miles City Community College and be the star for that team, averaging 24 points per game, making 80 percent of his free throws. The very next summer he was on a forest fire with one of the Indian crews, jumped some distance down on a rock, jammed both of his heels and could not jump or run, could never play basketball again.

If I had watched Belgrade play State School on that Friday afternoon, I did not watch the Panthers play Gildford the night before; Helena is close enough to Gallatin Valley that we could pick and choose, could run over to Helena in two hours to take in a game. My family elected not to watch the first game against Gildford, and as it turned out, I would never have the chance to watch the Broncs in person. Since beginning to write this book, I have been kicking myself the entire time (and it hurts!)

In that first game, Belgrade wore green and white, Gildford green and gold, but only Gildford was the greenhorn. The Broncs were facing the defending state champions, a team that was making its the fifth consecutive appearance at the state tournament. At first glance it appeared the overwhelming odds were in Belgrade's favor. The year before with largely a brand new team, the Panthers gelled at the right moment to win it all. True, they won the three games in the state tournament by a grand total of seven points, but they won, and now they were back with four out of five of their starters from the year before. They had Stan Craver, who had been the top scorer for the state champions and was an indefatigable worker underneath the basket. There were the Langston brothers; older brother Phil a three-year veteran starting point guard, and younger brother Denny, only a sophomore, athletic center-forward who was second team all-tournament selection as a freshman, and who with ice in his veins would sink two free throws with no time left to put the opening game into overtime against Outlook. He would go on to transfer to Class A Havre with his family and become all-state for two years with the Blue Ponies. After his high school career, he played four years for Pacific Lutheran University. The Panthers had Gene Cook who was short at 5'5", but everywhere on defense and capable of scoring when needed. And lastly there was a standout newcomer from Wyoming to the team, sophomore Larry Moore who was almost in the same league with Yelloweyes when it came to banging from long range. It seemed like Gildford was against a dream team that would only get better as time went on.

But in 1959, if Belgrade had acquired Moore, it no longer had the one starting player who had graduated, Roy Sharp, who had been the emotional leader the year before. Sharp was not a verbal person, not a leader off the court, but he led by his actions, had a knack for turning around a bad situation, and could step it up when the game was on the line. The team looked to him and he was no longer there. Not only that, little had been expected of Belgrade in 1958; that team crept up on everyone. Now in 1959, with the team largely intact, everything was expected of it. The pressure was on; Denny Langston could remember Craver telling him how the team had better win. It was altogether different from the year before. "I was just a kid, just a young kid. I wasn't an adult, had never been to college, I handled it okay, I guess, but it affected my play." For the Belgrade fans it was the state crown or nothing. Coach Howard Voiles had said the 1959 team was more talented than the previous year, but the chemistry just wasn't the same. As it turned out, Belgrade arrived at the state tournament, with not even the best record in District 8. For all its victories—Belgrade had a 22-5 record coming into Helena—it struggled with the Townsend Bulldogs, who had beaten the Panthers in three of four meetings, including championships at District 8 in Bozeman and the Southern Divisional in Red Lodge. Belgrade would not be an overwhelming foe for Gildford.

Still, it looked like it would be Belgrade's game. The Panthers led by one-point at the end of the first quarter, four-points by half-time and eight with the third-quarter buzzer. It was just a matter of Belgrade pulling away in the final period. But Gildford put on a full-court press, and Gene Cook and Phil Langston had trouble bringing the ball up the court. At the end of regulation the score was tied 56-56. In overtime Gildford completely took over, scoring five field goals by five different players before Belgrade finally sank a bucket with seconds to play. Some Belgrade players said they should have defeated Gildford, that they didn't "bring their A game" to the first match. Flatness, on the other hand, said, "We weren't nervous about playing Belgrade, but we didn't play very well, couldn't get the lead out of our butts. We didn't have a coach to pump us up except to say, 'Go kill 'em boys!'" Several Belgrade players did acknowledge that Miller had been "amazing." Larry Moore said, "The big kid just tore us up, Miller had long arms and he could jump. And he was a good shooter. We fouled him three or four times and he made every free throw."

Gildford had escaped from what it thought was its toughest match, at least until it might likely confront Townsend in the final. But first Gildford had to take care of a team from far western Montana, the Superior Bobcats.

Superior is just off and easily seen from Interstate 90, roughly halfway between Missoula and the Idaho line. It is the county seat of Mineral County but, of the fifty-six counties in Montana, Mineral

County is number fifty-four on Montana license plates. In other words there aren't many people in Mineral County and its county seat isn't a very large town. I have traveled by Superior countless times over the years coming from Oregon to visit various members of my family in Montana, venturing into the town itself but once. Even then I had no plans to go there, but during Christmas vacation in 1984, as our family traveled back home in a blizzard, I veered too close to the edge of the road and ended in a ditch. After being pulled out by a roving tow truck (for twenty dollars), we decided it would be wiser to stay the night in the nearest town, which happened to be Superior. Luckily at this mid-evening hour we found a motel room, and the next morning walked out into a wonderland as beautiful as anything Montana has to offer. Superior sits in a canyon along the Clark's Fork of the Columbia River; the snow can really dump in this neck of the woods. The area seldom gets wind so the snow just piles up.

Superior had always had a connection with the woods in one form or another, but in the mid-1950s the town got an economic boost when Diamond Match Company built a large mill four miles east of town. The company had closed its mill in northeast Washington and transferred a number or workers to Superior. A good percentage of the people worked at the mill, and the transfers from Washington increased the size of the high school to the point that by 1959, the school had consistently over 130 students. Several of these transfers added to the strength of the basketball team.

One of these who would start on the team was forward Rick Jasper, whose father was a major person in management at the mill. The other starters were forward Jim Tamietti, Russ Brazill at point guard, Lou Forrey at off guard, and Virgil Whalley at center. If Superior were to ever win the state championship, this would be the year because four out of the five starters were seniors. Only Whalley was a sophomore. The Bobcats were lucky to have a deep bench with Gary Ballou (at center, the only member of the team over six feet tall), Butch Upsahl, Bill LaCombe, and Leroy McGillevray. Over the course of the season,

Superior had eight players who scored at least 20 points in a game.

Most of the time guards Brazill and Forrey were the leading scorers, but everyone was capable of putting up the numbers. Brazill once wrote an article titled, "A Team without a Star"; that is the way the team members looked at themselves, a team without a star. The article analyzed why Superior was winning; in Superior the businesses would shut down for both football and basketball. The teachers would talk to the players every day, tell them how good they were; the team had tremendous support from the student body, had great cheerleaders, a great pep band. When Brazill goes back to Superior, someone who had been in the fourth grade will come up to him and tell him he was part of that championship team. Brazill thought, "How could we not win? How could we let them down? We were a team without a star but had many bright lights."

The coach of Superior was Mac McLaughlin, who wasn't a great x&o man, but a real motivator who got the most out of the team. He stressed defense, turning Superior into a very good defensive team, switching back and forth between zone and man-to-man. When the Superior team members arrived at the state tournament they were shocked to find that many of their opponents were averaging 70 to 80 points a game while Superior averaged only 52 points per game. How could Superior compete against teams like that? They would find the other teams did not score like that against them.

Superior had a 23-3 record coming into the state tournament, but for all its preparation, cohesiveness, the support from everyone, and feeling good about itself, the team was still fortunate to be in the state tournament. It had lost to the Plains Horsemen by a healthy margin in the semi-final of the Western Divisional tournament, finishing in third place, and was granted a challenge match against Lima on the Monday following the championship. Superior defeated Lima and was now one of the eight teams in Helena.

As I have said, they took down Yelloweyes and State School in the first game on Thursday afternoon, and were now slated to play

Gildford on Friday night. Don Miller told me this was one ugly game; no one on either side could do anything right. I sat with him listening to a recording of the last part of that game, and could tell the play was sloppy, everyone shooting poorly, but for all that, Superior was ahead the entire game. As Brazill said, "We felt we were a much better ball club, in our own minds at least, and we would think things were going really well, look up and they were only two points behind. It was one of those games, we would play a little while more and think, well we are pulling away from them now, check the score and they were right there with us. It was that way the whole game. They were a solid team. They played well, played hard and evidently they were good because they won the next year." Cady thought Gildford underestimated Superior. "They were better than we gave them credit for. They were big strong kids." During the day the team had gone on their tour of Helena, "and by game time we were worn out and didn't play very well."

And so it came down to the last few seconds of the game. Superior was up by two points. Brazill brought the ball down, was feeling confident that no one ever stole the ball from him, and the guards on him would not. But suddenly, Miller came out, and with his long arms, reached around Brazill, flicked the ball, grabbed it, and was all alone, heading down the floor for an easy layup. The game would be tied and likely go into overtime. As he approached the basket, Miller eased the ball up; it rolled around the rim and went out! "I was mortified and can see it to this day," Miller said. But there was still time left. Flatness grabbed the rebound and was all alone for a shot from farther out. "I should have tossed it to Miller who was all alone under the basket, but I thought I had the perfect shot. I turned around and the basket was right there. But I missed it; that is the way it goes in basketball." Lynn Hayden remembered, "For Don to miss the layup was just horrible for him. The rest of them just felt bad. No one was going to boo-hiss. Everyone was quiet because he was such a cool guy. When he missed it they knew he was suffering the rest of his life. People didn't yell at the players, didn't yell at the referees. People just didn't do that."

Gildford had lost, but the tournament was not over. The boys had to get up the next morning for a game against Power. The Pirates were not expected to go far in this tournament, but had lost to Plains by only five points and defeated Medicine Lake the next afternoon. Now on Saturday morning the Pirates were in a good position against Gildford, which the previous evening, had lost a heartbreaker, with players physically and emotionally drained. In fact Power was ahead for three quarters in this morning game against the Broncs, was increasing its lead and taking control of the game. At some point in the fourth quarter Power was leading by 17 points when Flatness called timeout. He remembers none of the conversation, but as co-captain with Miller in the huddle essentially said, "This is my senior year and I'm not going to go out losing." He directed the team to a full-court press, said they would play man-to-man. The team had never played man-to-man. Freih, nor anyone else on the team, knew how to play man-to-man defense. Then according to Flatness, "We just caught on fire. We just killed Power. They just quit. They did. They just quit." Gildford won 55-50.

Gildford was feeling more upbeat about its upcoming contest in the consolation match against State School and George Yelloweyes. There was no mistaking State School would be a difficult match; the Beavers had lost to Superior after being in mental disarray. It beat defending state champion Belgrade the next day. And then in the morning it defeated Townsend by nine points, the same Townsend team that many thought would capture top spot in the tournament. As for Yelloweyes, his point total for the three games was 26, 46, and 31. Gildford would have its hands full with this one.

But right off Gildford managed to have Yelloweyes figured out. Toward the beginning of the game, Yelloweyes was coming down the floor, Cady running with him to set up, looked out the corner of his eye, thought Yelloweyes was going to shoot, and then got lucky; Yelloweyes shot, but Cady jumped and caught the ball before it had gone three or four feet out of Yelloweyes' hands. That had a psychological impact on the State School star. He never did well after that. Gildford then had a 1-2-2 zone with Welsh out front meeting Yelloweyes, Cady and Nelson on the sides, and Miller and Flatness underneath the basket. Welsh pretended to let Yelloweyes get by him then he, Nelson and Cady would box Yelloweyes in so he couldn't shoot. Yelloweyes ended with a miserly 16 points and Gildford won by a whopping score of 70-47.

Superior beat Plains 54-47, to win the championship, a game that was never in doubt. But Gildford came away with a few awards of its own: the Broncs got the sportsmanship award, the cheerleading award, and Roger Freih, whose main contribution had been deciding who would play and to cheer from the sidelines—"Go kill 'em boys!"—was named Class C coach of the year.

Roger Freih might have come back to coach the following year, but did not get along with Gildford District Superintendent Myron Loe. More likely Myron Loe didn't get along with Roger Freih. The disenchantment seems to have been related to Freih's teaching skills. Several students said he was not a good teacher. Cady, however, said Freih was not working under the best circumstances, had to work around the fire. Nevertheless, his contract was not renewed and Roger Freih would not come back to Gildford the following year.

Once again, Gildford was without a coach although it didn't seem to matter. The Broncs were poised to win it all in 1960; the new coach would practically have to dismantle the team to keep this from happening. The only question: who would be Gildford's opponent for the championship? It wouldn't be Belgrade; much of its best talent had graduated or moved away. Same with Superior. Power had a good program; maybe it could be Power. Moore was moving up. State School had some bruisers who had talent, learning their craft after landing in Miles City. State School was totally unpredictable because from one year to the next no one knew which players would be there. And then there were a few in the know who had other ideas, who thought the aspirant would be another institution like Gildford, which previously had never had much success in basketball. It just might be a small Catholic school, a school nestled in a mountain valley in southern Montana.

The Catholic Arm of Bozeman

I HAD A PERSONAL CONNECTION, HOWEVER TENUOUS, WITH HOLY Rosary High School in Bozeman. Rosary was only ten miles from where I lived. I would pass within a block of Rosary countless times as I rode into town with my parents or grandparents and later on my own when I had my driver's license. At one point I drove by nearly on a daily basis, but I wager I can count on two hands—minus a finger or two—the number of times I trod on the campus of Rosary itself.

I had forgotten the old square brick school had three stories, that it had a peaked roof, that a by-pass entrance was constructed so fans wouldn't have to tramp through the school to attend a basketball game. In truth I knew very little about Holy Rosary. I did not know the high school was confined to the top floor, leaving the bottom two for the elementary. I did not know that the high school had been established in 1924, and that the original building had been expanded in 1938, making it twice as deep from 3rd Street, creating the gym, auditorium and the by-pass entrance. I did not know of the academic eminence of Rosary, that the teaching staff—consisting mainly of the Franciscan Sisters of Perpetual Adoration—was second to none, that students consistently defeated those from larger schools in forensic competitions, that of the seventeen students who graduated from Rosary in 1961, over half were in the top 95 percent on their SAT scores. I didn't know any of this. What I do remember is the cramped gym in the basement where I watched Belgrade play Rosary from the balconies that stretched along the length of the floor on both sides.

I watched several games there, but on one infamous afternoon

Frank Spragg

when I was on Belgrade's eighth-grade team, I found myself on the floor of this cracker box, sent in to confront the young man I was supposed to guard, Tom Monforton. I met Monforton out on the perimeter, where he proceeded to drain a shot before I had a chance to gain my bearings. From then on it was a case of trying to guard what I could no longer see until Coach Langston mercifully pulled me out. I shouldn't have been discouraged. I would later find out that Rosary dispensed with every team it played that year by 30 points or more, including Emerson (Public) Junior High which represented the entire city of Bozeman. And that Tom Monforton in future years would be named first-team all-state twice and eventually nominated for the Class C Hall of Fame.

But that afternoon fiasco became a one-time personal incident. Most of the time, honestly, unless Belgrade involved Rosary in sports, the school never entered my mind. I found this same mentality for many students at Bozeman High School, which lay not more than a mile west of its parochial counterpart. All said and done, I didn't know any students at Rosary. It was this tight little enclave, out of sight, out of mind, until something was scheduled with the school. The school didn't really enter my consciousness until I wrote in my memoirs how the Rosary basketball coach in 1961 exacted his "revenge" against Belgrade. The Rosary players said no, that is not the way it was, and they were right, but it seemed like a good story anyway and was the basis for my beginning this book.

IN MAY 2012 I WAS WALKING NEXT TO A PARKING LOT ON 3RD STREET in Bozeman, heading north toward Main Street and the Roman Catholic Church, which was undergoing renovation and expansion. As I moved along, I looked down to my right and noticed a small concrete marker designating this piece of real estate, this parking lot as the location of Rosary High School before it moved into its new quarters in 1962. The school was on the corner of 3rd and Babcock with the main entrance facing 3rd Street. Had the main entrance still been there as I walked by, and had I elected to turn right and walk in, I would have found myself at a split level, one set of stairs going up to the second story, the other stairs down to the first.

Deciding to go up, I would have found myself at the beginning of a hallway with classrooms on each side for the fifth and sixth graders, a hallway leading straight back to an auditorium with the stage on the left. Assemblies and theatrical productions were held here, with folding chairs constantly being put up or taken down for one event or another. In one corner was a small kitchen to aid in such events, but normally, the students ate lunch at the main dining hall in the basement of the church. The women put on the lunches; there was no subsidy from the government. The church basement was used also for awards dinners, proms, Sno-balls, and Sadie Hawkins dances.

Going up one more flight of stairs, I would have arrived at the third story, leading to another hallway with three rooms on each side. There were rooms for science, office skills, the library, religion and other basic classes; this was the home for the high school of eighty plus students, nearly three times the size of Gildford but small nonetheless. It was here that students gave respect to the venerable sister cadre, gleaning information that would help take them far in life for a group its size.

Back down at the main entrance, if I went down the stairs, I would see more classrooms for the elementary grades before coming to a door leading to the balcony of the gymnasium in the basement. It was in this space directly underneath the auditorium where history was made in 1960 and 1961. It was unlikely that I or anyone else would walk down to the main floor from this inconvenient location. Usually everyone entered from the by-pass entrance on the right end of the building still facing 3rd Street but next to Babcock. From there if people went down the stairs they would be at the south end of the floor with the boys' (home) locker room on the right. If they did not go down the stairs but straight ahead, they would find themselves at the door of the girls' (visitors') locker-room. This outside entrance was the only ready access to the main floor of the gym. Needless to say, if a fire broke out in the gym during a packed house, players and fans alike might as well curl up and say goodbye.

THE FRONT SECTION OF THIS BUILDING WAS OLD,—FORTY-FIVE YEARS old in 1960,—but not the original Catholic school in Bozeman. That school preceded the local parish, even the diocese in Helena. According to research by Tom Diamond:

"In 1880, an Irish-Catholic woman, Miss Annie McLaughlin, at her own expense, built a one room frame building at 302 North Bozeman Avenue and opened up a school known as St Agnes Academy. She taught the basic four 'R's, reading, 'riting, 'rithmatic, and religion to many who became Bozeman's leading citizens. Annie McLaughlin was a many-sided individual: an expert musician, brilliant scholar, gifted teacher, artist, cattle rancher, and a big-hearted, two-fisted fighter who stood up for her rights, and invariably got them. It was said, if many of the old time settlers of this Catholic faith have passed on their faith to their children, they owe it in large measure to this extra-ordinary woman, who Sunday after Sunday, gathered the little ones around her, and unrecompensed, taught them the fundamentals of their faith. She taught classes here until 1887.

"It sounds like a Sunday school in the normal meaning of the term, but apparently on those Sundays McLaughlin taught the children more than religion. There is no record of what happened to McLaughlin or why she quit teaching. Continuing with Diamond's research, "After the closing of the Academy, a Professor Rowdy took up Annie's work, and opened up a Catholic School in the Farmer's Hotel, which then occupied the site of the old city library on North Bozeman Avenue. The hotel burned down two years later, and the school ceased to exist."

By this time the diocese in Helena had been established, and soon thereafter the parish in Bozeman. For many years there was no school, but the idea of a school never left the minds of the parishioners. In 1915 when rancher John Cahill left his 200-acre ranch to the parish, it was sold immediately by Father August D. Leithham, making $15,000 available for the express purpose of building a school. The school was designed and after Bishop John P Carroll in Helena approved the plans, ground was broken in September. On October 10, Bishop Carroll laid the cornerstone. By 1916, the three-story brick school of "Romanesque" style was completed with a five-room home directly to the north on 3rd Street purchased for a convent. The cost totaled $23,389, with the balance of the money needed to complete the project coming from the parishioners.

But the school could not open. The Sisters of the Third Order of St. Dominic had agreed to staff the school but were forced to pull out because of a personnel shortage. Finally, in September 1919, the new school opened grades one through eight under the care of three teachers of the Franciscan Sisters of Perpetual Adoration from La Crosse, Wisconsin, with a fourth sister arriving as their housekeeper. The order had been established in 1849 by a group of "tertiaries" (members of a monastic third order, usually lay people) of St. Francis who emigrated from Bavaria. Over the years the sisters were known throughout the nation for various forms of charitable and missionary work.

At Rosary, these sisters had duties beyond secular education. They were also there to serve the priests. They would take care of the garments, get the altar ready, and place the cloth over the altar topped by a secondary runner of the appropriate color for the liturgical season. For example if the season was Advent, the color was purple; for normal celebrations, green; for the High Season, gold. Of course if there were a funeral, the color was black. The sisters handled the priests' vestments, an article they wore over their clothing, seeing to it that the vestments were laundered, pressed, placing a plastic cover over them to keep out dust, setting them in the room where the priests would change just before mass, making sure the chalice was there, that the tabernacle (a small container made of gold) into which the host (unleavened bread) went was placed in the sacrament room before mass began. The sisters did not prepare everything for the mass—much was left to the altar boys—but the sisters trained the boys for this service, which was still held entirely in Latin.

The sisters lived a restricted existence. Some said the priests were considered to have a pipeline to God for administrative purposes; the sisters did not have this pipeline, which they were to accept and made a point of getting along with the priests. They were to be frugal. If they needed to travel somewhere, they were at the mercy of others to drive them. They had very structured hours. They could never go to the basketball games, because they were expected to be in the convent by nightfall. This did not imply that they were not fans: they listened to radio broadcasts assiduously, often helping the team notate statistics.

If the sisters had many duties to keep them occupied, their main function was to be the backbone of school education, which they fulfilled admirably for many years. The students had a certain reverence for them and rarely caused them trouble. There had been many luminaries among the sisters over the years and this light would not dim in 1960. At any time during that period there were thirteen or fourteen sisters at Rosary, the majority of them teaching in the elementary school. Several have been singled out to me: Sister Patrina, an office-skills teacher the students thought "older than God" but also "sweet and warm hearted." She also taught history and Dick Ward, for one, thought she taught him more about history than he ever learned in college. There was Sister Celestine, who had been school principal but also introduced the students to music. She would bring her record player to school and have the kids listen to musicals. She was also considered excellent in Latin and English (Latin was the only foreign language taught at Rosary). One name that came up often was Sister Mary Linus, who taught science, physics, and upper-level math, who was considered outstanding by the students. She could have taught college, one said; after all, she had received her doctorate from Notre Dame. She would stay after school and prep students who were about to take SAT exams.

But the sister who had the most overall impact on students may have been Mary Michael Costello, "Sister Mary Michael" as she was called, or "Mother Mary Michael." She taught English, put on plays and musicals, and taught speech. She had also recently been made principal. The students loved her; she was easy going, unflappable and kept the ship on a smooth path. Many of the nuns were awestruck by the priests, but Mary Michael was not. She intermingled with them, speaking with them as equals rather than superiors, even with Father Mackin, who was the head pastor at Rosary and considered aloof by most.

Perhaps it was her unusual receptacle of wisdom. George Gallagher remembered one particular experience with her: he had to take a shop class at Bozeman High because it was not offered at Rosary. Bozeman had originally set the class up for the last period of the day, but because of schedule conflicts, it was moved to one period earlier. Bozeman knew about the arrangement, and Gallagher and his fellow Rosary classmates knew of the arrangement, but Mary Michael was not informed, or so Gallagher thought. After shop and mechanical drawing, instead of going back to Rosary, he would go to the pool hall for an hour before arriving back at Rosary just in time for basketball practice. At the end of the year Gallagher told Mary Michael about his caper, thinking he had pulled one over on her. She said, "No, you didn't pull one over on me; I knew what you were doing and as long as you stayed out of trouble I decided to let it go." She was that way, pragmatic.

I had heard so much about Sister Mary Michael Costello and now, on a sunny January afternoon, I drove into Oregon's Columbia Gorge to meet her for a one and only time. She lived at a convent for the Franciscan Sisters of the Eucharist, a beautiful old Spanish-style mansion. The place had cost $1 million to build in 1916, sold when the husband suddenly passed away, fell into disrepair under several ownerships, and had been abandoned for seven years when the Catholic Church purchased it at a steep discount in 1975. The sisters living there with much toil, along with generous help of others, largely restored the property to the beautiful residence it is today.

I knocked on the door and was let in by one of the other sisters who immediately introduced me to Sister Mary Michael, as she preferred to be called. She was ninety-four years old, moving slowly with a walker, motioning me into an adjoining room where I could conduct the interview. Touching her chair, she sat down carefully and we began to talk. Sister Mary Michael may have looked frail but her mind was razor-sharp, her hearing intact. She had been at Holy Rosary for six years ending forty-six years before our meeting, but could recite the name and describe each student of the 1960 and 1961 classes as if she had met them yesterday. She could give detailed experiences from her early life, discourse on complex liturgy, and in general answer with ease any question I threw at her.

In a way, Sister Mary Michael made me think of Mother Teresa. She had known from an early age she would heed the call to serve God, to take the vows of sisterhood. She would live a life of simplicity close to poverty but she proved to be a shrewd administrator, always getting things done, getting along with everyone. She had been a principal at Rosary, then became a *provincial*, which was like a regional manager over all the convents in Oregon, Washington, Idaho, and Montana. She had helped negotiate the purchase of the mansion where she now lived. If she was Spartan in her own life, she had no compunction about acquiring materials or services for others or for the general good. When her fellow sisters were hesitant about approaching people for a project, she would say, "You don't get anything if you don't ask."

During the entire time I was there she had a good word for everyone, and I could feel that she meant it. She had a deep conviction that everyone had a job to do and though everyone might not be likable, you had to learn to get along with people and respect them, to "make things work, go with the flow."

Sister Mary Michael grew up in Spokane, Washington, one of

seven children, living across the street from the convent and from St. Francis Elementary, where she went to school. Then she went to Mary Clift High School, an all-girls Catholic School in Spokane. Her father was somewhat religious, which translated into having integrity, always doing the right thing. He had an important job keeping the trains moving from Spokane to Missoula, keeping charge of the rails and the bridges. They had to be in perfect order because there weren't any airplanes when Sister Mary was young; the trucking industry was in its infancy, so railroads in those days, as she put it, "made the West."

Her father let members of the family do whatever they wanted, was supportive of whatever they wanted to be. That meant supporting his wife who was deeply devout in the church. She made sure that all of the children attended Catholic school and she prayed that one of her sons would become a priest. Several children and grandchildren took the vows. Sister Mary Michael said, "She prayed for one and got all of us."

Sister Mary had thought about becoming a nurse, but there was a great need for teachers in the schools at the time, a need to keep the Catholic schools going. There were no lay teachers in Catholic schools; they were all sisters. These teachers had done a great job, in Sister Mary's eyes, of training students to do the right thing. That was the impetus for her to take the vows; she wanted to do the right thing. But where would she be trained? There was the Provident Sisters at Holy Names, an order in Spokane, but she knew nothing about them; the only order she knew was the Franciscans because they had been her teachers all the way through grade school and high school.

When Sister Mary desired to be in the Franciscan order, she went to La Crosse, Wisconsin, because that was where the Franciscans were trained. She moved into a large convent with one thousand other young women who came mainly from Iowa, Wisconsin, and various other states in the Midwest. This was a training convent, a temporary place where the sisters lived until they took their vows and were sent to missions all over the world.

The first year was *postulency,* which was a form of boot camp. The girls were broken down into groups of thirty-five and it was with this group that each girl lived, worked, and socialized during the first year. The girls got up at 5:30 a.m. and were in mass by 6:00 a.m.. They were asked to say certain prayers during the mass; the pastors had been asked to say these prayers but they became too busy and asked others to say them instead.

For most of the day, the young women were in regular classes, but they also studied the Bible and theology. They also had to chant the Office twice a day, which was a set of scriptures usually out of the Book of Psalms. They each had to make their beds, clean the living area, and wash the floors. Some of the women worked in the kitchen. Sister Mary never worked in the kitchen except for washing dishes. There was no physical training; work was considered physical training. All were in bed by 9:00 p.m. Sister Mary would continue all her life to retire by 9:00 p.m. Most of all, the women had to live together, live with other women they might not like initially but would learn to like.

The word *postulency* meant each woman was asked to *come in,* to be a part of the order. If the order didn't think a woman was going to make it, did not fit in, she was not asked to come in. As rigorous as the training was, only 10 percent did not make the grade after the first year.

The second and third years were called *novice.* The first year of novice was very strict; each woman would work outside the convent during that year. The training was all religious; no regular classes on English, math, or the like. Instead it was all religious training, more theology and study of the Bible. There may have been a thousand women at the training convent, but only 100 were in the convent at any one time; the rest were outside working.

During the third year, the women were *missioned* somewhere. They would sign a form, which was a directive to go to a certain parish and teach a certain grade, the same idea as student teaching. Many assignments were close to La Crosse but some were not. A woman might be sent as far away as Spokane.

Finally, after the third year, each young woman took the vows and became a sister, a part of an order. They followed a book of rules, approved in Rome, which was called a *constitution* (the rules were the same throughout the order but could be different for different orders). Part of the training was to learn the constitution. Like the army, it was very structured.

Sister Mary's first assignment was to teach at Aquinas High School in La Crosse. It may have started out to be a temporary assignment but she stayed at Aquinas for seventeen years. Aquinas was a large high school with 1,200 students, and was considered a *diocese* school because it was administered by the diocese. Sister Mary taught English, speech, and drama. She had a stage crew that built the scenery, and every year put on a big musical or play. Two hundred and fifty kids were involved and did a fantastic job, according to Sister Mary. The school put on *Brigadoon,* and *Around the World in Eighty Days,* among others. The school had a very good orchestra directed by a sister who was "fantastic" at music.

And then one day, Sister Mary was reassigned to Holy Rosary. The school needed someone to be the principal, to be the mother superior and to teach English. They picked her because she could do all that. She taught English because she achieved a master's degree in English from Marquette University. She considered teaching her main job, teaching four classes of English. She taught speech and drama, directing plays during the evenings, the only one who did. Sometimes she got help from Montana State, which would send a drama intern to help out.

Being a principal was on the side. It was an adjustment for her to go from a large school to a tiny school but she loved Rosary. She not only taught English but speech and sent several students to speech contests.

The school had four priests, all who she thought were very good men. The head priest was Father Paul M. Mackin who she liked very much. She loved working with his assistants, Father Jim Burns, Father M.J. (Joseph) O'Donnell, and Father James McCarthy. The parish owned the school, so the principal person in the school was the head priest. Father Mackin was in charge of the money and had the responsibility of paying the sisters. They were there to serve the priests and worked with them, but Father Mackin for the most part left the sisters alone. Sister Mary Michael never had a problem with him. She never had a problem with any of the priests. But she did not think they had a special pipeline to God. In fact they were not considered above other people but merely administrative heads, like the father of a family. They made sure the bills were paid and that everything was going OK. It was a good relationship.

On a typical day the sisters would get up early and pray for a half hour, have breakfast, be off to mass for another half hour, then off to school. In 1962, when the new school was built outside of town, the sisters had to ride to school, but prior to that, the convent was conveniently located next door to the school. School started at 8:30 a.m. and lasted until 3:30 p.m., after which the teachers prepared for the next day, corrected papers, and so forth. There would be dinner, prayers again at 8:00 p.m. and then bed.

Sister Mary said as an English teacher, you had to be ahead of the students, or "you were sunk," especially if the students were reading novels or short stories. At one point she had a set of identical twins in her class, one of whom called her years later when she was living in Portland, telling her he needed a job. Sister Mary said, "You can have the job if you can diagram a sentence. Which he did." He went on to thank his teachers at Rosary for teaching him to diagram a sentence and for giving him a foundation in grammar.

Sister Mary liked Rosary especially because at such a small school, the kids didn't get lost. She had said, "This was my nicest assignment, and I was so lucky because everyone cooperated and were always the best that they could be. With about eighty students and with four classes going on at once, in such a small class, the kids received plenty of attention." She said the kids should have been at the top of the percentile, and she was inspired by students who were unusually bright. Many of her students received doctorates or became attorneys, physicians, and the like. At Rosary she didn't have to worry about sex, drugs, and guns. She didn't keep track of dating habits but as long as the students were happy, that is what mattered. It was a happy time.

She said people in the parish were very supportive, very good about helping when they could. When the Northwest Accreditation Association sent someone by to inspect the school, some of the mothers would get together and put on a luncheon for them. This was the kind of cooperation she had.

In addition to teaching, being principal, and preparing for mass, Sister Mary was the mother superior. This meant that she was head of the house, head of the convent. She made sure the other sisters were paid, that there was enough food in the house, that rules were observed. The priests had nothing to do with that. Because a sister could be mother superior in a school for no more than a certain period of time, she was assigned to be provincial for the Pacific Northwest.

I concluded my visit with Sister Mary Michael and left. I hoped to visit her once more but never did. She would have been ninety-five years old on August 7, 2011, but passed away in June.

Sister Mary had mentioned the priests. The most recent addition, Father McCarthy, was brand new to the parish, new to his vows, and looked even more youthful than his considerably young age. The students had not had the chance to know him as well as the others. A tragedy would befall him much later in life, when he became the unsuspecting victim of a gas leak. At his home in Butte and while sitting in his bathtub, he lit a cigarette which set off an explosion, killing him and destroying the home.

Father James Burns was universally loved by all who knew him. One student said Burns was a really nice guy and liked the kids. He was the one priest girls could talk to if they had a problem. He was approachable; people often invited him to dinner, invitations, which he would accept if at all possible. He would take the kids on outings: Joe Cahill said, "On one occasion three of us rode with Burns to a meeting in Helena. He took us to a hot springs south of town and told us to stay there until he returned. It was a fun little trip." Burns also taught a religion class known as *Apologetics,* which meant learning how to defend the principles of the Catholic faith and in this he went by the book. There was the right doctrine and everything else was wrong; it really wasn't open to discussion. Yet, kids overlooked that because they liked him personally. Several girls wanted Father Burns to officiate when they married.

The other assistant priest, as likable as Burns and a real character, was Father M. Joseph O'Donnell. Like the other priests at Rosary (except for Father Mackin) he came from Butte. It seemed that nearly all the priests originated from Butte in those years. He was short, tubby, but no one ever gave him any guff. He liked to walk downtown with black leather gloves, stop in at the B & B Café—the worst café in Bozeman, where all the sleaze hung out—and be as gentle as a lamb. But if anyone was bullying, acting like motorcycle gang wannabees, he would settle things down. They listened to him.

As with Father Burns, O'Donnell liked people and they liked him. He taught religion classes at Rosary but also directed plays, and those associated with them said he did a great job. What is most memorable about Father O'Donnell was his sense of humor. He loved humor and could be funny himself. Once during a high mass on Sunday, Father O'Donnell walked along the aisle sprinkling the congregation with holy water, holding a short brass baton with a sprinkler head at the end. On his left walking with him was an altar boy who held the water vessel, his "ammo" as he called it; on his right another altar boy held up his vestment so his right arm and hand were free to hold the brass baton. The three reached the beginning of the aisle at the entry door and were just beginning to turn to go back up when the entry door flung open. Standing there was a young woman with her daughter; she was embarrassed for being late. O'Donnell's and the woman's eyes met; without a word, he dipped the wand into the holy water and, with a grand flourish and flick of the wrist, gave her a shot of holy water point blank in the face. Chuckling, he turned back up the aisle and resumed the procession to the altar. Diamond, one of the altar boys, said, "If this scene had been shown in a theatre, it would have won an Oscar."

O'Donnell loved a good practical joke even if he was an unwitting part of it. Which happened when several Rosary students pulled off a Christmas abduction caper. Every year the city displayed a nativity scene in the city park near the cemetery; included in that scene of course was the display of several sheep. At exactly 9:02 p.m., a car pulled up from the east to meet several boys hidden near the nativity scene. All the sheep were shepherded out of the manger and tossed into the car, with one placed at the home front door of each boy's girlfriend. The next day the *Bozeman Daily Chronicle* wrote about this "malicious act" that had happened the night before. Part of the prank was for the boys to confess their misdeed to Father O'Donnell, trooping to the confession booth where he was holding court. It must be remembered that confession in the Catholic church was a solemn affair, all done in the strictest confidence; the priest was, after all, between heaven and hell. In the confession, the priest sat in the middle of a closure; people would speak through a veil and could only see the dim outline of the priest inside, as in the same way he could only see them. The priest would try to say a rosary in response to a confession or perhaps give counsel, but often he was so rushed he would tell the confessor to say a few Hail Marys or Our Fathers. The confessor would then be in the good graces of God and the priest would go on to the next person. For a priest to express levity during confession was highly unusual.

The boys timed it so they would all go to confession together. Often O'Donnell acted like he wasn't listening, but he was listening this time. The first boy, Jim Murphy, confessed that he had stolen a sheep from the city nativity. O'Donnell said, "YOU DID WHAT?" Murphy repeated his transgression. O'Donnell asked if the sheep had been returned. Murphy said yes; his girlfriend got the police to return the sheep under a "don't ask because we won't tell" agreement. O'Donnell responded "Your penance is to say one for me." When Murphy was finished, his fellow cohort, Ed Seitz, came up to the box and confessed. A chuckle was heard from the confessional. Then Seitz was followed by Joe Kearns, Ron Brooks, Jerry Monforton and Rick Ritter, all giving the same confession. By this time there was a thunderous roar of laughter from the confessional booth. Father Mackin from the next booth came over to see if everything was all right. Father O'Donnell assured him that everything was normal. O'Donnell was dying to share his story with Father Burns but could not because of confessional secrecy. Only months later did the boys let him off the hook and shared their story of "wild criminal mischief."

BASKETBALL ARRIVED AT THE HIGH SCHOOL IN 1938, BUT THE BULL-dogs, as they were to be known, were largely living the same history as Gildford. Generally the success rate was middling followed by more middling. The team did win the district tournament in 1944 but after that, through the 1950s, the Bulldogs were nearly always in the middle of the pack, usually beating Wilsall, Clyde Park and Willow Creek, but generally coming up on the short end against the likes of Belgrade and Three Forks.

In the mid 1950s, the team was coached by Joe (Jumpin' Joe) Kelly who generally had more wins than losses. He was followed by Joe Doohan who coached at Rosary for one year, and who was highly praised by many students. He had a passion for forensics and estab-lished the speech and debate program at Rosary, defeating schools in Class A and AA. In sports, Doohan started a football program which understandably did not do well in competition because everything had to be instituted from scratch. He also loved track and field, a sport many other coaches tended to neglect. Naturally he was also expected to coach basketball which was not his favorite sport. And he didn't have much to work with. He only had one senior, J.C. Maney, and the juniors had little experience. Still, for all that, he came away with a 9-12 record.

It seemed Rosary was destined to always be ordinary in basketball, but there was a quiet groundswell in the lower ranks, an indoor version of what was taking place in Gildford. During these years in the early fifties, there was a group of young kids that would stand on the sidelines during the high school basketball practices; when there was a break in the practice and the high school kids were off the floor—maybe for a time out in scrimmage, or to listen to the coach— these youngsters would run out onto the floor, play around and shoot baskets. There were John Wantaluk, Paul Weber, Mike Murphy, Dick Ward, Frank Seitz. They would go out on the floor and were constantly chased off by the coach. But whenever coach wasn't looking and there was a break in the action, they were back out on the floor. They called themselves the original gym rats.

Chief among them and one of the earliest of the gym rats was a runt of a kid named Tom Monforton. He had come from pioneer stock on both sides of his family. The Monfortons had come to Gallatin Valley from France via Ontario Canada. The first to arrive was Henry Monforton, who settled near the Four Corners area west of Bozeman and donated land for the present day Monforton School, which was named after him. He also chipped in five thousand dollars to help the diocese buy the land for the new Bozeman school in 1915. His brother Remi followed in his footsteps and settled at the mouth of Gallatin Canyon. Remi's son Ernest improved the ranch, raising registered Herefords but also some wheat. Ernest was the father of Tom Monforton, and it was at the mouth of Gallatin Canyon where Monforton would spend his formative years.

The Monfortons had always been Catholics and it was natural that the kids would attend a Catholic school. Tom had eight brothers and sisters; he and his brother Jerry, one year younger than he, brought up the rear of the family. The Monforton boys had all been involved in basketball through the years: father Ernest was an avid fan, never missed a game, was a principle financial supporter of the team, and with the mouth of Gallatin Canyon ten miles from Bozeman, the Monforton family would not head home for the day until basketball practice was over. As his older brothers were out on the floor practicing young Tom, in only the first and second grade, would watch, darting out on the floor to take a few pot shots of his own when the players were off the court until yelled at once again by the coach.

Monforton and the other boys grew into the nucleus of a team that entered into a city-wide basketball tournament for the sixth grade league, which included all five public elementary schools in Bozeman plus Rosary. But Rosary had very few sixth graders so the team was made up largely of players from the fourth grade— of which Monforton, Weber, Murphy, and Wantaluk were members—and the fifth grade which included Ward and Seitz. Rosary won the tournament, which did not make the tournament officials happy; here a bunch of underage pipsqueaks were taking off with the trophy. The next year the officials would not allow any boy younger than the sixth grade to be in the tournament. Monforton was forced to sit out a year. When he was in the sixth grade and once again eligible, Rosary roasted every team it faced.

This dominance would not end with the sixth grade. When Monforton was in the seventh grade Rosary beat every team it played until it ran up against the Livingston All-Stars at the end of the season. Livingston had Francis Ricci, already 6'5" and Jay Sumner, both whom in high school would take Livingston to the state Class A title, upsetting Anaconda and legendary star Wayne Estes. Livingston beat Rosary twice, but only by one point each time. For Rosary it was a combination of good things: good coaches and an exceptional group of young kids playing constantly together in the gym. Monforton, like other kids his age, when he wasn't playing at the school, was playing somewhere at home—in his case with a hoop down in the basement.

It was with this legacy that Monforton and others entered the eighth grade. Seitz and Ward had moved on to high school, but now brother Jerry was at Tom's side, the two of them making a devastating guard combination. Weber, Murphy, and Wantaluk made up the front court. Another boy was also on the team, Dennis Tierney—a backup of sorts. The eighth grade team beat every team in the valley by an average of 30 points. No one could even begin to challenge them this time, including the Livingston All-Stars.

But the prospects did not look good when Tom Monforton became a freshman. John Wantaluk transferred to Bozeman High. Paul Weber's parents moved to Billings, where he would star for Billings Central both in football and basketball. Dennis Tierney moved away to Wisconsin where he became a state all-star in basketball. It looked as if Rosary would move back into its accustomed role of mediocrity.

The Kid from Chicago

O UR GENTLEMAN IS AN AVID PLAYER OF HANDBALL. TWO OR THREE days a week he arrives at The Ridge in Bozeman for a go-around with fellow players, several of whom have competed against him for years and are considerably younger than he is. Picking up the sport in college, he went on to win state tournaments, mostly as a doubles player, when he lived in Billings, then Helena, and now Bozeman. He is lean and fit for a man in his late seventies and along with a nimble body has a sound mind. He can recite episodes going back six and seven decades with astonishing recall. For the skeptics, I have visited with him on three separate occasions, sometimes recapping the same subject matter, and with each question he has given me the same, albeit differently worded, answer. Of the four coaches who stood on the sidelines for either the 1960 or 1961 Class C championships, he is the only one still living. Because of that and because he is naturally loquacious, I know far more about him than his fellow coaches. Which is unfair, I suppose. But Neal Joseph Christensen had a compelling background leading up to his years with Holy Rosary High School, something small-town bumpkins in mid-century Montana could hardly imagine.

HIS GRANDFATHER, NELS CHRISTENSEN, HAD COME AT AGE FIFTEEN from the Copenhagen, Denmark, area as an indentured servant, working through his youth for the Virginia family that purchased him. As he became an adult, he worked his way cross-country, finally landing in Oconto, Wisconsin, where he started a trucking business. He became a wealthy man, spreading out to own a brewery, warehouses, a Ford garage; he was one of the first stock buyers of the Green Bay Packers. Then he lost everything in the Great Depression. His kids were left with nothing.

Neal Christensen became a grandchild of the depression. He was born in Albany, Indiana, on April 16, 1933, but his father, Henry Christensen, worked in different locations, taking his family with him, working all types of odd jobs, earning as little as fifty cents a day. Often he had government jobs, Civil Conservation Corp. work where he had to travel. Then one day Dad got a job in the insurance industry as an underwriter. The family would land in the South Side of Chicago.

The Christensens led a frugal existence in Chicago; Neal slept in the bedroom, Mom and Dad on a Murphy bed in the front room. As a kid he always had a job, shining shoes in bars, delivering papers, manning a Kool-Aid stand. For shining shoes he got a nickel, for selling a large cup of Kool-Aid, three cents. To sell Kool-Aid, he would line up his orange crate as close as possible to the commuter train where people got off after a day's work.

But not too close. There were maybe ten slots for selling Kool-Aid along the street and the older bigger kids got the closer slots. You had to be accepted because the South Side was a tough place. His parents were strict in some ways, his mother a devout Catholic, but they did not corral him from being out on the streets. He never got into real trouble, never went to jail, but he was constantly getting into fights. It was a way of life; there were gangs. Christensen was part of a gang that had thirty kids. And yet his parents were not concerned.

Chicago was very segregated in those days. The blacks lived about a mile away but that did not keep Christensen from battling them on a regular basis. He grew up full of prejudice. His uncle was a cop on the take from Al Capone and said the only good n— was a dead n—-. Everyone he knew talked the same way: give them an inch and they will take a mile. Curiously he never actually knew any black people until he went to Michigan State University. Through athletics there he came to know blacks and became good friends with many of them. By the time Christensen moved to Montana, he had grown out of his prejudice. To him Indians were just like other people. Asians, blacks, whites, Indians? It didn't make any difference to him.

Life may have been a challenge in Chicago, but there was always room for sports. When Christensen was young he lived about one and a half miles from Comiskey Park. He and his friends would jump on street cars with grates on the windows. They would grab onto the grates with their hands, their feet on the axle covers, and ride to Comiskey Park to watch the White Sox. About five or six times a summer the group would take a combination of commuter trains and subways across town and watch the Cubs in Wrigley Field. When he wasn't watching baseball, he would play ball on the local sandlots.

Sports had been a family legacy. Christensen's dad was the leading scorer on the La Crosse State Teachers College (now University of Wisconsin-La Crosse) basketball team his senior year. He played against the future coach and legend John Wooden when Wooden was at Purdue and later against him in the industrial (semi-pro) leagues. Few people remember that Wooden was a great basketball *player.*

Christensen would always play basketball and baseball during his formative years, but his first love, the sport he thought was his ticket to the future, was football. As a freshman at parochial Mt. Carmel High School in Chicago, he had been only 5'2" and 120 pounds, but by spring break he had shot up to 5'6" and 130 pounds, and by summer 5'11" and 170 pounds. At Mt. Carmel, he had reason to be excited; he was playing with an unusually gifted group of players, five of whom would go on to play for Notre Dame; two of those would be co-captains for the Fighting Irish in their senior years. Mt. Carmel would go on to win three straight city championships (there was no statewide football championship in Illinois) and was arguably considered the greatest high school football team Illinois had ever seen.

Then Henry came home and said, "Neal, we're movin'. We are

moving to Jackson, Michigan." He had bought into an insurance agency there. Christensen was devastated and protested, "But Dad, I can't go!" He had grown up on the South Side and had all his friends. But there was no discussion. They were going and that was it. And Mom insisted he go to a Catholic school. So he would attend St. Mary's in Jackson, which was a much smaller school than Mt. Carmel.

They moved before school began, and Henry introduced him to the coach. The coach asked him what position he played; he said running back. Christensen was the fastest kid in school, had a great running game, and within weeks, he was on the varsity. One day the coach came up to him and said, "Neal, I want you to play end." Christensen had never played end. "You are fast, hold onto the ball well, and I need an end. You aren't going to start as a running back but you could start as an end." Christensen played at this position for two years and got to like it. The team was a part of the Southern Michigan Catholic Conference—teams coming from Kalamazoo, Lansing, Battle Creek, Ann Arbor—a tough league to play in. The next year they thought they could win the state Class B championship.

Then Henry had trouble at the insurance agency. He told his son they were moving back to Chicago. The coach in Jackson said Christensen could live with him. He would make sure he studied, would make sure he stayed out of trouble. Christensen had been written about in the newspaper. He protested to his father, "Dad, this isn't right!" But he knew his dad had to work. He had been taken for a ride by the insurance company he bought into in Jackson. So Henry moved to Chicago to start work and it would be Chicago where Christensen finished out his junior year.

He had wanted to go back to Mt. Carmel, but a new rule was put into place which said a student had to live in the area of a particular Catholic school for one year before he could play for the school. The situation looked discouraging financially, but Henry was certain his son could get a scholarship. He didn't know where Christensen would play but he *had to play*. Dad and Mom found a school west

Frank Spragg

of Chicago in Elmhurst called Immaculate Conception that was willing to take Neal on, and it was at ICHS where Christensen would play his senior year. He was voted most valuable player on a team that was co-champions of the Northeast Catholic Conference and he had great teammates, several again, who would go on to play ball for major colleges.

After graduation in 1951, Christensen had a tryout with Notre Dame but nothing came of it. Instead the coaches referred him to Xavier University, and the folks down there were thrilled to have him; he could easily play at Xavier, they told him. They offered him a scholarship and Christensen was set to head south. Then Michigan State University came into the picture. The coaches there called him over along with another boy who had played tackle at Immaculate Conception. They told him he could become the next Sonny Grandalius; Sonny had been an All-American running back at Michigan State. Later Christensen learned that every kid who came to check out Michigan State got the same talk.

The entire staff would be there, would treat the recruits like royalty, but the principal man extending a hand to Christensen and his fellow aspirants was Clarence (Biggy) Munn, the head coach at Michigan State. "Don't call me Mr. Munn," he would tell everyone he met, "Just call me Biggy." He was likable, he was personable, and he had an absolutely brilliant football mind. With everything else on his plate, Biggy managed to find time to teach a class on football for anyone who wished to take it. In that class, Christensen said, he learned more about football than he ever wanted to know.

Before Biggy Munn came along, Michigan State was a backwater school, considered the cow pasture platoon by folks over at the University of Michigan in Ann Arbor. In fact, before the name change, the school was officially known as Michigan Agricultural College. Unlike the other major state universities in the Midwest, Michigan State wasn't a member of the Big Ten Conference. Even if the Spartans were a top-ranked team, they could never go to the Rose Bowl.

But Coach Munn would change all that. He was part of a new breed of gridiron coaches after World War II, when universities ballooned with so many students coming aboard on the GI bill. Coaches no longer just directed teams, they built *programs*. Biggy Munn elevated recruiting to an art form. When you talked to him, he convinced you he had the greatest team in America. And when kids came to Michigan State, they didn't just hear about the great Sonny Grandalius—Sonny gave them a personal tour. It was all top-drawer, leaving a deep impact on any prospect who stepped on campus.

To see the entire Michigan State football complex was an experience of wonderment. There were several locker rooms, one for the varsity and one for the freshman, which was huge because there were so many players. When Biggy gathered his army of veterans and recruits at the beginning of the preseason— 300 in all—he would sit atop his tower watching five scrimmages at once. Regularly he would tell one of his assistants to send this player up to the main scrimmage or that one back down.

Coach Munn didn't care what a player did off the field—get drunk, carouse, do dare devil stunts, overeat—as long as he came to the practices and performed. If he didn't perform, he didn't play. It was as simple as that. Munn ran a football factory, and if you couldn't do the job, someone else just as good as you would take your place. It was a numbers game.

Biggy had changed how football was played. He installed the multiple offense, combining the two major formations of the day, the T and the single wing behind an unbalanced line. Opponents never knew what Michigan State was going to throw at them. In previous decades the Spartans had never won many games, but by 1951, they were undefeated. In 1952 they were national champs.

Christensen was given his uniform and equipment and told to go out and play; he had no idea which team he was on or who he was playing with. And then, as he put it, "They just started beating us up." No one was ever cut during the preseason; the staff didn't have to. The winnowing was so brutal that, by the end of the first week, a third of the players were gone. After two weeks, half the players; they couldn't put up with the punishment. Kids in the dorms would get up in the middle of the night, pack their bags, and vanish before dawn. One boy Christensen played football with in high school, who was burley at 6'3" and 220 pounds, was called up to the varsity and lined up against Don Coleman, who weighed only 178 pounds but was an All-American offensive wing tackle, so quick and strong, he could pop seams of two or three dummies in a week. He beat the friend up so badly, he lay in his bunk that night crying; Christensen came in and asked what the matter was.

"Someone died in the family?"

"I can't play again, Neal, can't ever play football again."

"But Bill—."

"No," the friend said, "I'm serious." He quit and never came back, never played football again.

When Christensen first talked to Munn, he came away thinking he would be the next All-American running back, but when he started practices, saw how the other players were bigger, tougher, faster, he realized how far away he was from stardom. Christensen had scored ten touchdowns his senior year in high school, but now he talked to one player who scored ten touchdowns in one *game.* Christensen remembered catching a pass one day in a split scrimmage and Jimmy Ellis, All-American safety, ran right up and took the ball away from him. It didn't help that Biggy was standing just a few feet away when it happened. *"How do you expect to play if you let someone take the ball away from you!"* barked the coach.

Christensen swore he would never quit, but he was getting beat up in the scrimmages, wasn't getting much encouragement, in fact didn't think he was even being noticed. The folks at Xavier had told him Michigan State was too big for him; the team was three or four deep in every position and he would never get to play much. If he came to Xavier, he might even get a starting position as a freshman, certainly as a sophomore. If he were willing to come down they would pay his way.

On a Thursday at the beginning of the season, Christensen up and left Michigan State, traveled to Xavier, worked out with several players, and with almost no observation, the staff told him that although he would be ineligible for a year because of transferring too late, he would be under full scholarship. So he went back to Jackson, Michigan, for a few days, hung out with friends, and went back to Michigan State on Tuesday to work out and stay in shape and the staff there didn't even know he had been gone. They called out his name to be defensive halfback; he played in several scrimmages, intercepted a couple of passes, tackled some people. At the end of the week, this guy walks up and asked, "Meat or fish? You are on the freshman team going on a trip to Ann Arbor. Meat or fish?" Christensen chose fish and stayed at Michigan State. That season, he didn't start but was in a great deal, playing about a third of all games. He was playing defense and by all estimates playing well.

By spring practice, Christensen was playing for the varsity, slated to start as a defensive back in the biggest showcase game of the spring: the Green-and-White spring practice game. He had not known what he was going to do after high school—be a butcher or a milk truck driver—and now he was playing for a nationally recognized football team! Michigan State was in the middle of what would become a twenty-eight game winning streak, (they would win the national championship that next fall), and now, in the spring of 1952, he was on this team. His parents and girlfriend came over to watch the game and he did well; although he didn't intercept any passes, he made numerous tackles. At the end of the game, Henry asked the coaches if Neal still might be better off going to a smaller school where he could play more. He was told Neal hadn't been a very good football player when he came here, but he was now. They told him he was on full scholarship. There were ample people in his position (including All-American Johnny Wilson) so he couldn't suit up that year, but he would play in all the scrimmages, do all the sprint drills, the calisthenics, go to all team meetings, travel with the team. It was a form of redshirting, although they didn't call it that in those days. He had a great time during his sophomore year and learned a great deal from Jimmy Ellis on how to cover people. In that fall of 1952, Christensen was certain he had the glory world on a string. It was just a matter of showing up for practice.

Then on the morning of January 4, 1953, he woke up, turned on the radio, and found his life turned upside down. The news said that all colleges were going to the one-platoon system; all players would have to play both offense and defense. Suddenly if teams had been three deep in a position, now they were six deep. Very talented, even All-American players were leaving major schools in droves (Jimmy Ellis at Michigan State suddenly found himself third on the depth chart), wandering around the United States like vagabonds seeking a school that would accept them. Murdo Campbell, who played for University of Montana, remembered four or five kids from University of Washington coming up to the coach asking to play, asking for a scholarship. Some stayed at Montana and became some of the best players on the team, some were forced to move on; careers all around the nation were going in the dumps.

To throw salt into an already open wound, laborious new rules were put into place for substitution. A player could go in a game or come out only once a quarter. If he came out in the middle of a quarter, he could not go in again until the following quarter. (If he came out at the very end of a quarter, say the first quarter, he could still go back in at the beginning of the second quarter.) Coaches and referees hated the new rule. Only a computer-brained person could remember who had been in, who had come out, and when it all took place.

Even with all the upheaval, Christensen, in the summer of 1953, decided to stay at Michigan State. He figured he was a fine runner, had good defensive skills, and could make it both ways. And yet he found he couldn't. One day he learned he was fifth on the depth chart. He didn't know what to do.

By 1953 Michigan State was in the Big Ten, had the best record in the conference, and was entitled to go to the Rose Bowl to be played on New Year's Day in 1954. All the main players were taking a break for a while. But the coaches called in Christensen, along with another kid who was a linebacker and a year behind him in school, and told them to keep practicing; *one* of them would travel to the Rose Bowl in Pasadena. Neal was shocked; he didn't even know he was being considered. Normally at Michigan State, if a player was doing well, the coaches were always talking to him: Hey Jim, how's it going? How are your classes going? No one was talking to Christensen.

But now people were thinking of him. Christensen called his dad and said, "Dad, I have a chance to go to the Rose Bowl!" But at the end of the last practice, they took the other guy. Michigan State would travel with 45 players to the Rose Bowl and Christensen found himself number 46. On New Year's Day he would watch television and see the big blond linebacker joining the rest of the team, coming out of the tunnel onto the field.

Christensen went to see Duffy Dougherty, who had taken Biggy Munn's place as head coach at Michigan State when Munn became Athletic Director. Christensen had known Dougherty well, liked Dougherty and knew that the coach liked him; he even had Christensen come over to his home and take care of his yard. But now, Dougherty said, "Neal, I'm really glad you came by. If we had the two-platoon system you would have started at Michigan State. That is how high we are on you. But now we don't have any room for you. We have Travis Buggs, the Indiana state high school sprint champion who is a year behind you in school, but one slot ahead of you on the depth chart. I'm going to have to cut the part of your scholarship which includes your room and board." Dougherty told Christensen he could try but he would be better off going to a smaller school where he could play and get a degree. It was an emotional conversation but he took Dougherty's advice. After Christensen went back to his apartment off-campus, and after packing all his belongings, it hit him that his career at Michigan State was over and that he would never be back. He broke down and cried.

LIFE LOOKED BLEAK, BUT CHRISTENSEN HAD OTHER INTERESTS; HE was in ROTC and loved it. He thought about going to Drake or South Carolina; each had ROTC, but both schools were on the semester system and Michigan State was on quarters. Christensen didn't want to have to drop out of ROTC until the next semester started.

Meanwhile, it just so happened that Tony Storti, who was the head coach at Montana State College in Bozeman, and Brick Breeden, athletic director and basketball coach, were in the Chicago area recruiting at Christensen's old school, Immaculate Conception. They were looking at Joe Bender, a 6'5" basketball center, but in the conversation, the coach told Storti and Breeden about Christensen and his situation, adding that he was one of the best athletes to ever come out of ICHS. The Bozeman folks called Dougherty, got his OK, then called Christensen and offered him a full scholarship. They also told him that Montana State had ROTC and was on the quarter system. Christensen told them, "I'm comin'!" He had never been west of Chicago.

Christensen flew out, got off the plane and was immediately taking part in spring practice. There were no eligibility rules in those days, especially with the switch in the platoon systems. At the beginning of the season, in late August, Christensen started playing and in short time developed a muscle spasm. From then on he had to slowly work his way up, got almost no playing time at first. Eventually he played significant ball, lettered, and had some really fine games.

Christensen loved Tony Storti. Before Storti came along, the Bobcats had been consistent losers. He built the program, kept building it until, near the close of the 1954 season, Montana State was 8-0 going into the last game against arch-rival University of Montana in Missoula. Storti was a fired-up kind of guy, had incredible energy, wanted to win so badly, and now was given a telegram that if the Bobcats beat the Grizzlies, they would go to the Cigar Bowl in Tampa, Florida.

The Bobcats were terrific in the first half. A running back named Don Edwards, who had a scholarship offer at University of Wisconsin but turned it down, was rolling down the field at will racking up 100 yards rushing before halftime. Then with just a few minutes to go before the half, he was banged up with a concussion and out for the rest of the game. Montana State was never the same after that, losing the game by four points. Storti couldn't hold it; he went "wacko," started climbing up the tower holding the time clock. When the other coaches and players pulled him off, he went into the locker-room and started tearing the place up, throwing everything all over. When the players were finally able to enter the locker-room and clean up, they were sent to a dance where they encountered their fellow players from the University of Montana. It became a very awkward situation, with the two sides not interacting at all. Finally the Bobcat players boarded a bus and were back in Bozeman by 3:00 a.m.

The next fall, Montana State had a new football coach, a man by the name of Wally Lemm. He was no Tony Storti, and Christensen disliked him intensely. The two had come to know each other, not through football, but basketball.

NEAL CHRISTENSON HAD ALWAYS BEEN AROUND BASKETBALL, HAD played constantly on the playgrounds when he was in grade school. When he became a freshman in high school, he was still only 5'2" but in Chicago, both the Catholic and the public schools had an unusual system for competition; if a boy was over 5'8", he played for the varsity, or if he was freshman or sophomore, the "bantam weights." If he was 5'8" or shorter, it would be the "lightweights" for the older kids, "flyweights" for the younger. The flyweight team Christensen played with as a freshman went 26-0 against other teams in the inner-city area.

On "Measure Day" every boy in the city was sized to see if he would be with the varsity or the lightweights, the bantam weights, or the flyweights. If boys found themselves on the straddle point, they would rather be the big honcho among shorter talent than the other way around. Kids would walk the streets of South Side Chicago carrying bowling balls, aiming to shrink an inch or so. Of course it never worked.

It was a moot point for Christensen because by the time he became a sophomore, he had shot up in height and weight. When he transferred to St. Mary, he was considered quick and fast, always a starter. The coach called him over during one practice and said, "Neal you are the best driver I have ever had and you aren't driving. What's the matter?" He started driving the basket again, scoring twenty points a game in the 1948-49 season. In 1950 he was with a team that was ranked third in the state and won the Southern Catholic Division in Michigan. When he transferred to Immaculate Conception for his senior year, he was with a mediocre team but he continued his high-volume scoring and was written up in the *Chicago Tribune*. At the end of the year he was first team all-conference guard, and honorable mention for both all-Chicago and all-state.

Even when he was on the cusp of being cut at Michigan State in football, Christensen was recruited by the coach to play basketball. But for Christensen at the time, if there wasn't football, there was nothing. And so when he came to Montana State, he was primed for football. Spring practice at Montana State was nothing like the real deal at Michigan State. The players didn't venture outdoors but stayed in the old Romney gym and worked out, doing various kinds of drills to keep in shape. After "spring practice" was over, Christensen continued to be the gym rat, working out, using the swimming pool, playing handball, whatever activity caught his eye. One day he asked the basketball coach if he could scrimmage with his team. The coach said yes. His name was Wally Lemm.

After watching Neal for a couple of days, Lemm walked up to

him and asked,

"Who are you? Where did you come from?"

Christensen answered that he came to MSC to play football. He had been here since March 31 (the conversation took place sometime in April).

"Where did you play?"

"At ICHS in Elmhurst, Illinois."

"I coached at Lake Forest," Lemm told him; Lake Forest was near Chicago. He knew the conference and knew that Christensen played basketball there. Neal told Lemm he was an honorable mention all-state player.

Lemm said, "Do you want to play here? I will give you a scholarship." Christensen told him he already had a scholarship. "Do you want to play basketball anyway? You will start here."

So Neal started playing right away in the spring. He played in the Blue-Gold scrimmage. Then he went off to ROTC camp at Fort Lewis, Washington. It was rugged basic training which kept him in perfect shape for football the next fall.

But football ate into nearly all of the preseason basketball practices. And then Christensen asked Lemm for an additional week off to let his "football legs" adjust to "basketball legs" (apparently something every guy has to go through when he is a both-sport player). This meant that Christensen did not join the basketball team until just before the first game against Wyoming. Lemm had known from the beginning that Christensen was going to play football, but the reality of the situation must have stuck in his craw: Christensen didn't play against Wyoming. After that he hardly played. He and Lemm didn't connect, almost never spoke to one another. He thought Lemm was a poor coach. And the road trips were dreadful. Montana State was still NAIA (the organization for small colleges) in those days. They would travel down into Wyoming and all around the Rocky Mountains in two stretch station wagons; the coach drove one, the trainer drove the other. Each station wagon had five players. It was all sleep or playing cards in a cramped space. After Christmas, he told Wally this just wasn't cutting it for him; he hadn't been that interested anyway. Lemm said OK. He wasn't very verbal.

Christensen was walking across campus that spring when his good friend, Jim Argeris (who in 2009 was inducted into the Montana State Football Hall of Fame) came running over to Christensen and said,

"Wally wants to see you and he is not happy. He won't give you a scholarship."

"How come?"

Argeris couldn't give a reason. So Christensen went to see Lemm.

"I'm cutting your scholarship," Lemm said.

"For what?"

"I'm just cutting it; that is all you need to know."

"But you can't cut my scholarship; I lettered in football. I have a scholarship in football."

"I can."

"I don't think so."

Christensen went to Breeden, who was his advisor. Breeden said Lemm wasn't cutting his scholarship. Christensen said he didn't know what the deal was, and Breeden didn't know either. He was given his scholarship.

Lemm ended up getting fired as a basketball coach but was rehired the next season as the head football coach after Storti quit with a nervous breakdown. So Christensen was faced with Lemm again. The team finished 4-4-1, with the same boys who in the previous season under Storti went 8-1. There was rampant dissension, with the team split down the middle. Christensen ended up having a terrible year, not getting much playing time, not even getting into some games. To this day Christensen doesn't know for sure what happened, why Lemm had it out for him. Then Wally Lemm was fired as the Montana State football coach. From Montana State he went to the pros, where he eventually became American Football League Coach of the Year with the Houston Oilers. The only thing anyone can say is that he found his wrinkle and it worked for him.

WHEN CHRISTENSEN PLAYED BASKETBALL, FATHER BURNS AT HOLY Rosary had watched him. He knew Christensen because he went to church at Rosary. After Christensen quit over Christmas, Father Burns approached him and said, "I know you aren't playing anymore. Would you be interested in coaching our grade-school kids?" Christensen said sure. At fifty dollars a month, it was almost as much as his scholarship. After school started up in January 1956, he started coaching the junior high-teams.

Immediately he noticed this 4'6" Monforton kid who could shoot the eyes out of the basket. He had Mike Murphy, John Wantaluk, Paul Weber, Dennis Tierney, Frank Seitz, and Dick Ward; he couldn't believe the speed, toughness, knowledge and especially the character of these kids. As already stated, Rosary ran through the competition for the two seasons Christensen was there. The Livingston all-stars defeated Rosary twice the first season, but the next year, Rosary turned the tables and humiliated Livingston 85-10. "It got embarrassing after a while," Christensen said. He tried tactics like slowing the pace, but some opposing coaches were still angry. A few fans didn't like humiliation coming from a Catholic school.

Life was good at Rosary, but Christensen had his heart set on becoming a career army officer, already having an eight-year obligation with the ROTC. He had a two-year active duty stint, but all through the service, the kids were on his mind; he had visions of them winning a state championship, thinking how great that would be. He started to realize that what he really wanted was to become a coach.

He was also getting a nudge from the military. There was no war at the time, and the program he was in was trying to get rid of officers as fast as it could. Even guys with eighteen or nineteen years of service were getting riffed. With no war, no one dying, a career in the army wasn't looking good for Christensen. Father Burns contacted him again in the spring of 1958, when the contracts for the teachers came out. He said, "Neal, I have your number. Are you going to stay in the army or what?" Christensen said he was thinking of getting out. "If I send you a contract, would you sign it?" Neal said he would.

Then in July the Russians went on military maneuvers, headed for the Middle East with five divisions. The Pentagon thought a war could be imminent and the entire military was frozen; no one could get out. School at Rosary would be starting in a few months and no one knew what to do. Then suddenly all Russian divisions turned around and headed back north. The freeze was off; Christensen got out, called the Father and said, "I'm on!" He left the army on August 28 and was in Bozeman by September 3, 1958 just before the beginning of school.

When Christensen stepped into the corridors of Rosary High he was told for the first time that the Bulldogs had a football program. Football had been resurrected only a year earlier by previous coach Joe Doohan. Christensen decided to use some of the knowledge he had gained from Biggy Munn's football class, adapting the multiple offense to eight-man football with an unbalanced line, one lineman to the left of center and three on the right with a quarterback and two running backs. He found a great group of players; Mike Murphy was as tough as any kid he had ever seen. And then there was Tom Monforton. At first he wouldn't let Monforton play because he was too small, he didn't want him to get hurt, wanted to save him for basketball. But Monforton kept bugging him, "I want to play!" Against Sheridan, Rosary was faced with two 200-pound running backs, both of whom were trampling them. Tom stepped up and said, "I can stop those guys, Coach." So Christensen put him in and immediately he made an unassisted tackle. Soon he became quarterback because he could pass, was smart and was the leader of the whole group. Rosary that year had a 4-3 record, which sounds reasonably good except they were beaten by Belgrade 54-6 and Townsend 55-0. (Townsend would beat Belgrade 19-0 and eventually win the Western Division/Eight Man State championship.)

When the coach stepped out onto the court at the beginning of the basketball season, he recognized some of his gifted players from days of yore, now sophomores and juniors. He still had Tom Monforton and Mike Murphy, who would be his two guards. Monforton was quick, had great court sense, and was as sharp-shooting as ever. Murphy was really an underneath kind of guy and would move to forward the following year. Some of his other players from junior high, as we know, had moved to other schools; Monforton would say, "It was that way at Rosary, we kept losing kids." There were promising signs: junior Dick Ward was not a great scorer but as Christensen would learn the following year, would be a tiger on defense. Freshman George Gallagher was already adequate at center, and junior Frank Seitz, who stood out in junior high, could come in as either forward or guard. But these players were still in reserve status; because Christensen had three seniors left who were fully aware of the talent coming up, who knew Christensen had coached these kids and wondered aloud if they should even bother to try out. Christensen announced this wasn't the way it was going to be on his team. All would try out, and the best players would be the starters. The seniors were slow, couldn't be suited to the fast break or pressure defense, but they were tall: Joel Dubois was a good shooter and the other two—Arlen Bittner and Larry Ritter—were good rebounders and tough around the basket on offense. These three seniors would become the initial starters, along with sophomores Monforton and Murphy.

On defense, Christensen preferred man-to-man. He had grown up with the notion that you had a man to guard and he was your man. But he switched to zone at Rosary because of the slower players. These seniors also forced him into a deliberate half-court offense. The team improved as the winter progressed and ended the regular season with a 16-8 record. The high-water mark was stepping into the cramped gym in Townsend, home of one of the premier teams in Class C. The Broadwater County High School had its big center, Bob Hoppe who

Frank Spragg

in the spring would become state Class C high jump champion, and all-star guard Pete Carson. The coach put Monforton, only 5'5", on 6'1" Carson which seemed a mismatch, but Tom kept Carson from dribbling and frequently stole the ball from him. Christensen also put a four-man zone on Hoppe, rendering him ineffective. Rosary won the game, and the home fans sat on the benches after the game in silence. The Rosary kids were all fired up; they had defeated a great team on its home court against all expectations. Later in the season, the Townsend boys came back to Rosary's court with word that they were going to smack it to the Catholic boys real good. But Rosary won again, with Monforton driving in to score with a half minute left for the victory.

Coach Christenson also had his big snafu during this inaugural season: facing forlorn Willow Creek, he decided he had reserves who worked hard, yet didn't get to play very much; why shouldn't they have a good workout and start the game? Immediately Willow Creek jumped out to a twelve point lead. The normal starters kept looking at him; when was he going put them in? Finally he did; the starters made quick baskets and the score was tied. Christensen again thought he had the game in hand so he started the reserves again in the second half and kept them in for the entire third quarter. Now Rosary was down by 20 points. In the fourth quarter, he again put in the starters, who almost evened the score but fell shy by one point. In the days following the game, Christensen received anonymous letters telling him he didn't know anything and should get out of coaching. He learned a good lesson: you shouldn't feel sorry for anyone.

In the district tournament, Rosary ran over Clyde Park in the first game, only to meet the other Bulldogs from Townsend in the semi-finals, who this time were taking no chances. They steamrolled Rosary and went on to win the district tournament. Rosary fought back, winning the next morning and again that evening over Manhattan in the consolation match. The Bulldogs now had a chance for the first time in many years to go to the divisional tournament in Red

Lodge *if* they could beat Belgrade in the challenge game on Monday evening. Rosary had not yet faced Belgrade in the tournament.

Then on Sunday evening, center Arlen Bittner had his appendix taken out. He would be out of the ballgame; freshman George Gallagher would take his place. Gallagher would be a valuable contributor to the team in the future, but in 1959 he was no Arlen Bittner. As it was, Rosary nearly had the Panthers on the ropes, but it was not to be. Belgrade won 56-51 and along with Townsend would advance to the divisional tournament in Red Lodge. Townsend and Belgrade would finish one-two again and would represent the Southern Division in the state tournament. As for Holy Rosary High School of Bozeman, its season was over, the players sitting at home forced to listen to coverage on the radio.

Enter McCloskey

On January 30, 1960, Gildford traveled thirty miles east to take on the Havre High School junior varsity, a preliminary bout before the Class A varsity game between the Havre Blue Ponies and the Sidney Eagles.[7] John Heberly, who was on that JV team, remembered how this gaggle of mostly freshman had no business playing the Gildford Broncs. The JVs actually jumped to a 3-0 lead and then Gildford turned it on, winning 63-33. "They just toyed with us," Heberly said, "They should have played the varsity. Miller could have played on any Class AA school that year easily." But the Havre varsity team would never have put Gildford on its schedule. Havre was considered good, even by Class A standards. It had ended fourth in the Class A state tournament, and it is unlikely the Broncs would have defeated them. But what if Havre lost? Gildford was in line to win the state Class C championship; Miller and company could presumably hold their own against teams in Class B, even Class A. For Havre the risk of humiliation was too great.

Gildford had the team. All it needed at the beginning of the season was a new coach who was worth a plug or two, and that coach came in the visage of Thomas Arthur McCloskey. Like Roger Freih before him, McCloskey had a myopic basketball background. In the photos of him with the Gildford team he looks tall enough, sturdy enough, but in fact all the time in high school and college he never played much basketball, never really participated until he started coaching. The players at Gildford thought he had been a "football guy" elsewhere; in fact there is a photo of him as a senior in the football section of the Havre High School yearbook. He weighed 175 pounds and was listed as a running back but was never a starter. For whatever reason—not enough support from parents, a late bloomer physically—he just didn't get an early jump on football. He would not run the gridiron extensively until later, in the military at Fort Bragg, California. In basketball, he played as a sophomore and then disappeared from that sport. All around, according to activities shown in the yearbook, he was never a Big Man on Campus but he always had his share of friends.

McCloskey proved early he had a knack for making friends. He had his pals on the block where he lived in Havre, including Philip Kaluza, who later would help him get his first job in Lodge Grass. From then on, except (sort of) for the Gildford position, McCloskey never actively sought employment; every job he would ever have in his entire adult life materialized because a friend with connections urged him to accept it. He had left Gildford because John Tietema, who had been superintendent of one of the neighboring schools on the Hi-Line had gotten to know McCloskey, liked him, and when Tietema took a similar position in Eureka, Nevada, he called McCloskey and told him Eureka needed a new coach. He could coach both football and basketball, and the pay was much better. McCloskey couldn't say no. Later, after McCloskey had been in Eureka, an attorney in Reno who had connections in Eureka recommended a job for McCloskey as a juvenile judge in Washoe County. Again he knew he had to make the move. He would be on that job for twenty-three years.

McCLOSKEY WAS BORN ON JANUARY 7, 1932 IN HAVRE TO JAMES Anthony and Pearl Hill McCloskey. Little is known of his early life because McCloskey and his only brother, John, have long since passed on. He has a sister Mikki who is still living but is almost impossible to pin down, not just by me but by nearly all her relatives including one who at one time was close to her. Lowell Miller's wife, Mary, lived across the street from the McCloskeys but barely knew Tom. She said,

"We each ran in different circles."

McCloskey's father, Jim, had worked in Havre for the Great Northern Railway as a locomotive mechanic. Because of his position, he was never forced to travel as did many who worked for Great Northern. Pearl was a stay-at-home mother until after Tom entered the military and Jim died after a three-year battle with leukemia. She then went to work for Buttreys in the bedding department, selling sheets, pillow slips, and related items. Like his counterpart at Rosary, McCloskey's mother was a very devout Catholic and saw to it that he be enrolled at St. Jude's School in Havre. When McCloskey married his wife Joann, it would be in a Catholic church.

The family had lived on 10th Avenue across from the old Sacred Heart Hospital in the original part of Havre. From all reports, McCloskey had an agreeable home life, getting along well with his siblings: John, five years older, and Mikki, ten years older, the age difference possibly making it easier. Dad not only worked for the railroad but owned a ranch seven miles out of Havre near Fort Assiniboine. Tom would comment often to Joann about the many times he and John picked rocks from the soil on the property, rocks which were ubiquitous in the area.

When he enlisted with the military after graduation from high school in 1949, it was a joint action with several high school buddies. He was in Korea for nearly the length of the war, leaving early so he could be at the bedside of his dying father. McCloskey had seen traumatic action in Korea, but no one knew any details. "He would never talk about Korea," Joann said, "not ever." After visiting his father, he returned to the military finishing at Fort Bragg before receiving an honorable discharge in March 1953.

If McCloskey was good with people, it went hand in hand with hard work. Money from the army helped him get through college at the University of Montana, but he always worked part-time running a beer truck in college and during the summers, traveling back and forth with a truck from Havre to Great Falls. He was able to completely pay for his own education.

On Christmas day in 1956, young Joann Svendsen, who was only a junior in high school, traveled from her home in Hogeland seventy-five miles southwest, to visit her aunt and uncle in Havre, something she did many times. During that evening there was a gathering where she met McCloskey. Her aunt's (by marriage) brother, who had been a college friend of McCloskey's, was at the gathering, and introduced Joann to Tom. She liked him from the beginning. He asked her to dance and she found him to be an excellent dancer. Some weeks later, when he was at Northern Montana College, he drove her over forty miles east to Harlem where she could visit more of her relatives. During that drive and back, they had long conversations and built a deep friendship. They would marry in June 1958, after his graduation from college, and eventually have four children.

McCloskey had graduated in history and PE and landed his first job in Lodge Grass in the fall of 1958. Both Tom and Joann liked Lodge Grass, liked the hunting in the area, the beautiful scenery and the people he was working with. Joann said Tom got along with everybody. He loved teaching and coaching, especially football, which is probably where he got his football reputation in Gildford. Joann said if she were given the choice to start out again, she would not have turned down their experience in Lodge Grass.

Moving to Lodge Grass was an introduction to the unfamiliar Crow Indian culture. Soon after they arrived, in late summer, Tom and Joann would have their windows open at night and hear the pounding of drums used as backdrop for peyote parties, the established means of stimulation for the Crow Indian people. In the middle of the winter, people would jump into the river and then swiftly move inside a tepee and warm up by sitting on hot rocks. Even without the cultural adjustments, life was not easy for the McCloskeys in Lodge Grass. During the winter, Tom had to make long basketball trips throughout southeastern Montana. Also even if Lodge Grass was in the middle of a reservation, by no means were all the students at Lodge Grass Indians. There were many white kids at the school, which created ethnic conflict, especially among the girls. Then the newly married McCloskeys took in a teenage Indian boy for three months so he could have a place to stay and play basketball while his father found another home. With the struggles, the inconveniences, and being so far away from the Hi-Line, Tom and Joann decided if he could find a job closer to Havre, he would take it.

McCloskey had connections for the position, only this time it was through Joann. The superintendent of Gildford, Myron Loe, had the same position in Hogeland all four years Joann went to high school there. He had taught her business math, typing, shorthand and was a personal friend of her father. Over the years, her mother had babysat Loe's young daughters. Loe had liked Joann and she thought he was a great teacher. With McCloskey's personality and his wife's influence, it was not long before he found himself passing the interview with Loe and becoming the new history teacher and coach at Gildford.

The kids at Gildford took to McCloskey immediately. They liked his humor and enthusiasm. Throughout his life, young men and women felt comfortable with McCloskey; they could confide in him and he would show empathy. When he taught at Eureka, Nevada following his stint at Gildford, a yearbook was dedicated to him with this inscription:

> We the 1963 Sctari staff are very proud to dedicate our year-book to Mr. Tom McCloskey. His helpfulness, guidance, and enthusiasm in school activities, inspired many throughout the school year. He has the admiration and respect of numerous people, because of his wonderful sense of humor. Because the school year was filled with the inspiration with which [he] surrounded us, as a warm friend and inspiring teacher. We the 1963 Scutari staff affectionately dedicated this year-book to you Mr. Tom McCloskey.

Later when McCloskey was a juvenile judge in Reno, many a

troubled teenager who had nowhere else to turn, could always bend the ear of the amiable judge. He was a good listener and very compassionate. He had left teaching and coaching in Eureka because one his football players, Angelo (Butch) Tognoni, had died in a mysterious football accident. McCloskey was in no way responsible and no one blamed him, but he felt such grief that he had to get out of coaching for good. Before long he had his county position in Reno. He had been hired in Reno because of his gift with people. Everyone liked McCloskey. He had networked his way into his jobs at Lodge Grass, Gildford, Eureka, and Reno. People said you just felt comfortable with him; he was absolutely unpretentious.

McCloskey loved the kids in his own family, and they loved him. He was easy-going, didn't like to be the disciplinarian. Joann always had to be the bad person. He was like that as a teacher, too; the kids could easily get him off subject, get him to talk about sports. He was one of the kids; there was no doubt about it. He would pull jokes on them, hiding socks or some other silly thing. And they had no compunction about trading jokes back. When he was the shop teacher, for example, kids would sneak into the circuit breaker and shut off the electricity so none of the machines would work.

McCloskey loved to hunt. In the Gildford area, this translated into hunting rabbits, often at night with flashlights, often after a basketball game. He would take kids and stay out until 1:00 a.m., usually his two young sidekicks, Chris Pappas and Ken Whitaker. One wintry night the three went into an area near Pappas' farm, an area with which Chris was well acquainted. At one point McCloskey started to drive down a hill on a narrow side road going through strips of fields. Pappas warned him not to go down there because of snow conditions, but McCloskey went anyway and got stuck in the snow. Now he had to back up in reverse, and it was up to the boys to take scoop shovels out of the back of his pickup and dig a route so McCloskey could gain some traction. As the boys were slaving away, periodically McCloskey would roll down the window, blow out a puff of cigar smoke and ask, "How we doin', boys?" Pappas said, "We could have killed him."

McCloskey often asked the boys to go hunting with him, as he saw it, to keep them out of trouble. But for his regulars, it became a joke. On a Thursday night, the night before a game, Pappas and Whitaker would make conversation where McCloskey could hear them: "Hey, maybe we could hook up with some guys from Rudyard and get some booze........." They weren't going out for any booze; they didn't know anyone who had booze. But McCloskey would hear them, and that evening would come over to the Whitaker home where Pappas and Whitaker could always be found and say, "What are you doing tonight, boys?" He thought they would be out late and screw up the team. So he had it all figured out. He would take them rabbit hunting and have them back by 9:00 p.m., thinking it was too late for them to plan anything else. He didn't realize he was going through this "protect the boys" ritual for nothing.

On one occasion after the basketball season, McCloskey took Whitaker and Noel Preeshl elk hunting down by Lincoln because he heard there was an elk herd there. They stayed at the old hotel in Lincoln, where all sat at the bar and McCloskey ordered them a drink. The legal drinking age was twenty-one, and Whitaker and Preeshl were barely eighteen, but McCloskey didn't care. They all got something to drink, but no one shot any elk.

In his first year at Gildford, McCloskey involved himself in two actions, which quietly co-existed: he continued to smoke his beloved cigars, and he bought a brand-new red Dodge Dart. He would smoke cigars as he drove down the road but there was no more to it than that; certainly a puff of smoke could never be confused with the roar of an engine.

Or could it? Pappas, always up for fun, kidded McCloskey, telling him he just might do something to his Dart, warning him to be on the lookout. On a hideously cold winter day when the temperature outside was something like minus-thirty degrees, McCloskey, Pappas, and Whitaker were off to Hingham in McCloskey's car for basketball practice. McCloskey had to leave the car briefly for some reason, and while he was gone, Pappas and Whitaker filled his cigars, which he kept under the visor, with "loads" (tiny devices that explode when ignited) and then quickly retreated to their seats before McCloskey returned. When McCloskey got into the car and started driving away, he grabbed a cigar and lit it. The loads went off but were defective; instead of exploding as they were meant to do, they just crackled loudly.

McCloskey, confused by the noise, stopped the car, turned and looked at Pappas and Whitaker. Ken, sitting by McCloskey in the front seat, should have been given an academy award for composure because he kept a straight face. But Pappas, sitting in the back, couldn't help himself. He burst out laughing.

McCloskey was not amused. "PAPPAS!!! —WHADJA DO TO MY CAR??"

Pappas did not respond. He was shaking, his mirth scale off the charts.

"GET OUT! YOU'RE WALKIN' BACK TO GILDFORD!!"

Pappas didn't budge, so McCloskey got out of the car, walked back, and attempted pull him out. Luckily the car was a two-door, so Pappas was wedged in; McCloskey couldn't move him. Still he didn't lack for trying. "I thought he was going to pull my arm off," Pappas said. Finally McCloskey gave up, got back into the car and drove away, fuming as he headed down the road. He didn't fully cool off until the next morning.

McCLOSKEY, IN ADDITION TO TEACHING HISTORY AND SHOP, TAUGHT PE and oversaw Gildford's bare-bones sports program. There was of course no football team; track lasted a few weeks, braved with primitive facilities and equipment. Any baseball was pickup intramural. Which left only basketball. But very good basketball. At the beginning of the 1959-60 school year, Cady remembered walking into a bridge club in Hingham where one of the men asked him, "You guys going to win state this year?" "I thought he was crazy," Cady said. "We knew we could play, but we didn't think about our chances for the coming year. We learned from the Superior experience; you play one game at a time." This was not false modesty. Gildford would be without Lawrence Flatness who had graduated. He had been the bruiser rebounder inside that Gildford needed alongside Miller. Cady, who as a third year starter, would have to try to fill his shoes.

McCloskey knew little more about basketball than Freih, but he was an organizer, a motivator, a presence. The players responded to his plan: the best path for winning, he thought, was to simply get the kids in shape. They would run around the gym endless times and if they slowed down, he would run up and give them a good shove in the rear with his foot. Sometimes he had them do laps around the building, or even to the cemetery and back, each leg a mile long. The boys did fine going out, but coming back, their tongues would hang out, so Pappas and Whitaker would slip into a ditch on the way out when they thought McCloskey wasn't looking and stay there until the rest of the kids came back from the cemetery and jump in among them. Of course McCloskey knew what was going on and made them do extra laps around the gym area.

The coach got the kids in shape because, unlike the year before, they would be primarily a running team. Opposing players have said that Gildford had four guards and a center. If Gildford didn't have as much beef under the basket as the year before, a.k.a. Flatness, every player, including Miller, would run the fast break. Miller himself acknowledged he was "all over the floor." In game situations, McCloskey kept to nuances, having his boys key on one opposing player or another but that was about it. He never had a grand plan, instead left it up to the players to use common sense. The big difference was that he made the game interesting, kept the players focused. "He didn't let one player get ahead of another so to speak," Miller said. "Make it a team effort; get the ball to the open man." It was important to

McCloskey that the players were up for a game. And he wasn't one to get on referees and didn't let his players do that. Miller said, "He was a very positive person."

Ken Whitaker came in frequently as a sixth man, but otherwise, McCloskey used his subs sparingly. Mostly he used Miller, Cady, Pappas, Dave Welsh, and Ron Nelson. Pappas usually brought the ball up the floor if the team needed to settle into a half-court offense. The off-guards were Welsh and Nelson, although Nelson often brought the ball down in place of Pappas. Every player, with the exception of Pappas, was capable of prolific scoring. This is what made Gildford so dangerous: Miller and Cady were great rebounders, and the team was off and running, especially with Miller grabbing the rebound and tossing it to Welsh, who was already more than halfway down the court for an easy two. If Gildford was fleet-quick, Miller was the difference over other quick teams; he was tall, he could jump, and he was fast. One of the Darby players who ran against Miller in the state tournament said he was like "Michael Jordan" out there.

Gildford also had another player, Noel Preeshl, who sometimes started at the beginning of the season but was forced to quit after four games. He was a stocky kid, good for rebounding, and could help out in a number of other ways. But in the latter semester of the previous year, Preeshl was forced to drop out of school for personal reasons, and under the rules of the Montana High School Association, was not allowed to play sports the following semester. If he had stayed out of basketball until the spring semester, starting in February, he would have been on the team when the team needed him the most. But the Gildford administration had not thought everything through, and Preeshl started playing with the team beginning in November.

According to Preeshl, the coach of Joplin, Jim Corr, noticed what was happening and looked into the rules. When he reported it, the end result was that Gildford was forced to forfeit the first four contests, games the team had won by an average of 20 points, all, of course, on opponents' courts.

It would prove to be a minor distraction. The Broncs put up good numbers— 65.8 point per game—and won the fourteen remaining games in the regular season by an average of 22 points. The average would have been greater if not for one other team in District 11, the Chester Coyotes, who gave Gildford trouble. The Coyotes had some good big players; in one game between the two schools, Gildford won by five points and the second game by a single point. In that latter game, however, Miller had sprained his ankle and was forced to sit out for much of the evening.

The District 11 tournament was the next step to be played February 18-20, again in the gym at Havre Central. Gildford won the first game against Inverness 68-46, a contest never expected to be a challenge; Gildford had beaten Inverness by 30 points the one time the two teams faced each other during the regular season. The semi-final against Oilmont was predicted to be more difficult; the school at the western edge of the district had given the Broncs more competition than most, but even in those two meetings, Gildford won each by at least 11 points. This time Gildford won also, not handily, but never in trouble either, 54-46. And finally the title match against arch-rival Chester. Surprisingly, Gildford ran away from the Coyotes, 61-49. Chester didn't have to play a challenge game, so both teams would advance to the Northern Division tournament, to be held March 3-5 in Lewistown.

Gildford was the heavy favorite to win the tournament; its first game to be against Moore, the same team the Broncs faced in the opening game of the division tourney the year before. Moore basketball was a program on the upswing, with two very good juniors, center Fred Yeager and forward Ron Tilzey. In 1961 Moore would be a team to be reckoned with, would go nearly undefeated until the state tournament, but in 1960 the Bulldogs simply weren't as good. Gildford easily defeated them 66-47.

In the semi-final, Gildford faced old nemesis Power. Chris Small was back, leading a team that was a much improved over the year before. Small put Dennis (Buddy) Williams on Miller and instructed him never to leave Miller for a second. How did Williams control Miller, something no other center was ever able to do? "He stood on my feet all night," Miller said. In the waning minutes of the game, Miller fouled out and Whitaker took his place. Whitaker had never been out on the floor much in any game; he certainly wasn't going to fill Miller's shoes. For one thing he was three inches shorter and hardly up to Miller's skills as a center. But now, with just a few seconds left in the game and the score tied, Whitaker found himself open for a shot. He took the shot from the perimeter and missed. But the ball bounced off the rim and backboard right back to him. He looked for someone to pass the ball to but no one was open except him. So Whitaker tossed the ball up again, with no time left, and it went in. Gildford escaped against the toughest team it faced all year. The final score was 65-63.

Not surprisingly, Gildford was matched up again against Chester for the championship. But Chester would pose no problem in division play just as it had not in the district. The final was an anticlimactic 78-67, closer at the end than for much of the game. Chester, not having to play a challenge game, would advance with Gildford to the state tournament in Helena. Fans in District 11 wondered if the two would meet a third time for the state championship.

Not if boys in blue-and-white from Holy Rosary could help it.

Down to the End – Part 1

At Rosary, the makeup of the team was much different from the year before. In that 1958-59 season the front line, made up of Joel Dubois, Arlen Bittner, and Larry Ritter, was competent but slow, necessitating a half-court game. Now those three had graduated, and Rosary would go through a metamorphosis like Gildford; in 1959-60 the Bulldogs would be smaller but quicker. Tom Monforton and Dick Ward were the guards. Ward had started for the team at the beginning of the previous year, but was then dropped to reserve status. He was not a scorer like Monforton, but a terror on defense. He and Monforton would often double-team a player and steal the ball from him. At forward positions, Christensen had Mike Murphy and a new starter, Ken Schweitzer.

Schweitzer was born in Havre, and moved with his large family to the Denton area when he was two years old. His father farmed near Denton until he saved enough money to purchase property just north of Bozeman and send his children to Rosary for their education. Ken entered his new school as an eighth grader, but was not a basketball factor in junior high; in fact Christensen didn't even remember Schweitzer being there when he coached the eighth-grade team. As a sophomore he still played JV ball for a time and if he advanced to the varsity, was eighth or ninth man on the team, getting little playing time. He still was not terribly memorable as far as Christensen was concerned. The only reason that can be given is that Schweitzer had not achieved his full growth, was still short and scrawny.

By his junior year Schweitzer had grown to his full height, just shy of 6'0", filled out and one afternoon in practice, Christensen started noticing Schweitzer, how smooth he was, how good a shooter he was, that he was a good team player. Christensen decided to start Schweitzer for the coming game and, as Christensen put it, "he never came out." He not only started but was blossoming into a finesse player who could score in abundant numbers, often from long range, and would team up with Tom Monforton as one of the two top scorers on the team. After he left Rosary, he played for Montana State.

Murphy would prove to be one tough nut underneath the basket, in effect a power forward. If he grabbed onto the ball, no one was going to take it away from him. He had also started the year before, mostly in a guard position. And finally there was Tony Gaffke at center. Gaffke was a senior, had never played much his three prior years in high school, but suddenly he emerged with an unusual style of play, awkward-looking but effective. Coach Christensen chose him as a starter over sophomore George Gallagher, who had seen significant play at the center position as a freshman. The other four players on the first string were serious and generally quiet. Not Gaffke. He was the team clown who would loosen everyone up.

No player on Rosary was very tall; Gaffke and Gallagher were slightly taller than the others at 6'1". Gallagher's playing time was reduced, but he could come in and make a huge difference. In a divisional tourney game against Joliet, Rosary went wild in the second quarter, scoring 30 points and Gallagher had been a big part of that surge. Another reserve getting significant playing time was senior Frank Seitz as backup forward/guard. Seitz had been a crucial part of the junior high team when Christensen coached there in years past. He had not improved like some of the others but had his moments. He was instrumental in winning a game for Rosary in Three Forks. Joe Cahill was another reserve forward who was not going to beat out Schweitzer and Murphy for the forward positions, but was valuable to the team. Christensen had great confidence bringing Cahill in off the bench. Jerry Monforton, another sophomore, came off the bench as the third guard. Jerry would be a starter the following year, and as a senior would score over 25 points a game for Rosary. For now, however, his skills were not yet up to the speed of his brother's and Dick Ward's.

Because of the players he had, Christensen made two decisions that would govern the team as much as possible in every game: first he would have his boys running; Murphy and Gaffke were the rebounders, with the other three off and down the floor. Just as importantly, Christensen would have his team play almost exclusively full-court, man-to-man defense. Ward and Monforton were out front with the other three not far behind. All five of the starters were considered excellent in the press. But then Christensen, like McCloskey, got his players in top shape.

At Rosary the gym, as we know, was cramped; by the time the season was one third over and Rosary obviously a very promising team, Christensen realized he must do something to try to accommodate all the fans who wanted to see a game. They were all trying to get into the gym and there was no room. Particularly when Rosary played Belgrade or Manhattan, people would be out in the street, not able to get in; officials from Rosary were trying to work their way down the goofy stairway of the bypass entrance, explaining to people outside what was going on while the game was in play. So Christensen went to Bud Purdy, who managed the Field House at Montana State, and made a presentation to him, how the year before in the district challenge game against Belgrade, the crowd gave a standing ovation for Tom Monforton; did Purdy remember that? The excitement that was going on? By having Rosary play teams as a preliminary before a Bobcat game, MSC would increase its attendance. People up and down the valley who would not normally attend a college game would be there. Purdy went along with the idea, and Rosary played opening act to Montana State games. Thousands in attendance saw Rosary play, and it helped the Bulldogs prepare for the District 8 tournament, which of course was to be played at the Field House. At that point, Rosary only had five regular home games left, and they were all played in the Field House. Christensen got flak from other coaches in the district, saying if Rosary can play there, so should their teams. Because of coaches speaking up, some other teams from the district also played in the Field House during the regular season.

It was good that Rosary could prepare in the Field House because no basketball facility in Montana could be more different from the typical small gym in Class C. To begin with, the floor was regulation-size, but that was nothing compared with other features of the huge cavernous Field House which covered nearly the length of a football field. The seating capacity was for 10,000 fans, but when the battle for the World Middleweight Boxing title came to town, well over 12,000 people crammed into the building. The floor itself was built in sections for removal when the Field House hosted a rodeo or other events, and when the floor was there, it sat on dirt ground like a thick postage stamp fifteen feet away from the crowd. The floor was different in other ways as well. It had more spring than the average high school floor, and because it came in pieces, had dead spots which the players had to be aware of and become accustomed to. And shooting became an adjustment also, because the hoops at each end were backed by vast amounts of empty space. Any team in District 8 would have given its last jock strap to be able to play a game there before the tournament.

During the regular season, Rosary played 19 games and lost four, two of them to Catholic schools in non-conference play. Rosary lost one to Anaconda Central away in a gym that was the loudest it would play in all season. Not that the fans were any louder, but the wall on the opposite side of the bench was bare of anything but concrete, and sound reverberated off it in spades. The other loss was to St. Leo's in Lewistown. Christensen knew the coach at St. Leo's and though Lewistown was some distance from Bozeman, the two agreed to a home-and home-series. St. Leo's won in Lewistown, the game played at the historic Civic Center where for many years the Western

Invitational tournament was held each summer, with players coming from all over the United States. Rosary won at home by 18 points.

For the upcoming District 8 tournament, Rosary had no real competition except Manhattan. At Belgrade, most of the starters had graduated or moved away. Also, Belgrade acquired a new coach fresh out of college who was concurrently learning the art of coaching while trying to rebuild a team. The other power from the previous year, Townsend, had lost its two big stars, Bob Hoppe and Pete Carson, to graduation. As for Manhattan, the Tigers had beaten Rosary in a preseason invitational game in Manhattan, a game Christensen disputed because of what he claimed was trickery by Coach Jim Bouchan (pronounced *Booshon*). Bouchan overinflated the ball so it bounced with greater intensity than Rosary's boys were used to. Also, Christensen insisted that one basket was shorter than the other. The referees agreed with him, but the final score did not change. When the Bulldogs got Manhattan back in their own gym, they pounded the Tigers 75-45. In the very last game of the regular season in Manhattan, Rosary won 53-46. Against every other District 8 team, Rosary won by an average of over 20 points per game. Rosary even trashed Belgrade 69-32, a team that would end the season much better than the loss indicated.

But there was one loss to a conference opponent, Wilsall, which was an embarrassment. The game was played in Wilsall's storied old log gym, always a challenge to any visiting team no matter how good. On this night, Rosary had more going against it than the gym. According to Christensen, the Wilsall custodian had waxed the floor with material that made the floor so slippery, the players could hardly stand up. Christensen watched the JV game and saw players on both sides falling all over the place. He told the Wilsall coach the floor was unacceptable; for safety reasons, he could not put his players on a surface he characterized as dangerous. So the coach coated the floor with rosin, which was supposed to make it less slippery. And it did, but whoever ran on it created a dust cloud that was knee-high;

hence Christensen called the match the "Powder Puff Game." The contest was even down to the very end. Rosary finally got ahead by one point with twenty-five seconds left on the clock, so Christensen called a time-out. He told the boys, "We are lucky to stay in this game. You guys are good ball handlers, you are not about to lose this game. *Don't shoot the ball!* We are a point ahead. Run off the clock!"

Monforton took the ball out of bounds and threw it to Gaffke, who immediately took a shot from the top of the key. Wilsall got the rebound, and one of its players dribbled the ball the length of the floor for a layup and Longhorn victory. Christensen grabbed the players afterward. "Tony, what did we talk about in the huddle? Why did you shoot the ball?" Gaffke said, "Coach, it hit me, if I hit the basket, we win by three points. (There could be no three-point response in those days.) Christensen said, "Tom, why would you pass the ball to Tony?" Monforton agreed he should not have. Christensen said, "I was angrier at Monforton than Gaffke because Tom was smart and should have known better."

Rosary ended the regular season against conference opponents with a 14-1 record, three games ahead of Manhattan with its 12-5 count and four games ahead of Belgrade, which finished 10-5. Because of this, Rosary drew a bye in the district tournament not playing until Thursday against the winner of the Willow Creek/Gardiner game. The Bulldogs would have had to come down with a collective case of sleeping sickness to lose to either one of these ball clubs, especially Gardiner, which ended at the bottom of the league with one win and 11 losses. During the regular season, Rosary had beaten Willow Creek 67-46 and Gardiner 73-34.

As expected, Rosary played the first game against Willow Creek, jumped off to a 15-3 lead in the first quarter, 25-10 at the half and cruised to a 51-40 victory. The second half was garbage time. Against White Sulphur in the semi-final, both teams had woeful shooting in the first half, with Rosary leading only 14-12. But in the second half, Rosary finally clicked with its fast break and full court press and ran away laughing 54-25. In the other semi-final, Manhattan barely eased over Belgrade 44-43, holding on to a one-point lead for a full minute. Manhattan in the final would be more of a contest for Rosary than the two previous teams but not by much. It appeared Rosary was in a fight for its life: At the end of the third quarter, Manhattan led 36-34.

Then Rosary turned it on in the fourth quarter, Gaffke hit a hook shot, Schweitzer a push shot, and Rosary was on its way. The final score was 53-42. Manhattan defeated Three Forks in the challenge match giving the Tigers the honor of accompanying Rosary to the Southern Divisional tournament in Red Lodge. It would be the first time Rosary had advanced to the division tournament since 1944.

The 1960 Red Lodge tournament, of course, was known for the huge snowstorm that clamped a vise on everything. People were not able to go out of town until the following Monday. As for Rosary, the team shrugged off the snow and went to work. In the first game against the Colstrip Colts, runners-up in District 5, it looked like Rosary was going to take care of the Colts easily in the first quarter, but then Colstrip led by Dale Harris, roared back to lead 29-27 at the half. The Colts couldn't seem to miss. Then Rosary got its machine going early in the third quarter and won easily, 57-43.

Next up for the Bulldogs in the semi-final were the Joliet Jayhawks. Coach Don Steele preferred the same system as Christensen, an up-tempo, good-transition game, steals, layups, brought on by stingy defense. Joliet always hoped to get the ball before it reached the center line. The Jayhawks had Dick Lohof and John Jensen at guards, Jerry Kanaub at forward, with John Jensen, Bob Weber, Tom Kress, and Ted Cooney trading off at the other forward (Jensen also played guard), and Ron Hagen at center. In a way, Joliet had two teams, because when Hagen was in there he was effective but slower, forcing the team to play a half-court offense. When Hagen was taken out, Joliet reverted to the running game. Joliet had lost four games thus far, including a loss to Roberts in the District 6 championship. In the first game Joliet had beaten Lavina from District 7.

It was said that if Joliet could score 70 points, it could not be beaten, and on this night the team scored 69. But the Jayhawks had never met a team like Rosary, a team as quick as it was. During this game at least, it was no match for the Bulldogs. At the very beginning, Joliet fell behind and could not catch up. Rosary could always counter what Joliet threw at it and crushed the Jayhawks with its full-court press. There was a stretch in the first half when Joliet could not get the ball across the half-court line. The final score was 89-69. Rosary would advance to the final against a more familiar team: for the fifth time it would meet Manhattan.

In the 1959-60 season, Rosary seemed to always have Manhattan's number. This match began much like their other contests, tied 12-12 at the end of the first quarter. Then in the second quarter Rosary went on a tear scoring a staggering 30 points and by halftime was leading 42-22. The game was essentially over. In the third quarter the point difference remained the same, and the game ended 68-51. The Manhattan players were so distraught by the loss that when they met Colstrip the following Monday night for the challenge game, Colstrip walked all over them, winning 76-56. Colstrip had led nearly the entire game. It would be Rosary and Colstrip going to Helena from the Southern Division.

OF THE EIGHT TEAMS GOING TO THE STATE TOURNAMENT, NONE HAD ever won a championship. State School and Brockton were coming from the Eastern Division, Corvallis and Darby from the Western; Colstrip, after winning the challenge match, joining Rosary from the Southern, and Chester and Gildford from the Northern.

Chester, as we know, was in the same District 11 as Gildford and had always been a top contender in the district. Chester made it to the district championship once again in 1960. But the Coyotes had never before made it to the state level, and with a 17-9 record, were not expected to do particularly well; in fact four of those losses had been to Gildford, with the Broncs seemingly able to gain the upper hand more easily each time the two teams met.

The name "Chester" was given to the county seat of Liberty County by the first telegraph operator in honor of his hometown in Pennsylvania. Most people from Gildford would say Chester is thirty miles west on Highway 2, official guides say it is twenty-seven miles, but Don Miller measured the distances between each town from Gildford to Chester and came up with thirty-two miles. I'll go with thirty miles. It is an easy number to remember.

Chester to a large degree has the same land (although less rocky) and the same economy as Gildford, but was founded much earlier, with the post office opening in 1891. Located on Cottonwood Creek, the Chester area had been a favorite stopover for cattlemen driving their herds to Minot, North Dakota, before the coming of the railroad. When Chester lost its fight to become the county seat of Hill County, the townspeople agitated for a new county and were assisted in their efforts by "champion county-splitter" Dan McKay. Motivated by business opportunities and working on the optimistic outlook of locals at the time, McKay, a lobbyist and "civic booster extraordinaire," persuaded people in Chester, for a fee to guide them through the legal and political process to form a new county. On February 11, 1920, the legislature approved the formation of Liberty County, land taken away mostly from Hill County to the east, but also from Chouteau County to the south. In 1921 Liberty County was enlarged when more land was taken from Hill County. Again Chester was in a contest to become the county seat, this time becoming victorious by defeating neighboring Joplin in an election.

Much of the early growth of Chester can be attributed to two men: Brown B. Weldy and Charles Baker. Weldy owned a "ramshackle hostelry" called the Prairie Inn, a temporary shelter for settlers until they could become established in the area. Weldy was apparently a man of many talents: a land locator, first postmaster, merchant, justice of the peace, and newspaper editor. Put it all together and it could be said he was *the* booster of the town. One historian noted, "Weldy seemed to be the sort of person that made you think you heard an enthusiastic brass band in the background when he spoke and the urge to fall into step was overwhelming."

Charles Baker started out as a traveling merchant, selling clothing and wares in covered wagons along the Canadian border. Later he and partner Alex Wright purchased the Chester Trading Company, which apparently sold everything. That is what the sign said on his store: "We Sell Everything"; if there was a buyer for it, they sold it (assuming they could first find it and acquire it). His pride and joy were his tiled meat cases, so much so that whenever a burglar snuck in, Baker chased him away unarmed, because he didn't want to damage his meat case in a shootout.

Largely because it was the county seat, and more or less halfway between Havre and Shelby, Chester became a hub and could survive more easily than its neighbors. It had a larger school and became a dominant force in District 11, but in 1960, it was going to state for the first time and considered one of the weaker teams.

Chester obviously had good players; several Gildford players agreed Jerry Heikkela was the Coyotes' toughest player, a strong kid who at 6'1" played forward. (He would have the misfortune of passing away not long after he left high school.) 6'1" Norman Bruce was the other forward, 6'2" Ed Green at center, and Bob Nordstrom and Lance Lambott, both 5'8" were the starting guards. Chris Pappas from Gildford said Chester "had super good players, played a lot like Gildford did; they had a couple of guards, if you didn't guard them, they were going to beat you." Norman Bruce might have been the top scorer, but for the most part the scoring was even among the starters. Chester's disadvantage was that, while it had some fairly tall players, none of them could match up with Miller or other players of his talent.

The team had been coached by Dave Curtis, who had been there at least four years. Bruce said, "In this day and age, he probably wouldn't be a good coach. But in those days we thought he was a good coach; all the kids liked him." Nordstrom added, "Curtis was a good coach.

The team had an up-tempo game, tried to run and gun, liked to score." The question was how Chester would perform against higher-caliber competition in the state tournament.

THE SAME COULD BE ASKED ABOUT THE COLSTRIP COLTS FROM THE Southern Division. The Colts had stumbled into the state tournament through the back door, were considered long shots in Helena. And though Colstrip and Rosary were from the same division, the two schools otherwise had almost nothing in common.

Colstrip sits near low-lying hills covered with an attractive mix of forest and prairie, just north of the Northern Cheyenne Indian Reservation in southeastern Montana. South of town is a sandstone formation, which General Custer crossed on the way to his death at the Battle of Little Big Horn. The team was lucky even to be in the state tournament. It began by losing to Rosebud for the championship of District 5. Luckily it didn't need to play a challenge game there, but right off in the first game of the divisional tournament it lost to Rosary. Then the Colts worked their long windy road through the losers' bracket, defeating four teams—including Manhattan in the challenge game—to make it to state.

Colstrip was also lucky to be at state for another reason. In 1960 it looked like the little town was going to dry up and fade away through a reversal of fortune. Colstrip may be in ranching country, but the town owes its existence to coal. In the 1920s a huge deposit of coal was discovered in the area, coal owned by Northern Pacific Railway and used to run its engines. Northern Pacific not only owned the mineral rights, it owned the settlement near this large layer of lignite conveniently located only a few feet beneath the rocky surface. NP named the settlement *Coal Strip* or Colstrip. It was hence a company town with virtually no business infrastructure, no grocery store, no bank, restaurant, or just about any other retail business you can name. If people wanted to shop, they had to travel over twenty miles into Forsyth, or for big shopping, a much longer trip to Miles City or

Billings. Still, in the 1950s Colstrip was thriving; the Foley brothers who ran the mine took good care of their employees. The mine was non-union, but the workers were paid higher-than-union wages.

Suddenly in 1959, train diesel engines came in and Northern Pacific no longer needed coal. The company sold the mineral rights to Montana Power, which sat on the mine and did nothing with it for eleven years. Most people left town because no one had work. Colstrip was rapidly disappearing, down to 100 residents by 1960. Bailey Eagen, who was on the Colts' squad, remembered having thirteen students in his senior class.

Being relatively close to the reservation, Colstrip always had several Indian students on the team and every year would play teams from the reservation. One school from this nation, an ignoble host for visiting teams, was Busby, not just the team members but also the referees and the crowd. Fans came in, tore up the dressing rooms, and threw objects at the visiting team bus. Winning was so important to them, they didn't care how they achieved it. They hired local referees who made ridiculous calls, who essentially rigged the game.

Several coaches in District 5 gathered and agreed this had to stop; if Busby carried on like this again, the opposing team would walk away from the game. Again Colstrip traveled to Busby to find their refs up to the same old tricks. That was it; before halftime, the Colstrip players walked off the floor. The Busby fans were enraged, abusing the Colstrip boys, shouting at them, throwing objects at them from the time they left the dressing room until they reached the bus. The fans couldn't stand it that the other team wouldn't play. But as additional teams also walked off, the effect was powerful. By 1960, no opposing school had problems with Busby.

This would be Colstrip's first trip ever to the state tournament. The team had been to the divisional tournament several times, the one just experienced in Red Lodge being one of the most memorable for reasons other than basketball: the terrific snow storm dumped several feet of snow, forcing the Colstrip team (along with everyone else) to be stranded, holed up in the same digs with other players, such as those from Rosary. On Saturday night, when Colstrip found it would be playing a challenge game on Monday, the coach and players decided not to make the relatively short trip home on Sunday only to turn around and fight the snow coming back on Monday. The decision paid off; Colstrip won and was off to Helena.

Colstrip had had an excellent coach two years before who had pushed fundamentals. But he took a job in Hysham, and the boys were left with a new coach who frankly didn't know much about basketball and mainly let the boys play. The starting lineup began with Kermit "Oly" Flatness, a big burly guy at center who ironically was related to the Flatness family in Gildford. Unfortunately his cousins had all graduated, so he would not face them when Colstrip played Gildford in the first game of the state tournament. The other starting players were Bailey Eagen at guard, Benny Limberhand and Ray Harris at forward, and a smattering of other players who rotated starting at the other guard spot.

The team had no system, which was good in only one way: opposing teams never knew what Colstrip was going to do, what defense it would play; the players might run some kind of zone for a few plays then suddenly shift to man-to-man for no apparent reason. The offense often used was called a "double triangle," really another name for the standard triangle offense. One player would be out front with two on the sides, one on the free-throw line and a drifter underneath the basket. The idea was to pass quickly enough to get a shot open for someone. The team also used a unique offense called the "circle"; one player would rove around the free-throw line while the other players moved around him in a circle. The circle worked well because the team members mostly free-lanced, were quick enough to make it work. If the system fell apart, the player holding the ball would simply throw it to someone open and let him create his own maneuver. Mostly the Colstrip offense was undisciplined; the team played mostly one-on-one. Which got them into trouble with any team that *was* disciplined. Like Rosary or Gildford.

THE TWO TEAMS REPRESENTING THE WESTERN DIVISION WERE COR-
vallis and Darby, both from District 14, only twenty-four miles from
each other and longtime fierce rivals. It was common tradition, for
example, when Corvallis came to Darby for a football game, for all
the saw mills and logging operations in the woods to close. The bosses
were all local, good people to work for, and would say, "Just shut 'er
down boys, we're going to the game." The Corvallis folks came in a
caravan stretching four miles. There was hardly enough room for fans
to watch the game. When the two played each other in football or
basketball, the contests were always a battle throughout, with only a
small margin of victory for the winner.

Though relatively close to each other in distance, the two towns
supported distinctly different economies. Darby is close to the south
end of Bitterroot Valley in far western Montana, up where the valley
narrows, not far from where the two forks of the Bitterroot River join,
one tumbling from the Sapphire Range to the east, the other originat-
ing west from the Bitterroot Range along the Idaho border. Darby
sits on shallow rocky soil supporting some ranching and mining, but
during the 1950s it was considered a wood-products town. In fact
the ground where the town sits was once covered with yellow pine
before it was cleared for settlement in the nineteenth century. In 1960
there were four sawmills and a large planer mill either in Darby or
the surrounding area. The town itself had a population of 500, which
was average for a Class C town in those days.

Down in Corvallis, the valley is three times as wide, with rich loam
soil running ten feet deep. The area was dominated by small farms,
averaging 80-160 acres, many for dairies, but also used for growing
hay, grain, barley, even corn. In the foothills were cattle ranches, also
small by Montana standards, running a section or two. Because the
farms were small, many rural people in the Corvallis area also worked
a second job, commuting to nearby Hamilton, the county seat of

Ravalli County. In addition to government jobs Hamilton also had the area hospital and the Rocky Mountain Lab, which originated in the 1920s and gained notoriety for a vaccine curing Rocky Mountain fever.

Living in farm country, it was said by folks in Darby, that the Corvallis kids were "fed better," likely taller, bigger. It was certainly true that Corvallis had a moderately tall team in 1960, taller player-for-player than other teams in the state tournament. The team was also slower and did not try to race up and down the floor with quicker opponents like Brockton or Gildford. The players used a deliberate offense and a three-two zone defense "99 percent of the time."

Corvallis had balanced scoring from four players who usually managed to get into double figures. If anyone scored the most points, it was 6'3" center Bill Engler. Others on the team were 6'2" Ronnie Wurtz at forward with the other players trailing down to 5'9". Chuck Stevens at forward, with Jim Hull and Tom Richards at guard, filled out the starting positions. The coach was Max Blodgett, who was the descendant of a pioneer family in the Bitterroot Valley (a beautiful canyon dropping down from the Idaho border was named after the Blodgett family). When I asked if Blodgett was a good coach, the answer was "Yes, but a coach is only as good as the players he is dealt in a small school." In Blodgett's case, he was either a very good coach or had a phenomenal string of luck with talent. The year before in 1959, he had taken Plains to the state Class C championship, losing to Superior, a team it had defeated in the divisional championship. In 1962 Corvallis, with Blodgett as coach, would win the state championship. My feeling is this: no coach in a school with thirty students can consistently win year after year. But Corvallis had 140 students, and with that many, the unusual coach can produce a consistent winner. Casey Keltz proved that with Townsend in football, winning 34 games in a row. Belgrade became a Class C dynasty in basketball throughout the 1950s. At any rate, Corvallis had a very good record in 1960, losing only to Class B Hamilton in the regular season and to Darby for the District 14 crown. Still, no matter how good Corvallis was that year, it always had trouble with Darby.

Darby did not have nearly the success as Corvallis during the regular season, but coach Walt Anderson didn't care. He believed in experimenting during the season, finding what worked and what didn't, generously using all the players on the bench and doing what was necessary to bring the team to peak for the tournaments. The kids appreciated his intelligence, his diligence in studying every opposing team and adapting a style of play that would work against that opponent. Still, Anderson mostly played an X-shaped offense with two guards out front—Bill Barringer and Calvin Greenup—Larry Matteson at high post and Richard Green and Pat O'Brien roving underneath the basket. The idea was for the guards to get the ball to Matteson, who would in turn dump the ball off to the boys under the basket. Green was the tallest at 6'5", but was mainly a rebounder (Green continued to grow after high school, shooting up to 6'8"). The star and top scorer on the team was Pat O'Brien, who averaged 20 points per game (He tossed up 38 in one match). He was not a great outside shooter but was mostly underneath anyway and with that wide body of his, was very effective; if you could get the ball to him down low, it was as good as two on the board. That is the way Anderson wanted it because it worked well for the team.

But as it usually seemed to happen, when Darby played Corvallis, the players couldn't get the ball to O'Brien. This happened again when the two teams played for the District 14 championship in Missoula. Anderson was forced into a different strategy; he told the guards to shoot from outside, which they did, which they did very well. With Greenup leading the charge, Darby finally broke the mold and blasted Corvallis by 18 points. When the two teams met again for the Western Divisional championship in Deer Lodge, Darby again took control until Green and O'Brien fouled out. Darby's only other player of any height, Matteson at 6'1", tried to handle the Corvallis big players underneath but couldn't do it. Corvallis won by eight points. Darby was forced to play Boulder for the challenge game on

Frank Spragg

Monday night but won easily. Darby and Corvallis were off to state, both for the first time.

IF DARBY WANTED TO CHALLENGE A TEAM AT STATE WITH WHICH IT had nothing in common, a good choice would be the Brockton Warriors from District 2 in northeastern Montana, one of the representatives from the Eastern Division. And yet unlikely as it may seem, Darby and Brockton had one connection: they were both coached at one time by Walt Anderson. Anderson had come directly from Brockton to Darby. Otherwise the schools were in many ways opposites. If Darby originated from the timber industry, Brockton sat in rolling, treeless prairie in every direction as far as the eye could see. The only trees were non-useable cottonwoods along rivers and small streams.

Brockton, over 400 miles from Darby, was in effect a different nation. If the players were, unlike the Tigers, short and speedy and traditionally known for passing skills, there was a reason: they were from the Assiniboine and Sioux tribes on the Fort Peck Indian Reservation. This rectangular forty-by-eighty miles chunk of land had been "given" to the Indians when the reservation was formed. But having been taken advantage of in business deals, the Indians in short time had squandered 35 percent of the reservation. The federal government stepped in and declared the 65 percent remainder a "land trust": in other words it was held in trust by the federal government, which held title; the Indians didn't really own it anymore, and therefore could not (and still can't) sell it or use it as collateral.

As would be expected, the school in Brockton was also sponsored by the federal government. There was no tax base for support; the government had to provide all the money. Which made it difficult whenever the local administration wanted an improvement such as a new building or program. Everything had to be approved by some distant authority with requisite strings attached. And it was hard to attract teachers to Brockton. There was no local culture to speak of, no art museums, music, good restaurants, theatres, plays, or social scene. There was no choir at the school; there was a band but few other electives outside sports. And yet, for all the drawbacks, in 1960 Brockton had a good cadre of teachers; the students considered themselves lucky.

The twelve seniors in the 1960 class at Brockton considered themselves fortunate to be in high school at all. The same class in the eighth grade had graduated thirty-eight students, that many down to twelve four years later, a shockingly high attrition rate. Many along the way had been killed in car wrecks and the like, but of the twelve who stayed, nearly all would go on to receive degrees from college. They would attribute their achievements to the teachers they had in high school.

This was the first time Brockton would be at a Class C state tournament and the first return to any state tournament since 1939. There was a connection with that 1939 team involving the Bighorn family, which was something of a dynasty in Brockton. Four Bighorn brothers had gone to the Chemawa Indian School in Oregon during the 1930s, picked up basketball there and brought it home to Brockton, where they helped build a team that went to state. In one game that year they defeated a team from Grainbelt 62-1. The elder Ernest Bighorn committed the foul that gave Grainbelt the lone point from the free-throw line.

That 1939 team was ultimately responsible for rule changes in basketball. After the Bighorn brothers graduated, they took on, storming through town, the Harlem Globetrotters. The Globetrotters taught the brothers a technique called the three-man weave, or a variation of it called the five-man weave. The elder Bighorns taught this technique to their sons who used it extensively in high school, helping to win many games. The boys could stay just inside the center line and weave back and forth, stalling a game for five or six minutes. Because of their slowdown, a new rule was instituted using hash marks painted on the floor three feet from, and parallel to, the center line. The players had to cross that hash mark in five seconds or be called for a technical foul.

In 1960, the Brockton team was partly made up of the younger Ernest Bighorn, his cousin Leonard, and another cousin (to both Ernest and Leonard) Jake, who was a reserve freshman. Two of the cheerleaders were Ernest's sister Jackie and their cousin Angela. The other starters on the team were Dave Brokaw, Fred First, and Gary Vaught. Players off the bench were Richard Wapple, who had a bad ankle and wasn't up to par, Aaron Martin, Archie Red Boy, and Kenneth Rakstad. Rakstad was not Indian but "he didn't know it." He had been raised with an Indian family since he was a baby.

The players were to a degree interchangeable in their positions. Dave Brokaw, the only tall player at 6'2" played both center and forward. Gary Vaught played mostly forward, Fred First played guard and forward, Earnest Bighorn at point guard, and Leonard Bighorn played center and forward. Brokaw, First, and Leonard Bighorn were the main scorers. Vaught and Ernest Bighorn generally didn't score much but were capable of doing so if called upon.

The coach, Lyle Shick, believed in an up-tempo game, including the fast break whenever possible. On defense, the team played a box-and-one zone or a variation of it called "sagging man-to-man"; either way the emphasis was on guarding the top scorer. On occasion Coach Schick would pick out the weakest player offensively on the other side and tell his players not to guard him at all. The team tended to gravitate toward the stronger offensive players and leave the weaker players alone.

The strategy seemed to work because Brockton lost only one game during the regular season, to Lambert. Brockton made it through the district, advanced through the divisional tourney to challenge State School Beavers for the championship. In that title match, Brockton trailed by five points with forty seconds to go, when a series of incidents unfolded, which would bring George Dyer, the tallest player for State School, to tears. Dyer came down the floor with Ernest Bighorn guarding him, Bighorn at one point in a position where he couldn't be seen by the referees. Dyer was a foot away from Bighorn when Bighorn did the flop and a one-and-one foul was called on Dyer. Bighorn made the first shot but beforehand told his cousin Leonard and Dave Brokaw he was going to intentionally miss the second shot, have it bounce to the left where one of them would get the rebound and put the ball back in. Which was achieved precisely the way the boys wanted; Leonard Bighorn grabbed the rebound and made the basket. Now Brockton was down by two. Almost immediately players from both teams tussled for a loose ball, and when a jump ball was called, Brockton got the tip and received possession; the ball was thrown to Fred First who made a jump shot with no time left, sending the game into overtime. Brockton won in overtime and would go to state as the champion of the Eastern Division. The defeat caused Dyer to sit down and cry, his mother sitting there consoling him. Ernest Bighorn by chance had known Dyer well. The players of different teams usually managed to acquaint themselves with others at this end of the state.

State Industrial School from District 4 did not have to play a challenge game and hence returned to the state tournament for the third year in a row. The school had very capable players in addition to George Yelloweyes who averaged 24 points a game. But alas, his double-digit outpour was not for the benefit of State School. Instead Yelloweyes lived on campus at the urging of his former coach Joe McDonald, and by special permission was free to come and go as he pleased, working his magic at nearby Miles City Community College. He was too old and no longer eligible to play high school basketball.

As one might expect, State Industrial School advanced each year with nearly an entirely new crop of boys. There would be no grooming of young talent at State School through the grades into high school, no anticipation for stardom in future years. The coach at State School began anew each year in every sense of the word with kids who had broken the law and were incarcerated at the school at the beginning of the basketball season. He could have an outstanding team, as happened in 1961 when the team won its first ten games, then lose his best talent, shipped home because their detention time at the institution had ended. And if the coach had good players, they likely had not been athletes previously at another school. Mostly they had not participated in school activities at all, had been on the fringe of society coming from dysfunctional homes, broken homes, in some cases nonexistent homes. Only 10 percent of the kids at State School had two parents living together.

Because of life at home, some kids were sent to State School for the slightest infractions, such as truancy or stealing a hubcap, sometimes in extreme cases for doing nothing afoul of the law at all. Life at home could be so dreadful, so destructive, that it was better for a boy to be in a place where there was some safety and structure. Montana had no halfway program for troubled youth in those days such as the Yellowstone Boys Ranch. There was no differentiated housing at State School for wrong doing, so a basically good kid who had taken a wrong turn was thrown in with hardened young criminals. Some of each could be on the basketball team.

The coach that year was Ward Fenton, who considered his two years at State School one of the highlights of his life. He had gone to high school in nearby Hysham, attended college at Rocky Mountain and Eastern Montana with a major in biology and a minor in PE, intending all along to become a teacher. He also had a background playing basketball at Rocky under Herb Klindt, considered one of the premier coaches in Montana, who had groomed some the most successful high school coaches in the state. Anyone under Klindt had a rockbound background in fundamentals.

After his graduation from Eastern, Fenton was working on the family ranch for the summer when he got a call from State School asking if he would like to come down for an interview. He drove over, had a two-hour look-around, said he would take the job, drove home, got his clothes, drove back, and started football the next day.

It was easy for someone like Fenton to think of coaching at State School as stepping into a cauldron of discord. After all, at age twenty-five, he wasn't much older than the kids. But he found the truth to be quite the opposite. The school had few activities outside of sports so sports became all-important. Nearly all of the sixty to seventy boys at the school tried out for basketball. If most could not make the main team, the school would find a place for them to play, perhaps against a Miles City High intramural team or a pick-up bunch from nearby Sacred Heart. At the end of the season all the boys who didn't make the main squad were broken into intramural teams for a tournament, each team coached by a member of the varsity.

Because there were no parents in the vicinity, Fenton didn't have to worry about folks looking over his shoulder. And unlike other schools, the kids stayed right there at the dorm, had to follow the training rules, could not go out and get into trouble, had nutritious meals, and would stay in shape. There was great incentive for a bas-ketball player to toe the line. He was at the top of the social order and if he got into trouble, his playing days were over. One night in Ekalaka, two boys on the junior varsity escaped and hid under a stairwell. It took several hours before the police found them. They were done playing basketball for the season.

Fenton found that if the kids liked him, he could mold them just about any way he wanted. When he arrived, the kids all had long hair, combed-back and greasy. He told them they couldn't play basketball with hair like that; they needed to get haircuts. They said, "But if we ask for haircuts at the cottage, they just clip it all off." Fenton said he would get clippers and cut the hair himself. He gave them nice short flattops and they liked it. Pretty soon every kid in school wanted Fenton to cut his hair.

He also made a change in the clothes they wore. The normal wear was blue jeans and denim shirts, washed in a big washer and never pressed, some badly faded. Fenton said, "You need to have new jeans and new shirts." They said, "But we don't have any money." Fenton proposed that if they were good enough to play on the team and had good conduct, they could go out on weekends and work. There were a lot of people in town who would hire the boys to rake lawns, pile bales, or any number of things. They did that, bought new slacks, a nice shirt. Then they started buying sports coats. They enjoyed dressing up and looking nice. Before long all the students at the school were doing the same.

It was easy to think that because the kids were so obedient in school, they were transformed once they returned to society. But again there was no safety net; they were flung to the wolves, so to speak. And so Fenton and the others at State School were in for a dose of reality. While it was true that some students did well—the quarterback for his football team became a college administrator; another student (whom I personally talked to) became an attorney. But only 10 percent were in the success category. One of his basketball players, after leaving State School, bounced around Montana, eventually becoming a bartender in White Sulphur Springs, where he beat a man to death. He spent the rest of his life in the state pen.

So even with all the incentives to stay in line, Fenton had to face the possibility of escape. The coach and his assistant followed a special regimen whenever the team played a game out of town. First of all, it was only the team and the coaches; no other students at State School were allowed to watch away games. When the team traveled, the two coaches supervised the boys and seldom had difficulties. If the team stopped at a restaurant or at a gas station for a bathroom break, everyone went together. The team was always kept in a group.

At these away games the Beavers had no one cheering for them, unlike other schools, which had parents and fans traveling with the team. It could be pretty quiet for State School at some of these games during the regular season. This would change for the tournaments. The district tournament was always held in Miles City, and if there was any room left in the gym for other students at State School, they could attend. If there was no room, as would happen during the championship, even if State School was in the championship, most of the students would have to stay back at the dorms and listen to the game on the radio.

At divisional and state tournaments, a different phenomenon occurred. There would be a "sympathy" support for State School. At the divisional tournament in Glasgow, there was no established fan base, but Glasgow was near enough to Miles City that many people knew Coach Fenton from college, knew him through coaching or were related to him in some way. Upon arrival, the State School boys had a spontaneous group of fans cheering for them. At the state tournament in Helena, the Helena High School cheerleaders took it upon themselves to create an ad hoc cheering section for the Beavers; an entire section of Helena students cheered for them, which was very effective and much appreciated by the players and coaches.

At home, State School had a strong support group. Here in their small gym, all the rest of the students managed to fit in somehow. There were fans around Miles City who came to the games; in fact State School had great support in Miles City. A newspaper reporter was there every week for interviews. State School received plenty of publicity in town, and as the team did well, more people came. Some local people came to all the games. Even if they couldn't come to the games, they followed the team closely, reading all the articles in the newspaper.

Fenton had had a successful football season, winning seven out of eight games, a marked improvement over the previous year when the team was without a victory. And now for basketball he would be starting with largely a new group of boys. All the newcomers had never played basketball before, at least not officially at another school. With all the boys to choose from, Fenton was bound to find those with natural ability, and he would have several. He had players such as Ray Wilson and Larry Trotchie, who played guard, and Emanuel Big Head at forward. But these players and others were in the shadow of his two stars, Gordon Wilkins and George Dyer. Not only were they big—Dyer at 6'2" played center and Wilkins 6'1" at forward—but they were rugged physical players who were tremendous rebounders and prolific scorers. Both were able to shoot from anywhere on the court. On any night one or the other could pour in 25 to 30 points. Dyer in particular could play inside or outside, could dribble the ball, could do practically anything a point guard could do. They were also aggressive on defense. Both Wilkins and Dyer came from the Billings area or at least had spent some time in Billings. Wilson was from Missoula, Big Head from Havre. Fenton's players came from all over.

Because all of his players had essentially never played basketball before, Fenton didn't have to correct any bad habits. They learned the correct fundamentals from the ground up. The coach installed an up-tempo game, using the fast break whenever possible. If that was not available, the team would set up in half court, often using screens with the objective to get the ball inside for a high percentage shot. But he had players who could shoot from outside. He did not have Yelloweyes, but he had players who could keep the other teams honest. On defense he used the 2-3 zone and man-to-man, but what worked very well for the team was a full-court zone trap, with the aim to snag the ball on the first inbound pass. He had players who were quick enough to make it work.

Through the season, State School lost very few games. But when the Beavers went to the district tournament, they lost to Broadus in the championship by a point. Luckily State School did not have to play a challenge game so entered the divisional tournament as the second-place team. Again the Beavers lost in the championship play-ing that notorious game against Brockton. After losing, State School again did not have to play the challenge game and would be one of the eight teams at the state tournament. Though this was the team's third trip to state in a row, as with the other seven teams in the tournament, it had never won. Maybe the third time around would be the charm.

As expected for the state tournament, the Helena High school gym would be packed with fans. Many schools indicated they would have a large attendance on hand. The smallest school would be Gildford, with 29 students; the largest Darby, with 160 students. Chester would bring its band. Every night there would be a dance put on by the Police Protective Association.

The initial schedule was as follows: on Thursday at 2:00 p.m. Gildford (20-4, really 24-0; 29 students) would match up against the Colstrip Colts (18-9; 61 students). At 3:30 p.m. the Brockton Warriors (16-4; 50 students) were scheduled against the Darby Tigers (16-6; 160 students). In the evening at 7:30 p.m. the Corvallis Blue Devils (24-3; 142 students) would tackle the Chester Coyotes (17-9; 118 students), and at 9:00 p.m. the Holy Rosary Bulldogs of Bozeman (22-4; 82 students) would meet the State Industrial School Beavers of Miles City (21-5; 76 students).

At 2:00 p.m. the Gildford Broncs and the Colstrip Colts met each other for the very first time. There would be a member of the Flatness family on the floor, only this time he was from Colstrip. After the first quarter, Colstrip was no match for Gildford. The Broncs led by only two at the end of the first period, went up by 11 at halftime. In the second half, Gildford staved off a short-lived Colstrip rally, and then cruised through much of the rest of the half, leading by as much as 18 points before winning 69-54.

One player from Colstrip, Bailey Eagen, said, "We couldn't rebound with them; they would pick it off the backboard for a fast break and we couldn't stop that. We were frustrated, talked it over in the huddle until we ran out of time outs. We didn't have enough horse power." For Gildford, it was an opportunity to play against a bunch of "little guys." Most of the teams it played against through the season were, on average, bigger than the Gildford boys. As Gene Cady said, "We were used to playing schools six times bigger, six times taller."

In the other afternoon game, a taller Darby team defeated Brockton 63-58. Brockton had led the game for three quarters but could never get enough of a lead to put Darby away. As Larry Matteson of Darby said, "Brockton passed well, they weren't all that tall, but they were fast and moved the ball well; they had crack shots from the outside, it was really hard to hold them down. We just wore them down underneath the basket." In the first evening game, Corvallis dispatched Chester 76-64, getting the first field goal and never trailing. Its largest lead was the final score.

And finally at 9:00 p.m. it was Rosary against State School. Throughout the district and divisional tournaments, Rosary never had trouble with anyone. But now they were dealing with a State School team that was different in makeup from the year before. Monforton said, "We couldn't rebound with them." Still Rosary got the first basket and never trailed, leading throughout the first and second quarters but never by much, maybe a basket or two. In the third quarter it seemed that Rosary was going to deliver its patented breakout game, leaving the competition behind. With its full-court-press defense and race horse-fast-break offense, that is what always happened. Sooner or later the opposition would fold.

But not this game. The Beavers kept hacking away at the lead in the fourth quarter and it looked like they were going to catch up. With just a few minutes left, Christensen decided to have his team go into a stall; State School was killing them on the boards. In hindsight, he wished he hadn't stalled. Rosary was normally good at free throws, but now State School was fouling, and Rosary couldn't drop its free throws. With thirty seconds left, Rosary had a scant three-point lead with State School in possession. Wilkins came down and made a jump shot, putting State School behind by a single point.

Rosary now had possession, but one of the State School players immediately fouled Murphy, who was not a good foul shooter. Christensen knew Murphy well enough to know that by the look on his face, he wasn't going to make the free throw. And Murphy missed. With time running out, State School came down and one of its guards, Wilson, threw up a shot just inside the half-court line. The ball rimmed around the basket and rolled out. The final score was 50-49. Rosary would stay in the winners' bracket.

The next afternoon in the losers' bracket, Brockton had little trouble with Colstrip, defeating the Colts 64-55. State School edged Chester in a goofy game 82-81 in which neither team could miss and which seemed devoid of defense. This time State School did win on a last-second shot.

Gildford was now matched in the semi-final against Darby, a ponderous game, which created little suspense. Gildford led the slower Tigers 15-8 at the end of the first quarter and was leading 46-27 at the end of the third. Matteson from Darby said, the problem was Miller: "He could dribble and handle the ball like a guard, a fantastic ball handler. He could take the ball from one end to the other or they would give him the ball and he could dribble through all of us and put it up on the board. And when he got inside, he could fade shots, could dunk the ball if he wanted to, he was terrible on the boards, he was so far up and higher than anyone else and he had such moves under the basket, we couldn't control him." Miller countered that he could barely dunk the ball and never tried to dunk in a game (it wasn't allowed). But he didn't dismiss the other accolades. The final score was 64-49.

Rosary was pitted against the other bigger, slower team from the Bitterroot Valley, Corvallis. Corvallis kept the game even 32-32 at halftime. But in the second half, Rosary pulled away, winning 67-55. Most of the Rosary players don't remember much about the Corvallis game. One Corvallis player, Bill Engler, remembers this: "It seemed like Rosary was unconscious. They couldn't miss. I didn't think they were any better than Corvallis, but Rosary shot really well that night. They shot over 50 percent and were hitting baskets all from all over the place. Tom Monforton was the one who killed us." The only positive note for Corvallis, unrelated to the game, was that Rosary guard Dick Ward married one of the Corvallis cheerleaders, having by coincidence met her in college. Brockton and Darby defeated their opponents in the morning games, met each other again in the consolation, and this time the smaller, quicker Brockton boys won decisively, 68-54.

It would now be Holy Rosary and Gildford for the championship. Many people did not see a disparity between the two teams; for others, Rosary was a clear favorite. Ron Nelson's relative in Three Forks had said Gildford couldn't stay with Rosary. Chester player Norman Bruce, remembered being out in the hallway of the Helena gym before the championship and overhearing fans talking. One said, "Rosary is going to run those cowboys right off the floor." Rosary's Coach Christensen planned on using the same fast break and full-court press that had worked so well against all the other teams with which Rosary had competed.

But one Rosary player, Frank Seitz, noted something different about Gildford: "They basically had four guards, four who had lightning speed, and Miller who was the rebounder." Dick Ward said, "The full-court press was not going to work against this ball club. They were a fast-breaking team and the full-court press wasn't going to work against the fast break." Ward would say after the game, "They had a big guy, 6'3" who was extremely effective under the basket. He really controlled the backboards. Gaffke was outmanned by this guy totally."

Rosary had other vexations: Ward and Murphy were sick during the tournament. Ward was extremely ill with the flu and had been out of school all week before going to Helena. Ward remembered at the end of the State School game, someone threw a pass to him and he didn't even think he could catch the pass. Murphy's sickness may be one reason he did not have good games.

And there was something else that was to interfere with Rosary's concentration, depending on who you talk to. At least one player, Ward and maybe Seitz, were involved in a speech contest. Christensen, who had great trust in the players, said he didn't know until 4:00 p.m. that Ward had been gone and was involved all day in speech competition. Ward insists that the competition did not take place during the tournament but rather the following Wednesday. But Monforton remembered his father being upset because the state had allowed speech contests to go on during the tournament. At any rate, the

Rosary folks would say that Gildford might have beaten them anyway, but they were not helped by the condition of some of their players.

In those years Nick Mariani, a broadcaster from Helena, arranged annually to have the championship game filmed. I was lucky enough have Don Miller and Tom Monforton each make me a copy. I have watched the film several times and wish I could say it was helpful. I know the people did the best they could with the equipment and skills they had, but the film would show action on one end of the court, and then jump to the other end when the players arrived. So I could never get into the flow of the game. But one thing I did notice, at least in the first half: neither team was playing or shooting very well. It seemed like a sloppy game. Nevertheless, Gildford jumped off to an 18-10 lead by the end of the first quarter and by halftime was ahead 34-25. During the intermission, Ward said he told Christensen that the full court-press wasn't working against this team. Christensen had been thinking about making a change but didn't do so until sometime into the third quarter. By the end of that period, Gildford stretched the lead a little further, 49-38.

In the fourth quarter, the dam broke loose. Gildford was starting to run away with the game. Welsh was settling into his familiar role of wide receiver, jetting down the floor while the shot was in the air, knowing that Miller or Cady would get the rebound. A few minutes into the quarter, Christensen decided to pull the plug and put in all the subs. Some of the starters complained; they were sure they still had a chance. But Christensen said no, victory was out of reach. Furthermore, these kids have been part of this championship team and should have a chance to play. Gildford walked away with an 82-52 victory, a Class C championship margin that would not be broken for many years. Gildford also won the sportsmanship trophy, and Tom McCloskey was designated Coach of the Year. (The cheerleading trophy went to Chester.)

The Gildford fans were ecstatic, as you can imagine, but hardly stunned. Just a few minutes into the fourth quarter it was clearly evident their team would win. Still everyone rushed out onto the floor, reveling in the moment. Lynn Hayden said, "[Fans] were hugging, screaming, everyone, the townspeople. Everyone was euphoric. Fans couldn't get enough of each other. After the game, we had a special dinner for the team. All the townspeople came. Everyone was going around laughing." The celebration lasted long into the night. But it was all clean fun. The parents and other adults went off to the bars, but the kids went to the dance or stayed at the motel. Nelson said he remembered driving around Helena with Welsh, both in a daze. It was hard for the people to realize this had really happened.

The next day, Sunday, a caravan of a hundred cars left Helena and headed back to the Hi-Line, going up U.S. Highway 87 from Great Falls towards Havre and meeting a huge group of people mostly from neighboring towns at Fort Assiniboine, six miles southwest of Havre. From there the caravan had a police escort take them through Havre and onto U.S. Highway 2, thirty miles west to Gildford. Once in town there was a large gathering with "the whole Hi-Line cheering for them." Hayden said, "Coach McCloskey tried to talk and didn't have a voice. Everybody was supposed to get up and talk and everyone was so tired they could hardly move." There were dinners and get-togethers during the week, some planned, some spontaneous, some sponsored by organizations, some by individuals.

The 1960 Gildford team had given the town reason for exhilaration. But there were two accomplishments it would never achieve: it would never play in the new gym still under construction, and it would never again play Holy Rosary. During the 1960s, both teams were not to be in the state tournament together; by the end of the 1970s, a rematch was impossible: one school closed down, the other merged with another school under a different name. The only way the teams could play each other was replaying the game over and over – in memories at school reunions.

The 1960 Gildford team, winners of the state Class C championship appearing with trophy.
Front row: Chris Pappas, Ken Whitaker, Gene Cady, Ron Nelson, Don Miller, David Welsh.
Back row: Gary Cady, Monty Borlaug, Rick Swinney, Richard Gummer, Coach Tom McCloskey, Wesley Whitaker, manager.

The 1960 Rosary team, runners-up in the 1960 State Class C championship.
Front row: Karen Kirwin, Betty Lou Gossack, Bitsy Murphy, Shirley Nash.
Back row: left to right: Coach Neal Christensen, John Huckert - manager, George
Gallagher, Tony Gaffke, Jim Heagney, Ken Schweitzer, Dick Ward, Joe Cahill,
Mike Murphy, Frank Seitz, Jerry Monforton, Tom Monforton.

Mary Condon was the
Montana Superintendent of
Public Instruction from1948-
56. Principal person involved
in fracas over accreditation of
schools along the Hi-Line.

The Gildford school board in the mid 1950s. From left to right: Murvin Hanson, Leonard Grimes, Ruth Tew.

Gildford school before it burned down in Jan. 1959. The gym sits directly behind the school and is not shown.

The 1959 Gildford team that took 3rd place in the 1959 State Class C tournament. Front row: Ron Nelson, Ken Whitaker, Gene Cady, David Welsh, and Chris Pappas.
Back row: Richard Gummer, team manager; George Trevor, David Saller, Don Miller, Lawrence Flatness, Jack Fried, and Coach Roger Freih.

The Holy Rosary school before it was replaced in 1962. The lighter front part of the building opened for school in 1919. The darker back part of the building including the gym was added in 1938.

Father Paul C Mackin, head priest of Holy Rosary from 1956-66

The 1961 Belgrade High School team, runners-up in the 1961 State Class C tournament.
Front row: Coach Chris Small, Manager Harry Armstrong.
Back row: Gary Cook, Larry Moore, Marvin Craver, Garry Hellyer, Tom Ver-wolf, Larry Karinen, Robert Otheim, Tom Saisbury, Leon Stiles, Charles Wright.

1961 Bulldogs. Standing: L-R Tom Monforton, Mike Cahill, Terry Corcoran, George Gallagher, Dave Noyes, Ken Schweitzer, Joe Cahill, Rick Ritter, Jerry Monforton, Bob Schweitzer.
Kneeling: L-R Manager Don Noyes, Coach Jim Owens, Manager Carl Johnson.

PART TWO

The Father, the Coach, and the Player

T HIS BOOK SHOULD END NOW, BUT IT CAN'T. I WON'T LET IT. HOLY Rosary was too close to my home and was favored to win the championship the following year. Along the way, it would develop a rivalry with my old school Belgrade that was—well— unrivaled. And this book was born because the new coach of Rosary had a unique place in my youthful observations. I just couldn't let it go.

When the 1960 state tournament concluded, no one had any indication that at the dawn of the following school year Rosary would have a new coach. Neal Christenson had lost the championship, but his best players would be back and he fully expected to return. Sure, Rosary paid a pittance in salary, but it would be crazy not to stay with this bunch. Winning would be good for the resumé.

Christensen loved being at Rosary for all the support he was receiving from most people, not the least from the nuns. The nuns were de facto servants, were not allowed to watch the games because they couldn't be out past nightfall. But they listened to the games on the radio, taping every game and giving the tape to Christensen the next day. He had learned a great deal about teaching from them and could analyze the game from the tapes. There were no video cameras in those days, only radio broadcasts. Some of the parents possibly filmed some of the games, but the school itself had no such setup. For all the lack of certain resources, Christensen was still happy at Rosary.

Then at the divisional tournament in Red Lodge, Don Zupan, sports editor at the *Billings Gazette*, approached Christensen and told him the basketball situation at Billings Central was not looking good;

he loved the way Christensen had his team playing at Rosary. The Bulldogs had just polished off Joliet in the semi-final, had for a period of time not even allowed the Jayhawks to cross the half-court line. It was one of Rosary's finest moments. Brent Musberger, the future famous broadcaster, was doing the play-by-play broadcast on radio and had raved about Rosary's play to radio listeners. Zupan himself was duly impressed. Red Lodge High School had contacted Christensen about a job, but the coach said he was not interested. Now, Zupan said the Central coach was going to be gone; he had contacted the booster group for Billings Central—known as the Roundtable —which contributed money and critiqued everything. Zupan asked Christensen if he would be interested in taking over the Central job. Christensen said he couldn't think about it with the tournaments on and, with the kids he had, would probably not be interested.

In the midst of the state tournament, Christensen forgot about the conversation with Zupan. But afterwards, over the weeks, he slowly got to thinking: Billings Central, another Catholic school, a larger Catholic school; that might be okay. He was also influenced by another source, the head priest at Holy Rosary, Father Paul C. Mackin.

Father Mackin had been born in Taylor, Pennsylvania, on July 10, 1908, to Michael and Catherine Mackin, had attended St. Thomas College in Scranton, Pennsylvania, Basselin College of the Catholic University of America, and Sulpician Seminary in Washington, D.C. In 1933 he was ordained a Roman Catholic priest in Scranton for the Diocese of Helena. He served at St. Mary's Parish in Stevensville for the summer of 1933 but that fall joined the faculty at Carroll College in Helena, and would remain there for the next twenty-three years.

Mackin had been an outstanding teacher at Carroll, had risen through the ranks and by 1956 was the dean of religion. When the current vice president passed away, the president of Carroll, Monsignor Vincent Kavanagh tapped Mackin to be the new vice president. Everyone agreed that no one could be more competent for the job, certainly no one more above reproach. But there was a small problem: Kavanagh had not cleared his decision with Bishop Joseph M. Gilmore of the Helena Diocese. Gilmore didn't appreciate that. When the time came for priests to be reassigned, the bishop, who had the authority, assigned Mackin to Rosary. He became the victim of ecclesiastical politics.

To a great degree, Paul Mackin was altruistic. He did what he thought was in the best interest of whatever he was dealing with, not bowing to political considerations. When his tenure was up with Rosary after ten years, he moved to the Missoula area, where he spent the rest of his life working with the poor. Certainly at Rosary he was an able administrator; not only was he over the church and the school, he oversaw raising funds and the construction of the new Rosary school, an undertaking that cost in the neighborhood of a half million dollars. He was dealing with his assistant priests, the sisters of the parish, the students, and the parishioners. He also taught a class at Montana State College and stood in as a teacher of math and religion at Rosary. He was a busy man.

Father Mackin could be a gracious host at Rosary for dignitaries from out of town or local powers who held the purse strings. He also tended to be a magnet for young men he thought showed promise. He had had his favorites at Carroll: students headed for a bright future, ecclesiastical or otherwise. Wags called them his "disciples," or more often his "twelve apostles." It became a great joke around Carroll; students would post the latest "chosen" on the bulletin board next to the school canteen, knowing it was an area Father Mackin would never frequent. If students weren't part of his sanctum, they were largely ignored. For most students (and adults, for that matter), Mackin would be remembered for his legendary reserve, no doubt a product of his East Coast upbringing. They would walk past Father Mackin in the hall and be considered *persona non grata*.

At Rosary it wasn't long before he had his new group of favorites. Some would help him count money after church on Sunday and then all would pile into the car and spend a couple of hours at the bowling alley. It was known that Father Mackin loved to water ski. A family would go to Hebgen Lake for the weekend, and Father Mackin would join them on Sunday afternoon. He worked this arrangement in an interesting way, assigning himself to a "mission" church, i.e., a satellite church known as Lady of the Pines in West Yellowstone. Taking care of mass there was considered a plum assignment; the three priests at Holy Rosary were supposed to rotate going to West Yellowstone during the summers, but because Father Mackin liked to get away and water ski, as head priest, he pulled rank and took every assignment to West Yellowstone. When mass was over, he would spend as much of the rest of the day as he could hanging on to a rope behind a boat. But for all the fun in the afternoon, when it came time to go back inside, he was not one to engage in animated conversation over dinner or for the rest of the evening. He was introspective, a thinker, not a talker.

He was a big bear of a man, intimidating to those who weren't in his inner circle. He never yelled at students but he had bearing such that all knew not to approach him lightly. This included every girl at Rosary. Father Mackin had the old-school attitude about women; they could be secretaries or teachers and that was about it. Some girls understood intellectually that Father Mackin was a "wonderful man," maybe in the same way Russians thought Stalin was a wonderful man. But he was considered scary. One told me she did not like him. She "quaked in her boots whenever she was around him." He was not personable but "gruff, forceful" in the way he talked to people.

Kids were intimidated by him not only because he was large and remote, but because he was brilliant. As former student Tom Diamond put it, in class he had a razor-sharp sense of humor and otherwise made it clear to the class that he was "very, very smart and we were very, very dumb." One day someone asked a "stupid" question and his retort was, "You boys are no more than a bunch of omedons. What is an omedon? Don't know? Well look it up." The students tried to find the word in a dictionary but came up short. "Can't find it?

Well, I will tell you. An omedon is someone who is not only ignorant but insists on remaining so."

These personality traits led to a dictatorial style of management. Father Mackin did all the hiring and firing and made it clear who made the final decisions at Rosary. There could be a discussion about something but once he made a decision that was it. If he overrode his assistants on the Lady of the Pines assignments he could do so in other matters as well. Young couples might prefer to have lovable Father Burns marry them, but Mackin said no. He was the head priest and he would perform the ceremony. End of discussion.

For all that, he was never one to discuss conflicts with personalities. Diamond, who in those days knew him as well as anyone, said, "He never said anything bad about any person; he really didn't. He never in my presence commented on anything about Neal Christensen at all."

Because Mackin might have had much to say about Neal Christensen. Anyone who had known both men previously could have predicted a meeting of oil and water. Christensen was the freewheeling talker who had sold shoes, Cutco Cutlery, cars, and insurance while in college, bright but not academic, anything but introspective, and above all, devoted to sports.

Father Mackin was not devoted to sports. He was not against sports. He had played golf regularly at Carroll, and as has been stated, enjoyed bowling and water skiing. He also supported team sports to some extent. He had been behind setting up a basketball game between Rosary Junior High and its Catholic counterpart in Butte. But he could see the sports program at Rosary getting out of hand and impinging on education, and Father Mackin was nothing if not a strong believer in quality education.

Christensen saw it differently, that Mackin was living in the Dark Ages. When he first arrived at Rosary, the basketball team had these "Neanderthal style" uniforms with small numbers, made of heavy wool, guaranteed to make each boy the laughing stock of District 8 if he dared to wear it on court. They were so bad, Christensen thought, he wouldn't wear them himself. Christensen went into Mackin's office and told him,

"I can't put a team on the floor with these uniforms; they must be at least ten years old."

Mackin couldn't see why the team needed new uniforms.

"The team needs new uniforms because they will be competing against good teams that *do* have new uniforms. It will make them feel better."

Mackin was unconvinced. "How much will the uniforms cost?"

"Six hundred dollars."

"SIX HUNDRED DOLLARS??" We can't afford that."

"We don't have a budget, so how can we afford anything?"

Mackin finally gave in. He told Christensen to go buy them. But according to Christensen it was all "nasty talk." He then went out and bought the uniforms and the kids looked sharp in them.

Christensen didn't like Mackin in general. As a health nut, he was put off by Mackin's chain smoking, his yellowed fingers. He didn't like the way Mackin could put him into a pickle. One day Mackin called him in about the conduct of Warren, the grade school coach. Warren was from Butte Central and was used to the Christian Brothers style of discipline. He would beat the kids, take balls out of the closets and throw them in their faces, yell at them, run them to death; finally high school kids started coming down, watched, and blew the whistle. Christensen noticed it too. The parents started calling Mackin and told him he needed to get rid of the guy.

Mackin said to Christensen, "Neal, you have got to fire Warren."

"Why should I fire him? You hired him. He isn't going to take this easy. He's a wild man."

"I know. I know what he is doing."

"You hired him; you have got to fire him."

"No, you fire him."

Christensen gave in this time. He was thinking, the grade school coach is 6'5", a brutal fighter, is going to go crazy and beat him up.

Christensen had been a fighter all his life, but he was no match for this guy. Finally Christensen screwed up his courage, called Warren in and said,

"Here's the deal. You are fired."

"Why?"

"Because you treat the kids too poorly. I didn't hire you; Mackin hired you but he asked me to fire you and I am just carrying out his orders."

Warren looked at him and said, "Okay." And then he left. He never came back and Christensen never saw him again.

With all the Mackin hassles, with the overtures from Billings Central, Christensen still had no plans to leave Rosary, at least not for one more year. He had a great group of kids both in talent and temperament. But soon after the state tournament, Mackin called him in once again and said,

"I want you to start deemphasizing sports."

"How do I do that Father?"

"I don't know, but just do it."

"How would I do that? Tell my kids not to play hard? Or not play the best players? Sorry, I'm not deemphasizing anything."

Some students at Rosary, especially those who were part of Mackin's coterie, saw the situation differently. They didn't get a sense that Mackin was trying to deemphasize sports at all. I mentioned earlier that the high school teaching staff was filled with Franciscan Sisters of Perpetual Adoration. But there was one lay exception to this in 1960: several classes were taught by the coach. Perhaps Father Mackin was drawn to something else: that Neal Christensen's classroom teaching skills were left wanting.

I must at this time address a question, which has been asked hundreds of thousands of times through the years, and at least once for sure in 1960 by a disgruntled fan: "Well, was he hired as a teacher or a coach?" Today, this problem in small schools has largely been solved by bringing in coaches from the community, often as volunteers. In

1960, that idea was mostly unthought-of. Instead the teacher-coach quandary was a fundamental issue, more so than many people would have cared to admit. Usually, in theory, the answer was teacher; that was why the person was hired and where he drew most of his salary.

The high school teachers were not paid enough but that did not stop us from high expectations. We wanted them to be electrifying, galvanizing, drawing us to linger after class for every last drip-drop of wisdom, after which we would rocket to the library for additional research on the lesson just taught, to declare the course the embodiment of our future careers, or at the very least, after we each were elected citizen of the year in our moderately large city, to stand before that banquet and say, If it hadn't been for Mr. X or Miss Y, we wouldn't be where we are today. Wasn't that what we wanted from our teachers? How many teachers could rise to that ridiculous standard? I say not many, and of those who did, few were also hired to be a coach.

The coach wore many hats. Aside from being a jock, he had to be a motivator, strategist, original thinker, military general, salesman, diplomat, nurturer, counselor, disciplinarian, full of patience and discernment, to fend off politics—which, if all attributes were fully developed, added up to genius. Above all the coach was a student and teacher. *But a student and teacher of sports.* This was expected on the college or professional level, but no one was expecting these prodigies to regale an audience on the intricacies of the Louisiana Purchase. The head may be up to the task, but the heart was not, couldn't afford to be. And yet, this in theory was supposed to play out in high school; the coach must be a show-stopper both along the sidelines and in the classroom.

Don't misunderstand me. Many a high school coach told me how much he loved the class-room, and I believed him. He loved the classroom because he loved education in general and loved kids. The kids loved him because he had been successful on the sidelines, a successful role model, and were now willing to run through a brick wall for him. And to be fair, some coaches were very effective in the classroom for the subject itself, particularly, say, science or shop. These were niche branches of learning the coach had long loved before he ever made the decision to go into education. And science, for example, required more skill than emotion, which the coach-teacher could plausibly switch to for a career. Good coaches often made great administrators but the problem came when the person had in reality been hired to be a coach, and now must be given *something* to teach in the classroom. The school couldn't afford to hire him for strictly physical education. And so the coach was faced with two focal points that didn't go together any more than sewing a hem goes with investing in cocoa futures. One coach explicitly told me he minored in social studies because he could not major and minor in sports.

There could be exceptions here, too. Joe Doohan at Rosary was passionate about sports *and* forensics. But he was single at the time and gave his life to the school for one year. By the next year he was off to graduate school. At Belgrade one afternoon, Tusco Heath, the assistant football coach and club boxing master, came into our classroom subbing for someone in history. During that one hour from his lips came the only two pieces of information I have remembered in the three years I attended Belgrade High School. He referred to authors Thomas Costain and Nikos Kazantzakis (I'm embarrassed to say I never read either of their works). Heath was riveting; there is no question about it. But the No Child Left Behind folks would have hated him. He went off on his own performance, leaving the lesson plan for the day instantly behind him.

The dilemma of coaching and teaching was compounded at Rosary. Not only was the coach to recount in detail the substance of the Louisiana Purchase, but explain with some expertise the principles of electricity, theories of Adam Smith, innards of a tomato plant, various forms of city government—all the while knowing that the most important game of the year was coming off Saturday night and every parent and booster would be watching.

And so it came back to Neal Christensen. He was not an effective teacher. One civics class he taught, according to certain students, was such a waste that they figured what the heck; at night they snuck into Sister Patrina's desk where they knew the answers would be, and filed them away for the next exam. The kids also claimed that Christensen didn't know much about biology. The joke went around that he didn't know, until they told him, that potatoes grew in the ground. He would come to class, hand out workbooks, and apparently sit there while the kids filled in the answers. But he was not just sitting there; he was scrambling to grade exams, make up new exams, and otherwise preparing as best he could for the next day. Or the next hour.

Christensen said he was given five "preps" (classes) to teach every day, which at different times included general science, biology, world history, American history, economics, civics, girls PE—and coach of all sports. During the basketball season he was coach of both the varsity and junior varsity. (In Christensen's second year, Rocco Percevelli, a former Bobcat football player, became an assistant coach over the JVs.)

He had had some biology at Michigan State and thought he could teach that, but he had no prep time. He could only give tests with multiple-choice answers because if there were tests with essay questions, trying to correct the exams was unfathomable. It couldn't be done. When he mentioned his circumstance to several of the coaches over at Bozeman High, they were shocked at his burden.

Christensen talked to the principal, Sister Mary Michael, about his class load, and she in turn talked to Father Mackin. But nothing changed. Finally he pleaded with Sister Mary Michael at the end of his first year to at least take away his science classes; he wasn't even endorsed to teach those classes, and she was able to eliminate them from his schedule. But even four classes was still an extreme schedule.

The one class where he thought he made a real difference was in girls' PE. He treated the girls like boys, ran them hard. They started complaining to Father Mackin and he told Christensen to lighten up on the girls, he was too hard on them. Christensen told him he had a degree in health and physical education and that his regimen was good for them. Mackin didn't agree, but four months later parents called Mackin and told him their daughters had never been in such good physical shape. Years later the girls still remembered that.

So when Father Mackin told Christensen to deemphasize sports, Christensen left the office and never talked to Mackin again. He was quite certain he would never see Mackin again and he was right. Father Donovan from Billings Central had called and asked Christensen if he was still interested in the job. Christensen said he would like to talk about it. Father Donovan and others came to Bozeman to interview him at Rosary. A couple of days later they asked if he would come to Billings and talk to the Roundtable, which he did. A few more days after that, they called and said they were offering him the job. Christensen said, "Okay, I'm coming."

CHRISTENSEN WAS GOING TO HATE LEAVING ROSARY BECAUSE OF THE players: the Monforton brothers, Ken Schweitzer, Joe Cahill, George Gallagher, and all the rest—certainly Mike Murphy. But in the end, Christensen would not leave Murphy, because Murphy would go with him to Billings.

Mike Murphy was a very mature young man, both physically and otherwise. His classmates said he began growing whiskers when he was only twelve years old. With his moderately dark hair and muscular attributes, he was unusually handsome. Many of the girls at Rosary wanted to "go with him," be his girlfriend. He didn't have to do anything to charm girls; he was quiet, respectful and the girls loved that. To some extent, he was naïve. When he moved to Billings and the girls saw this new kid and went "bananas," he would say, "Coach, when I walk down the hall, why does everyone look at me?" One senior girl at Billings Central who was unusually attractive and mature in her own right, who dated exclusively college boys and wouldn't give her high school mates the time of day, saw Murphy and immediately had a crush on him. But as was Murphy's wont, he did not return her affection (he was in love with a girl from Bozeman High School). He had that way about him that drew people, his quiet maturity, his demeanor; guys at high school and at Carroll College, where he went to school, just liked to hang out with Murphy. He was a leader that way.

Maybe part of what attracted people was Murphy's determination. He was conscientious to a fault at his summer jobs; he was dedicated to his school-work; he hoped to become a physician someday. One night after he began staying at the Christensen home, Neal got up in the middle of the night and noticed Murphy's light on in his bedroom. He walked up the stairs to see if everything was all right. Murphy was working on a geometry problem and would stay up until he solved it. Christensen tried to encourage him to get back to sleep because he had school the next day but Murphy would not be deterred. At 5:00 a.m., he finally cracked the problem and went back to bed.

He had that same determination in sports. Murphy was only 5'10" but he could rebound with players 6'3", 6'4", was determined he was going to get that ball and when he got it, *no one* was going to take it away from him. He could do that because he was unusually strong, but determination was part of his strength. When he was a football player at Billings Central and injured his knee, the doctor determined it was sprained, not torn, but his rehabilitation was going to need some work. So Murphy came to practice and started running up and down the stairs in the gym. When the other players left for practice outdoors and came back after two hours, Murphy was still running up and down. He soon put his injury behind him and came back to the team.

In his determination, Murphy could lose his temper. And the anger would lead to more determination. He had been employed during the summer at Restvedt Meat Market in downtown Bozeman, and one day when he came out from work, he noticed that his car had a big dent in it; someone's door had slammed into it. Murphy was furious, because no one would own up to doing it. He was determined to find out who did it so they would pay for having his car fixed. He had a big blue mark on his car which was one clue he needed. He was on the lookout for days, cars coming and going, and finally one day he found a car of that color parked in the parking lot; it was owned by an older man. Murphy followed him up to his home with the intention of beating him up. He confronted the man, who was only too happy to pay for the accident but later called the police. Murphy was taken down to the police station and Christensen was called on the phone. Murphy had to go before a judge, who let him off, but Christensen told Murphy, "A big strong kid like you threatening an old man like that; what were you thinking?" Murphy came to his senses and was deeply sorrowful. Once there was a theft in the locker room at Rosary, not Murphy's locker but that of another student. He became extremely angry; why would someone do that? He took it upon himself to be a sheriff at school, with a strong sense of righting a wrong. Shirley Nash, a classmate, remembered that Murphy would give everything his all. "He studied so hard; he would have troubles with some of his classes and he would get so mad if he missed something. If he missed something or didn't come out on top, he would be so mad. He would study harder than anyone I ever knew."

He could get angry in competition and when he did, opponents beware. If he missed, say, a block in football, the opposition would pay dearly for it on the next play. Sometimes his shortcomings led to mere frustration. His teammate Tony Gaffke was a gangly basketball player who made unorthodox moves, which threw off defenders. In one practice Gaffke drove across the middle to take a shot, Murphy jumped up to block it, but Gaffke faked, blew by Murphy and laid it in. Murphy went crazy. "I'VE BEEN PLAYING WITH THIS KID ALL MY LIFE, ALL MY LIFE AND HE DOES IT TO ME ALL THE TIME. AND HE DID IT TO ME AGAIN!!"[8]

In truth, Murphy was a good basketball player but not outstanding like the Monforton brothers or Schweitzer. He was a great rebounder and a tenacious defender, but he was only average on offense. He was not a particularly good shooter and terrible at the free-throw line. In big-game situations, he could choke. But in football, it was an entirely different tune. He was a running back, and when he got the ball, he would lower his head and run over people. He had been the main running back for the fledgling Rosary team and when he transferred to Billings Central, he and Christensen were enthusiastic that he could be part of a larger program. But the Billings Central coach wouldn't let him compete to be a starter on the varsity. So Murphy in practice played with the scrubs and was just running through the varsity defenses, "destroying" them according to Christensen. Finally the coach decreed this could not continue. So he had all eleven players gang up on Murphy and ripped up his knee, forcing him to miss games.

The knee injury did not doom Murphy. Instead he was brought down by the constant use of his head. Murphy was a brutal runner and blocker, was afraid of nothing, and would slam his head into players, not just in high school but later on, when he played for Carroll College. Mostly at Carroll he played defense, but he developed the same head-slamming style he had when he was a running back and finally, in 1964, when he was a junior, all the butting took its toll.

There is some disagreement as to what actually happened, but most accounts say Murphy was taking a shower one morning when he fell and sustained a concussion. He was lying there unconscious when fellow students discovered him, took him out of the shower, and put him to bed. He lay unconscious for the rest of the day and night. Why they did not do more is a mystery. The next morning, a Saturday, the priest came around, saw his door open, that he was quivering in bed and immediately called an ambulance. He was taken to the old hospital in Helena, was given an X-ray, and a large blood clot was discovered where he had hit his head on the shower floor. The doctor opened his head up, removed the clot, but could do little more because he was not a neurosurgeon. Murphy was taken to a room where he never regained consciousness. He started quivering again; this time he was rushed to Great Falls, where this time he was in the care of a neural surgeon. Another X-ray was taken and it was discovered that Murphy had an even larger blood clot away from the shower impact, a clot that had probably been in his cranium for years. (which is disconcerting because no one remembered Murphy having headaches).

But at Carroll, the coaches said Murphy was one of the hardest hitters they had ever seen. As Christensen said, "He hit people and they would never want to see him again. He had that kind of force." In the hospital, Christensen yelled at Murphy, pounded on his chest to try to get a response, but the doctor said stop. There was nothing that could be done. Murphy remained in a coma, never came out of it; he was in such good physical health otherwise that he lay there for a month before finally dying from pneumonia.

Maybe Murphy was so tense and determined in order to cope with being unwanted. His father had been killed in World War II and Murphy hardly had the chance to know him. His mother Aleta was a beautiful woman and no doubt had numerous petitions for marriage, but remained a widow, being devoted to her three children. She made sure they were actively engaged in a variety of wholesome activities. A childhood friend, Shirley Nash said Aleta let Mike hang out with her uncle, who engaged Mike in outdoor activities, hiking, fishing; Aleta and her kids became outdoorsy people. She had been responsible and attentive through the years, but when Murphy was a sophomore in high school, she met a man whom she would soon marry.

The man wanted a relationship with the mother but this did not include her son. When the new couple made plans to move to California, Murphy was not welcome to come along. It was sad because his mother was, in essence, choosing a man she had not known long over the son she had nurtured all his life. This might be understandable if Murphy had been an incorrigible pill. But if there was ever a boy a new step father could take to, it should have been Mike Murphy.

One day Christensen was standing in a hall at Rosary when

Murphy came up to him with tears in his eyes and wanted to talk to him.

Christensen said, "I can't talk to you right now. I have a class to teach."

Murphy said, "It's too important. I've got to talk to you now." His voice was cracking.

Christensen got someone else to take his class.

Murphy said, "This is hard for me. I'm really embarrassed; would you and your wife let me live with you? Mom is going to leave and go with this guy to California who she is going to marry and he doesn't want me. She said to ask you if you would."

Christensen thought, why didn't Aleta come and talk to me? She must have been too embarrassed to just up and leave Mike. Christensen told Murphy that he would have to talk to his wife. His wife agreed, because Mike was a great kid, would never cause any trouble. So Christensen called Aleta. "Is this story right? I hear you are going to get married." She said they could have her house rent-free. It was an older house in north Bozeman, near the old hospital. It was a good move for Christensen and his wife because when he first came to Bozeman they had rented a tiny apartment. Now they had this big old house and all they had to do was watch Mike, which was easy. For the rest of the time they were in Bozeman, they never had a real problem with Murphy.

The next year when Christensen decided to take the Billings Central job, it only made sense for Murphy to go with him.[9] He had bonded well with Christensen and his wife and had no other options. The Rosary team, which had high hopes for another shot at the state championship, was now not only without its coach but one of its starting players. Murphy was not the star, but he was integral to the success of the team. Players, parents, and a growing number of fans had reason to be more than a little concerned.

But something began to happen long before, even during, Christensen's first basketball season that no one thought at the time consequential. During practices, football players from Montana State would show up, players all with aspirations to be a coach. There were Bobcat basketball players also; Jim Murphy and Bill Epperly from the team were there, always seemed to be around, Christensen remembered. Epperly was Christensen's brother-in-law but otherwise all visitors were people he didn't know. Before long some asked if they could work with the players, work on fundamentals, have them go through drills. Christensen had no objection. He could use the help. His brother-in-law was foremost in giving assistance.

There was another basketball player that came down during Christensen's second year who introduced himself and said, before coming to Montana State, he had been a Class C ball player in Wibaux. He was different from the others, seemed to them vaguely intellectual—a correct assessment because he was a voracious reader—and didn't make a habit of hanging around other players and coaches. He was about 5'9" with blonde hair, who had been mostly a role player for the Bobcats. He didn't get much playing time at first but by the time he was a senior, saw significant minutes, often giving the team a needed boost. When he came to the practices, he proved to be likable, well mannered. He too asked to work with the kids and they grew to like him. Maybe it was because he was articulate, a great teacher, could communicate in plain terms that resonated with the players. His name was Jim Owens and little did he or anyone else know at the time that very soon after he graduated from Montana State, he would become the new coach at Holy Rosary.

The Savior from the East

EVERYONE KNEW JIMMY OWENS WAS GOOD. HE WAS ATTRACTIVE, personable, smart. And he was a true basketball guy: basketball was his first love. Most of all he was motivated to shine on the sidelines as a coach in a way he never quite could as a player. Certainly he was an exceptional player in Class C. Anyone on the court with him would tell you he could shoot the lights out from just about any position. He was the star of a team that should have won the state championship in 1956. But through an error in the coach's strategy, the team lost, and when Owens played ball in college he was never tall enough, never quite quick enough, relegated to reserve status as a role player. But now he could redeem himself as coach, and just down slope from where he attended college was a small parochial school with an exceptional group of players who needed his services. With these kids he had a real chance to grab the brass ring he had never enjoyed as a player. Before school had started in 1960, he was on board. He would be off to a sterling season.

James Dale Owens was born January 2, 1938, in what is known as The Big Open, that vast, mostly empty prairie in east-central Montana. His father, Gomer, worked on the Fort Peck Dam during the latter part of the Great Depression and because there was no place for families to stay at Fort Peck, Gomer's wife Lois Marie stayed forty miles away in the little town of Circle with her parents. Circle would become Jim's place of birth. Eastern Montana would remain the backdrop for much of his adult life. Some years after Rosary, for example, he would return to Circle and coach that basketball team to a state Class B title.

When Jim was two years old, Gomer had a chance to be part-owner of a Ford dealership/garage in White Sulphur Springs with his brother Hayden and good friend Fred Nopper (Hayden's wife Addie was Nopper's sister). Gomer had always been a mechanic and loved working on cars. He was happy to run the garage while the other two men continued to mostly farm. The business went well and Gomer loved his job, but when Jim was in the fifth grade his grandfather, Reece, asked Gomer and another brother Tom, to take over the gas station he owned in Wibaux. Gomer took up the offer because he could have greater ownership of a business and live near his parents. Over time, Gomer was able to add a garage to the gas station and enlarge the motel next door, his father had built. Jim would continue in Wibaux through high school graduation, always living with his family in quarters over the gas station until his last few years there, when Gomer built a new home for the family.

Jim was four years older than sister Mary Jane, eight years older than brother Frank, but the family was very close, not just the immediate family but extended family; there were frequent gatherings and Jim always looked forward to them. He loved fishing and hunting rabbits at night with his dad. He also worked for his father all through high school at the gas station. It didn't hurt that Gomer was a reasonable man, easy to get along with. When a raging teacher at Wibaux High School hammered on the locked door of the super-intendent's office with the superintendent quaking inside, Gomer, as president of the school board, was called in to settle nerves. Jim took on many of the characteristics of his parents; as a youngster he was always obedient, never giving his parents any trouble. He loved to read, which turned into a life-long passion. As an adult his favorite author was Ernest Hemingway. His sister Mary Jane said he was a contemplative boy, always thinking.

If Jim liked to read and think, much of it was about sports. Because as much as anything else, sports was a unifying factor in the family. Grandfather Reece had been a star baseball player. Gomer had starred in basketball when he was a high school player in Brockway. Sports had been a family signature, a tradition, and from a young age, Jim was an absolute enthusiast. He never wanted to miss a ballgame and he was encouraged by his father.

In White Sulphur, Owens was too small for basketball, but a fellow in town, Tom Watson, had all the small boys boxing and Jim joined in. When the family moved to Wibaux, there was no more boxing; Owens gravitated to the three traditional major sports, football, basketball, and baseball. He would excel in all three.

Jim had played quarterback, surrounded by exceptional athletes on his six-man football team. They would go undefeated and win the Eastern Divisional title in 1956 (no state champion in those days), the closest game against Rosebud 35-14. In the district playoff, Wibaux humbled Culbertson 43-0, the same in the divisional title against Medicine Lake 45-6. In one game during that season, Wibaux was so far ahead, the game was called. Owens played in the East-West Shrine game following the season.

Wibaux initially had no baseball team so during the summers, after working for his dad at the gas station, Owens would catch a ride thirty miles to Glendive to play for that city's Legion team. He almost never had trouble finding a ride; someone buying gas, as often as not, was heading that way. If he could not find a ride, he was determined; he would stand out on the road and hitchhike. If he had trouble finding a way home, Gomer would travel the distance to pick him up (Gomer only had to make the trip three times).

Owens had reason to be dedicated. He was always a pitcher, and a good one. Gomer had fixed a target out in the back yard where Jim could practice. He quickly became the dominant pitcher on the Glendive staff. The next year, Wibaux formed its own team. In one game against perennial power Billings (coming through town after touring the lower Midwest), Owens was pitching and in five innings, no Billings batter could touch him. Lois Marie was sitting in the stands and heard the Billings manager talking to two of his players, telling them, "That kid [Owens] is making a fool out of you." Billings managed to win by one run in that game. The manager later tried to recruit Jim.

But Owens' meal ticket would be basketball. As he had in other sports, he soon became the star. There is an article in the February 21, 1992, edition of the *Great Falls Tribune* talking about "Top Gunners" of Montana high school basketball, players who had scored 1,500 points or more in their high school career. Owens was eighth on the list, scoring 2121 points in four years, or 19.5 points per game. Owens had told reporters at the time, "I guess I wasn't much different than a lot of kids out in the boondocks. About all we did was shoot basketballs. What else were we going to do?"

Being a sports star, Owens would be more than popular in a town like Wibaux. As one schoolmate said, "Owens was outgoing in this small town with approximately 120 students in high school. There might have been a little bit of envy, because he was so talented. But he never wore that [arrogant] hat."

Wayne Marcus, who had long been a fixture of education at Wibaux and the junior high coach during the early fifties quickly saw Owens' talent. Over a two-year span, his team won thirty games in a row. In one game, the score was tied 20-20 at halftime. By game's end, Wibaux won 40-20; Owens had made all of the baskets. One day Lois Marie was sitting next to Marcus, who said, "I'm not going to let Jim graduate. He must stay in the eighth grade." Lois Marie (disturbed) asked, "Why, aren't his grades good enough?" "No," Marcus said, "I just want him to play basketball for me next year."

When Owens became a freshman, he was already a starter on a high school team made up mostly of seniors. That team went 17-11, a decent team coached by Willy Strange. When the seniors graduated, the team next year fell to an 8-11 record, a bunch of young kids lacking skills playing the likes of Ekalaka which had players that were huge, several of whom would go on to play college football. As teammate Eugene "Toby" Nistler put it, "We were still kids as sophomores playing against teams that looked like they had men." Strange taught two more years at Wibaux, but at the end of the season was forced from his coaching job. A lot of good kids were coming up, and the people of Wibaux knew the team needed someone else.

When Owens was a junior, that someone else was a new man in town whose name was Dick Cramer. Cramer was a firebrand, a gifted talker, a charismatic kind of guy. The girls in school were attracted to his good looks. He was also a coach of no small talent. Cramer was originally from the tiny hamlet of Ismay, east of Miles City, went on to graduate from the University of Wyoming and landed in Wibaux after coaching in Brush, Colorado. He wasn't the only standout in his family. His brother had been an excellent musician and band teacher at Fairfield High School, was known for taking every individual student and making them believe in themselves. Cramer would one day be Coach Jerry Tarkanian's assistant when the University of Nevada-Las Vegas won the NCAA basketball title in 1990.

Cramer had a flair for bending the rules. He had always been an English teacher, a good teacher, but an especially good teacher for student athletes. When someone asked him why he taught English, he said because that is the subject most players flunk. When one member of the Wibaux team failed a semester of English as a sophomore, in order to regain eligibility, he approached Cramer and asked if there was a way he could make the course up. Cramer said, "You have already made it up; your grade is in the office." Voila! The boy was eligible.

When Cramer came to Wibaux, he brought with him a senior student, Archie Burns, who at 6'2" would become a badly needed big man on the basketball team. But because Burns came with Cramer, he wasn't eligible. In short time Burns' father moved up, got a job on a ranch, and eligibility was restored. Or so the school thought. Sacred Heart also took in a boy from Baker with eligibility problems. Complaints from other schools were filed with the Montana High School

Association. In the end, Wibaux won its case but Sacred Heart lost.

Once Cramer got that problem behind him he could concentrate on basketball. It helped that Burns was more mature than the rest of the players; when team members got out of line, Burns would calm things down. But it was Cramer who really turned the team around. He broke everything down and started with fundamentals again. He "drilled, drilled, drilled," with lots of conditioning, plenty of wind sprints. Knowing the boys were still to some degree green on fundamentals and playmaking, he installed a slowdown game so that if the team ran a play and it didn't work, they could revert to the beginning and start all over again. The team had to be disciplined to accomplish it this way.

He ran a three-man weave with three men out front and two underneath, with no real center. They would run the weave until with a screen one could break for the basket. A similar play was called the "corner strings, give and go" because the middle was to be kept open for players breaking to the basket. Every play was a designed play. All the players knew where they had to fit in, where they would go, where they would be when the play was over. Dale Fasching, who was a reserve on the team thought the system was fun. Owens was always the center guard running the plays.

That year, 1954-55, Wibaux went through the regular season 19-0, outscoring opponents by an average of more than 21 points per game. In one low-scoring game, Wibaux defeated chief rival Terry 38-26; Owens had been out of the game with the flu. In another game it defeated Class B Circle 47-35. The Longhorns assured themselves the number one seed in the District 4 tournament when they defeated Broadus at the end of the regular season 74-21. The Longhorns were considered the overwhelming choice to take first in the tournament.

Wibaux started off breezing past State School 72-28 on Thursday night. But in the semi-final, the Longhorns struggled against Ekalaka, a team they had beaten 48-18 and 44-33 during the season. Both teams played well, and at times Ekalaka led, but in the end, Wibaux pulled it out 38-35 with superior free-throw shooting. Owens made 23 out of the 38 points.

In the final against Terry—a team Wibaux had defeated at home *without* Owens, and by 20 points on Terry's home court—the Longhorns frittered away a 10 point lead in the third quarter, a 6 point lead at the beginning of the fourth, and lost in overtime. This time Wibaux's charity stripe performance failed, while Terry was deadly at the free throw line. Also, Owens was shut down by Terry's tall defenders.

At least Wibaux could advance to the Eastern Divisional tournament in Glasgow without a challenge game. But in the first game of that tournament, the Longhorns lost 50-45, corralled by the taller Culbertson Cowboys who controlled the boards. The outlook for the rest of the tournament looked grim, but Wibaux managed to defeat Hinsdale, Terry, and Westby through the loser's bracket to grab third place. This time the Longhorns stayed awake against Terry, beating their old rivals solidly 62-45. In the Monday night challenge game, Wibaux bombarded Richey 88-73 to advance to the state tournament.

In the first game of the state tournament, Wibaux was matched against Belgrade, one of the most feared teams in Class C, with a 24-0 record. But Cramer had two weeks to prepare for the Panthers and was determined to be ready for them. He knew people in Gallatin Valley, had scouts out, learned who dribbled to the left, to the right, who couldn't dribble, who could shoot, who could—or could not—do this or that. For all his preparation, Cramer had something else going for him: Belgrade's star center Ken Jenkins sprained his ankle in the third quarter and was out for the rest of the game. Wibaux won 56-49.

On Friday night, the Longhorns this time were favored over the Stanford Wolves from central Montana. Wibaux regained the lead going into the third and fourth quarters, but Stanford made a push and ended up winning 56-47. The next morning, Wibaux ran into beefy Lodge Grass and lost 69-48. Wibaux had made a heroic march getting to the state tournament and through the first game, but in the end, didn't have what it took to get things done. Its final record for the season: 26 wins, 4 losses, all of them in post season.

Cramer had built a team blessed with a Jim Owens caliber of leadership along with a great supporting cast, a team that was in line to win the state championship in 1956. But before the school year was out, Cramer was to leave under a cloud. He had been at a bar in Terry, was jumped by some cowboy who didn't like Wibaux and wanted to remind the coach that Terry had won the district championship. He grabbed Cramer, worked him over good, and when the coach returned to Wibaux, he looked terrible. He intimated to the Wibaux kids that the Terry coach was involved in the brawl, and possibly some team members. He wasn't overtly enlisting anyone to make a trip back with him to Terry, but the kids were worked into a rage and wanted to haul over there and wring revenge for their coach. Again Archie Burns, who knew how Cramer operated, stepped in, defused the crisis, and there was no trip to Terry. But Dick Cramer was doomed with the administration for stirring up the kids. He was not hired back.

With the 1955-56 season approaching, Owens and company were back, minus Archie Burns, who had graduated. If Cramer had taught the kids fundamentals, one of the most important was rebounding, to "take advantage of disadvantage." This was particularly important because now all the main players were less than 6'0" tall. Cramer was gone and in his place was Don Kingery, who was already the school superintendent. Kingery had coached Poplar to the State Class C championship in 1951. Poplar was considered one of the best Class C teams ever, with three Indians who went on to play basketball and graduate from college, a rarity for Indians in those days. Kingery was more of a calm presence than Cramer, but like his predecessor was popular with the players. He was a friend to many folks, including Gomer Owens; he and Gomer often went hunting together.

Kingery adopted much of what Cramer had taught the players, but added an important ingredient: he installed an up-tempo, fast-breaking game. In his system, he was blessed with several players who were outstanding shooters. Owens shot the most, but everyone on the first string was a danger on offense. The best pure shooter on the team might have been forward Gary Helvig, who had better accuracy than Owens, but because he was not very aggressive, left the offensive show for Owens' direction. Owens and Harold Bakken were the guards, Helvig and Gary Barnaby the forwards, and Toby Nistler at center. The year before, the team would always play half-court, set-up and run plays. Now it was "boom, boom, go, go, go." The team averaged 68.3 points per game that year.

The Longhorns won all 20 games during the regular season, beating their opponents by an average of 23 points per game. This included three Class B teams: Fairview, Poplar, and Circle. With competition providing little challenge, it was natural for a team like Wibaux to fall into complacency. In a home game against Ekalaka, a team that should have been an easy touch, Wibaux won by only 3 points. But the real breakdown was against lowly Broadus. At home, the Longhorns had annihilated the Hawks 93-33, but when it came time to travel to Broadus, Wibaux was lucky to win 47-46, Owens making the winning basket with three seconds to go.

When tournament time came, however, the Wibaux boys got down to business. At the District 4 tournament in Miles City, Wibaux defeated all three opponents by an average of 25 points. In the championship, Wibaux took care of its old nemesis Terry 83-63. At the Eastern Divisional tourney in Glasgow, Wibaux again breezed through, beating its three opponents by an average of 23 points. The Longhorns had averaged almost 80 points per game over the two tournaments. With the championship win in Glasgow, Wibaux became the heavy favorite to win the state tournament in Bozeman.

The State Class C tournament was to be held at Montana State College, the last time it would be held anywhere other than Helena for the next twenty-three years. It was also the last time any tournament would be held in the old Romney Gym, which was soon to be replaced on campus by the brand-new, spacious Field House. I entered that old gym on Thursday evening, March 16, looking forward to cheering on Belgrade, which had reached State one more time and was vying for its first championship. This evening's first match up would be Belgrade against Moore, champion from the Northern Division. Belgrade had as good a chance of winning the championship as anyone, I thought; after all, the gym for years had been the venue for the District 8 tournament, a place with which Belgrade and Three Forks, the other District 8 entry, were thoroughly familiar. Not only that, Belgrade was only twelve miles away. Any fan who had the physical capacity to crawl out of bed would be at the game.

I knew the teams from Belgrade and Three Forks well, having watched them through the season, but I knew nothing of the other six teams in the tournament, certainly not Wibaux, which was a good eight-hour drive away. In the first game on Thursday evening, Belgrade rolled over Moore 70-40; I had good reason to feel confident. Then out came Wibaux against Twin Bridges. On the opening tip, Wibaux took possession and almost immediately Owens drove underneath for a reverse layup. From then on the Longhorns put on a clinic, hanging their poor opponents out to dry 80-58. The game wasn't as close as the score. It was also the high point of Owens' high school career. He scored 32 points on 16 field goal attempts, from all angles and distances from the basket, never missing a shot. Thirty of the points had come in the first three quarters. I sat there in shock, frightened that Belgrade would have to play this team the following evening. Belgrade had more height than Wibaux, but Wibaux was an ensemble, a finely honed machine. I frankly didn't see how Belgrade had a chance.

But the Panthers were a formidable team with a 27-1 record going into this match, the only defeat having been an upset by Three Forks in the Southern Divisional championship. The Panthers had defeated Three Forks twice during the regular season. Belgrade also had the advantage in this game of which I have already spoken: the

Panthers were home. Wibaux would be outgunned in the cheering section department. No doubt even Three Forks fans were rooting for Belgrade so they wouldn't have to face Wibaux.

As the players from Belgrade and Wibaux lined up around the center circle, everyone in the gym knew they would be witnessing something special, the de facto championship of Class C. As the Wibaux boys took stock of their green-and-white-clad opponents, despite being undefeated, despite the bravado in the locker room, knew in their hearts they had never run against a team like Belgrade. But then the boys from Belgrade, despite *their* forced show of confidence, had never seen a team like Wibaux. What was about to commence was a game, which anyone who watched it that evening, who listened to it on the radio, read about it in the newspapers or heard about it with great interest would never forget.

I WOKE UP ONE MORNING IN OREGON AND KNEW I HAD TO DRIVE TO Wibaux. Judith and I had driven by in 1994 on a trip to the Midwest, but had to be in Fargo by nightfall and couldn't take the time for even a short detour. Now I was reluctant to make the trip, because Wibaux is not the central focus of this book. And the little town is *out there,* so far from most of the central story. It is no accident that Wibaux's chief rival in any sort of competition is not Terry or some other team from its own district, not a team, in fact, from anywhere in Montana, but Beach High School, nine miles over the border into North Dakota. It has to be Beach, because no other school begins to be as close.

Wibaux was part of District 4, by far the largest area-wise, in Montana, an immense, sparsely populated land nearly the size of New England. Wibaux anchored the northeast corner of this district, Jordan the northwest, which then stretched all the way down to Broadus, not far from the Wyoming border. In addition to sheer distances by the flight of a crow, some routes from one school to another were grossly indirect, and because of this—for example Jordan trotting off

Frank Spragg

200 miles to Ekalaka—the team might stay somewhere overnight. Ekalaka and Broadus were closer to each other in distance, but to travel from one town to the other meant going over the least-evil back road, taking the Hammond turnoff on Highway 212 (from Broadus) and running forty-nine miles of gravel along Box Elder Creek before finally catching fifteen miles of paved road into Ekalaka. (The teams now use Highway 323, which was fully paved in 2011, from Ekalaka to Alzada. The route is longer but faster.)

People in this area have long been accustomed to isolation. When I traveled to Ekalaka a few years ago, I picked up a T-shirt with a road sign on it saying, "End of the World—9 miles. Ekalaka—12 miles." While still in high school, I drove to North Dakota to visit a friend, stopped in Jordan, and was told that cattle in the area could not put on any weight. Each bovine would begin to eat around a particular watering hole, munching in ever-larger concentric circles until just walking back and forth from the water hole to the remaining grass kept every beast slim and trim. A grand story, perhaps, but the point I'm making is that distance in this part of the world is king. People think nothing of hopping into the pickup and driving double digits, triple digits, for any old thing. But when they arrive at an event, they remember to bring everything they need, because a quick trip back home is not an option.

Wibaux was less isolated than some other schools in the district because it was on a major highway (even less so now; it is just off I-94), but the team had to put on multitudinous miles for every away game, miles multiplied in spades for the state tournament. And then when it was all over, these good folks had to endure the time and grind to arrive back home.

It was with great anticipation on a pleasant afternoon in May 2012, I found myself sitting across the table from Mike Archdale, longtime librarian for the Wibaux School District, and Toby Nistler, one of the players on the 1956 Wibaux team. They asked how my stay had been at the local motel. I said fine, except the man waiting on me in the front office was kind of flakey.

"KIND OF??" (laughter from both Nistler and Archdale). "KIND OF?" (more laughter). Everyone, of course, knows everyone else in Wibaux.

Toby Nistler and I had one more connection other than the Belgrade-Wibaux confrontation. He had played against the same Lodge Grass team I had watched in 1955. I mentioned one player on that team, Elwood (Woody) Schenderline, who I said looked like he was thirty years old. Nistler laughed. "Well he probably *was* thirty years old." We were referring to an area in the state—reservation territory—where keeping records was not a high art. For example in 1963, Darrell Hill was the undisputed star for a Hardin team that was one of the best in Class A, which ended up losing only two games all season.

Two years later, Hill and his brother were brutally murdered. This was a huge tragedy to be sure, but the newspapers said "twenty-two-year-old Darrell Hill" was murdered. Which meant that two years before, he was a twenty-year-old playing high school basketball.

Toby Nistler came with all his records and newspaper clippings, which were invaluable for information on the Wibaux teams in those years. He was a great source on the coaches and how the teams functioned. Mike Archdale's family knew the Cramer family when Dick (Ricky) Cramer was still a lad growing up in Ismay. Archdale also was a well of information on Wibaux past and present. Just down the street from where we were stands an attractive, painted red-brick two-story building that has long been an abandoned hotel, and because of excessive deterioration inside will probably never be restored. But it had been a lively place in its day. "Oh, I could tell you tales...." Archdale said, "John Steinbeck could have written a story about the hotel. The characters in Cannery Row were right there." My visit with these two gentlemen was illuminating; we sat and talked for at least two hours.

However, this was not my first scheduled experience in Wibaux. That morning the weather had been frigid, accentuated by a nasty breeze. I was happy to be inside the Palace Café on Main Street (also Highway 7) waiting for Marlene and Bob Blome (pronounced *Bloom*) to walk in and give me an introduction to the town. None of us knew what to expect. Marlene is considered knowledgeable on Wibaux history, but she had never been asked to do a tour before, and I had only a vague idea how the day should play out. I knew only this: I wanted to see the old gym where Owens played basketball and the motel and gas station his father once operated. Beyond that, it was a roll of the dice.

After an introduction to two lovely people, we seated ourselves in a booth, and Marlene began with background. Wibaux had been largely established by Pierre Wibaux, a native of France who was set up in the ranching business by his wealthy parents. Wibaux made a fortune during the hard winter of 1890 by buying cattle at bargain prices when other cattlemen were forced to sell, soon overseeing one of the largest ranches in Montana. The town had once been named Mingusville after a duo named Minnie and Gus who were early citizens, but in 1895 Wibaux exerted influence and the town was renamed after him. A statue of the master stands at the west edge of town.

After the orientation, I hopped into the Blomes' car and we ran the grid of streets, first stopping at the old Catholic church which, years before, had its exterior recovered with spherical pieces of lava, giving the edifice a beauty out of the Dark Ages. There would be other drive-bys: the trim white-framed building Wibaux considered his home office, the Box Car Museum, the Wibaux statue, and then we headed north on Highway 7 under the railroad tracks, and immediately on the other side and to the left was an old building with peeling gold paint, open windows, forlorn and abandoned. It was Gomer Owens' gas station-repair garage; the gas pumps and bay had long before been ripped out and hauled away. Just to the west of the garage was Gomer's motel, same paint color, still run by one more set of owners and looking very tired. It will probably claim the same destiny as the gas station-garage.

Bob suggested we drive to their ranch just out of town and view Marlene's garden, a symbiosis of trees, lawn, and artfully placed sandstone boulders. One of these stones, when seen from an angle, looks like a self-righteous matriarch, another the metatarsals from a tyrannosaurus rex and considering these prehistoric gadflies once roamed the region, my guess probably wasn't too far off.

After the garden tour, it was time for lunch downtown at the Shamrock Club. The night before, a woman told me I should eat at the Shamrock, that her brother owned it, and that the Shamrock had "the best steaks in the whole U.S." I didn't doubt her judgment, but since my new friends insisted on picking up the tab, I decided a common burger was just fine. Actually way, way *more* than fine. After taking on the house-sized "Western" burger and the deuce-and-a-half load of onion-laced potatoes that came with it, I thought the management would need a forklift to get me out of there.

At 1:00 p.m. the old high school of the 1950s was finally open for inspection, after being occupied during the morning by end-of-the-school-year activities. The original high school is now called the Wayne P Marcus Building; on another trip, I had the honor of interviewing Master Marcus himself at a Big Timber care center. He had been a junior high principal at Wibaux for many years, and coach at the high school in the 1940s. Upstairs in the building were the classrooms, used for storage now if they are used at all. I saw the door of the superintendent's office, scene of the notorious teacher-superintendent confrontation that Gomer Owens was forced to diffuse.

We traveled into the gym where the Longhorns played basketball before the new school was built, the home of Jim Owens and company. Used for elementary activities now, the floor is typically small; on the other side from the entrance, there is just enough out-of-bounds space for the teams to sit on benches. To the right is a bare wall, to the left a stage. All spectator seating is on both sides of the entrance, designed dark wood benches with wood dividers emanating a religious tone, more suited for a choir loft than a gym. There are six rows going steeply up the side; my guess is that 140 fans could comfortably sit there. But when Wibaux achieved notoriety, as it did in 1956, many more than 140 people came to the games. No one was turned away. Some could sit on the stage, but the rest of the overflow squeezed in, somehow getting their glimpse of glory. If there had been a fire? Hopefully, prayerfully, it was no more than enthusiasm from the players.

The Blomes now invited me to visit the present high school, which was completed in 1960. As we roamed the main hall, I could see every graduating class montage through the years, each student shown in a separate headshot. There it was, a photo of Jim Owens in the upper-right corner, as part of the 1956 graduating class.

We moved into the front lobby where the trophy cases were located. In 1979, one boy, Todd Leach singlehandedly led Wibaux to second place at the state meet for track and field. The girls had taken second at the state meet in 1977. But as we looked at the trophies, what was immediately evident (which I had been told about beforehand) was that Wibaux had been a powerhouse in football. The Longhorns had started the dynasty in the 1940s, but trophies were not shown in the cases until 1954. During the 1950s Wibaux had done well on a regional level, but from 1982 through 2001, Wibaux took either first or second place in the state Class C championship eleven times, placing first five of those times. The Longhorn dominance on the gridiron through the years has been remarkable; the accomplishments in basketball not as much. Still, basketball trophies were evident, and among them the trophy given to the team at the end of the state tournament in 1956. Many people who can remember that far back will say it should have been for first place. Unfortunately, if you were from Wibaux, it was not.

WIBAUX WOULD NOT GET OFF TO THE SAME FLASHY BEGINNING against Belgrade, as it had the night before against Twin Bridges. The team seemed nervous, uncertain, put into the unfamiliar position of falling seriously behind. Belgrade had jumped off to a 15-4 lead in the middle of the first quarter, ending that period with a still healthy margin, 19-11. But slowly and surely, Wibaux began to regain composure, to eat away at Belgrade's lead, until by the end of the third quarter found itself ahead for the first time, 46-45. The Longhorns had the momentum; it was a matter of maintaining composure and controlling the game through the final quarter.

Each team missed a free throw in the first seconds of the final period, and then Kingery called time out to make a fatal decision. With a one-point lead and nearly eight minutes to go, he would have his team stall. It began with Owens standing out beyond the top of the key holding the ball, keeping it for what seemed an unbearable length of time, then passing it to his teammate on the right wing who held the ball for an equally tedious length before passing it back to Owens. The procedure would then be repeated, this time going to the wing player on the left. Then to the right. Then to the left, the clocklike scenario droning on for six very long minutes.[10]

It seemed a Belgrade player could suddenly have jumped out and intercepted a pass for an easy layup at the other end, but Belgrade Coach Joe Lutz said no; he may have been afraid that, given the quickness of the Wibaux players, if Belgrade came after them, *they* would get an easy layup. So the Belgrade players stood back and watched as Wibaux made one pass after another. It was like the O.J. car chase: nothing was happening, but everyone knew *something* was going to happen; it was just a matter of when. By now fans were booing Owens, although he was just following orders.

Finally with less than two minutes to go, the Belgrade players were told to come out after Wibaux; Ken Jenkins fouled Toby Nistler, who missed his free throw. Belgrade grabbed the rebound and Jack Feddes scored a field goal. He later made two free throws, making the score 49-46. Owens made a long set-shot to bring it back to a one point margin. But then, with three seconds to go, Jenkins made a layup and the game was over.

Wibaux easily won the game the next morning for the right to play in the consolation game, but now the emotional tank was empty. In consolation, Wibaux lost to Twin Bridges 59-54, a team it had beaten by 22 points only two nights before. The season was a huge disappointment for Wibaux and Owens. As the *Wibaux Pioneer-Gazette* pointed out, "Wibaux being in a fourth place position does NOT mean it was only the fourth best Class C team in Montana. It will still go down in memory of all Wibaux fans and thousands of people who watched the team during the season as the BEST team in Class C basketball." That assessment was close to the mark. For the second year in a row, Jim Owens was chosen to be on the first-team all-tournament team.

His high school career was over. But life looked promising for Jim Owens; he was offered a full-ride scholarship to the University of Montana although he did not play much that first year. Meanwhile his girlfriend from high school, Marian Farmer, attended Western Montana in a quest for her teaching degree; she and Jim planned on getting married after the first school year was over. This did not set well with Grizzly head coach Frosty Cox. Frosty had a policy of not having married players on his team; marriage, to him, was a distraction. (In those years he was not alone in this opinion.) Owens was doomed in Missoula and he knew it.

He wasn't sure what to do. He was disillusioned enough that he didn't even finish his first year at the University of Montana. He came back to Wibaux and told his mother that if he couldn't get on with another school, he was thinking of going into the army. While he was home, Dobbie Lambert, head coach at Montana State, called him and offered him a full-ride scholarship. So Owens transferred to Bozeman and after his sophomore year traveled back to Wibaux to get married. The two of them moved back to Bozeman, where Owens would eventually graduate.

Lambert recruited from Montana but would get players wherever he could find them, married, single, in-state, out-of-state, fresh out of high school, veterans from the military. It was a hodgepodge collection of players that translated into a non-cohesive team. Lambert had been an assistant to Tex Winter at Kansas State, had tried to adapt his trademark triangle offense in Bozeman but it was never really effective.

As nice as Owens tried to be in high school, he understood that he was to a great degree the center of the universe in Wibaux. The same would not be true at Montana State, where he was again relegated to a reserve role. Lambert instead created his own center of the universe, which meant bringing in the first black player, Larry Chanay, to Montana State. Chanay was a nice enough guy from all reports, but everything revolved around him. During timeouts, for example, Lambert directed all his attention to Chanay; all the other players were just props. The role of these players was to get the ball to Chanay; he would put the ball into the basket. Whenever Jim Owens was out on the floor, he was to get the ball to Chanay whenever possible. And if Chanay was nice to some of the other players, he at first had it out for Owens, frequently taunting him. Finally Owens had enough and blew up. Chanay was always pleasant to him after that, but this in no way changed their relationship on the court. If Owens played at all, it was to be a role player, a feeder guy.

Not that there weren't other good players on the Bobcat team. Owens found himself immediately on the losing end for playing time against two other guards, Al Harris and Jack Tilley. These two renegades were nothing like anything Owens had seen in quiet little Wibaux. Ex-military veterans from Indiana, they smoked, drank, and caroused constantly. One player thought they were married but another said no woman in her right mind would have married either one of them. These two guards were more wild than most, but the party culture was a prevalent part of the team. Smoking was pervasive in those days; nearly all the players smoked. At one game in Indiana, Coach Lambert was angry and embarrassed because the players had been smoking in a hotel room, caused a mattress to catch on fire, and elected to dump it out a window. It all took place near a town where Lambert had coached high school basketball. But if most of the players smoked, drank, played cards, and engaged in all manner of street life, Jim Owens was not one of them.

To a degree, socially Owens did not fit in. He did not fit in also because many of the players were single and he was married. And being married with two kids while trying to play college basketball was no picnic. The family was trying to live on his meager scholarship money and Marian's occasional babysitting. Plus her brother was living with them, which, as Marian put it, was like "living on a dime." And the living conditions in the barracks where they resided were "just awful." It was a tough life for her, penniless, living in a dump, with Jim gone much of the time.

Owens, of course, was frustrated because he never got to play as much as he would have liked. When Harris and Tilley left, Owens might have been in line to be a starter, but in came Tom Sawyer, a transfer from Purdue, and Andy Mattson to take over the starting guard positions. Still, as time went on, Owens became more valuable to the team. His role was not only to come in and feed the ball to Chanay, but to give the team a needed scoring punch. As one of the other guards put it, "Jim had a beautiful set shot. He didn't even use his other hand. He pulled it off to his side and was deadly with it." Owens could jump start the team with his shot. In his senior year he had the fifth best scoring average for the team, but that wasn't saying much, 4.9 points per game, the fourth best overall scoring with 118 points. However his free-throw average was the best on the team at 79 percent. For all that, the team never did particularly well, having a middling record for the three years Owens was there.

For all his frustrations—not playing enough, having hardly any money, trying to spend time on his studies and with his family— Owens still had reason to be optimistic. One of the reasons he was straight-laced was that he was a practicing Catholic and in Bozeman was a Catholic school that was doing very well in basketball. Coach Christensen was open to all manner of people attending his basketball practices. Owens started coming and became a regular fixture.

Right after Owens married, he and his wife spent a summer in Beach, North Dakota where he coached the local baseball team. Owens discovered that he loved teaching and coaching, and now that he had a wealth of experience with basketball, he was drawn to Rosary. He went to the practices not only to watch, but introduced himself to Christensen and even asked if he might help drill the boys in fundamentals. Owens was fired up about coaching at the Class C level, had told Christensen that an all-star Class C team could beat any Class AA team in the state, an assessment Christensen had to agree with since he came from Illinois, which had no class system. One year in that state, a school—Hebron— with only ninety students won the entire tournament over a thousand other schools.

Over time not only the players, but the parents started noticing Owens. They noticed that he was good at what he did. Christensen was leaving; there was a vacancy for the Rosary coaching job, but the head pastor Paul Mackin had someone all lined up, a fellow from Three Forks named Dave Sauvageau. But the players and parents who held the purse strings rose up and said no. They wanted Owens to be the coach. Sauvageau had also approached Christensen for his support but Christensen thought Owens should be the new man. Jim Owens it would be.

That fall Owens kept the football program going with some degree of success. But as the basketball season approached, he began to survey his competition. He had remembered the humiliating loss to Belgrade in 1956, but over four years in college he had never given a minute's thought of revenge toward Belgrade. Now that he was at the helm of the Bulldogs, however, he had no choice. As he pondered his likely opposition for the state title, as he scanned the staggering reaches of the fourth-largest state in the union, with 122 teams spread out over fifteen districts, he had only to direct his eyes to the northwest and wonder if his biggest headache wasn't a mere twenty minute gun down the road.

Archrival

BELGRADE HIGH SCHOOL IS UTTERLY UNLIKE THE SCHOOLS IT competed against in the 1950s. It has grown…..no, let me start over…..it has exploded in growth. In the past fifty years, the number of students enrolled has increased 692 percent. It was once in Class C, then advanced to Class B, is now in Class A and is projected to be in Class AA in the near future. The *dropout* rate every year at Belgrade is greater than the total enrollment of some Class C schools. It is hard to imagine that Belgrade, with nearly 900 students once regularly competed against Willow Creek, which currently has a student enrollment of 14.

That said, its growth has not been matched by its basketball performance, which can best be summarized as all–over–the-place. In 1993 and 2004 Belgrade, by now in Class A, was in the state championship; in the latter championship, the Panthers lost in three overtimes. Through several other seasons, both in Class B and Class A, Belgrade made it to the state tourney. But just as often, Belgrade was mediocre and in some years—especially during the 1960s—abysmal. Usually during those years, neither the scores nor the overall records were listed in the yearbook. In a bizarre layout of information, in 1967 the junior varsity, with a 4-14 record, had all its games listed, but the varsity was absent.

Yet if any school could claim to be the Class C powerhouse of the 1950s, Belgrade would be the one. It had not won the state championship three years in a row, as Belfry had earlier in the decade, but it won two championships with two different coaches and with two completely different casts of team members. It might have won two other years if the star player had not sprained his ankle either before or during the tournament. If the Panthers had grabbed the big trophy only twice, they had been to the state tournament in '50, '53, '55, '56, '57, '58, '59, and came within a whisper of joining the elite in 1954. Had two teams been able to advance from the district, Belgrade might have reached the state tournament in 1951 and again in 1952. Quite a feat when you consider there were over 120 schools in Class C during the 1950s and only 8 could be in the state tournament.

With a dynasty like this, there had to be a number-one fan, a person more vocal than the rest, more devoted, a man who traveled with the team and became its statistician and hence its trivia master, a man who had a five-minute spot on the radio analyzing Belgrade and its opponents for the coming weekend and its predicted result. That man would be Wilbur (Buck) Curtis, the town barber, and it was Buck Curtis who informed me, as I sat in his barber chair, that during one stretch in the mid-fifties, Belgrade won 74 conference games in a row. You must understand, these did not include tournament games of any kind, preseason games, any "jamborees" during Christmas vacation, or games against Class B schools or schools out of the district. It was strictly against District 8 teams during the regular season. I decided to test Buck's claim by looking through all the school yearbooks of the period and must confess here that yearbooks were notorious for being riddled with errors. But according to my tally, Sir Buck was right on the money; from late-regular season 1953 into the beginning of the 1957-58 season, the Panthers put together a conference victory string of 74 games.

Under these circumstances, it was only natural that fans developed mega-high expectations. In the spring of 1958, there was a big send-off in front of Jensen's Fountain for the team going to the divisional tournament in Red Lodge. Someone placed a sign on the window of the Fountain that shouted, "GO BELGRADE! TAKE STATE!" Now, here was a team that had not yet won a game in the *divisional* tourney, had not even boarded the bus to go there, and someone was expecting them to "TAKE STATE!" The astonishing result of all this was that whoever put up the sign knew more than I did; in 1958 Belgrade *did* take the state championship.

THE LITTLE TOWN THAT HOSTED THIS JUGGERNAUT BEGAN IN 1886 as a siding on the Northern Pacific rail line running northwest from Bozeman across Gallatin Valley. A Bozeman realtor by the name of Thomas B. Quaw thought this rail location more central for bringing in and shipping out agricultural products in the growing valley's farm economy. Some mistakenly thought the town was named after Quaw—after his apparent middle name, Belgrade—when in fact the "B" in his name stood for Buchanan. This confusion is understandable because Quaw named his son Thomas *Belgrade* Quaw. The real source of the name is the capital of Serbia. A capitalist from that city helped celebrate the completion of the Northern Pacific Railway from the Midwest to the Pacific.

Belgrade is indeed more centrally located in the valley, enough that local promoters in the 1950s referred to it as "The Hub of Gallatin Valley," but the town is geographically central in one other unusual way: in nearly every direction from Belgrade is farmland with soil of high quality (not to the northwest, however, which has swampy, sour, hard-to-turn-over-soil).

But Belgrade itself lies in the middle of a roughly six-mile square of gravel between the East Gallatin and West Gallatin Rivers that is no good for growing anything, at least not anything that is alive. In fact a walk among the lands surrounding Belgrade in the 1950s was a believable introduction to nuclear winter. Yet, if this gravel bed has not been meant for crops, it is great for growing warehouses, office complexes, or most significantly, on the east edge of town, an airport. I liked to tell people from out of state that my tiny little town had its own airport—served by major airlines!—-neglecting to mention that the airport was there to serve Bozeman.

Following the railroad, the streets of Belgrade run catawampus with the world. So when I speak of north or south Belgrade I really mean northeast and southwest, or more accurately north-northeast and south-southwest. If the town was directionally off-kilter, the layout in other ways made sense in the 1950s at least in the northern half. On this side was a near-perfect symmetrical grid of residential development, with the main arterial Broadway running down the center. Perfect except that nearly all the streets were gravel and none had names. Or at least I didn't think they had; there were no street signs. Then one day I walked along and noticed that back in the Pleistocene Era, the sidewalk contractor had embossed the names of the streets in concrete at the intersections. So the streets indeed had names that are the names of the original streets in Belgrade today.

If the north half had order, the south half was a crazy quilt of not much. Broadway—perpendicular with Main Street or U.S. Highway 10—continued south past some grain elevators and a few homes, past the Federated Church, until it eventually came to a small subdivision, arced to the left, became Oregon Street, and headed back to the highway. In the center of this loop was a swash of scrubland, undeveloped, which could be used as a shortcut. One day I was doing just that when I came upon a lonely sidewalk with no street or anything else next to it. It went along, took a sudden ninety degree turn to the left, and ended as abruptly as it had started, a victim of aborted development.

Though Belgrade extended south and north, the center in every sense of the word was "Uptown" as we called it then, along U.S. Highway 10 through town. There were two blocks of retail, including two clothing stores, three bars, a grocery store, a drug store, a lumberyard and a bank. In the very midst of this, on the corner of Highway 10 and Broadway, was an implement store selling Oliver farm equipment. Normally you think of implement dealers on the edge of town with most of the tractors and other machines outdoors. But this store looked like an old-fashioned auto dealership, with everything inside. At least this brick building blended in with the other shops along the highway. Not so a small log structure cattycorner from the dealership, which represented the town library. It appeared comely, with fir trees around it, but seemed more suitable to a wilderness setting than the center of Belgrade retail.

The three bars—The Lounge, The Main, and The Mint—were toward the east end of the retail area (There was also a cocktail lounge on the very west edge of town known as The Hacienda, which later became the Beaumont.) The Main and The Lounge tended to be homes for serial drinkers, but The Mint was quite different. Like its namesake in Bozeman, The Mint was known as a watering hole for farmers to kibbutz and exchange gossip; it was a respectable place to be seen. But in one way The Mint was more notorious than the other two bars together. In the back room were poker games, and these games were not for fun and petty change. Big time personal possessions were won and lost in this back room; not just money but titles to land went to the victors.

Many of these storefronts on the highway were two-story, second floors in some cases for ancient dingy apartments where people still lived. One of these was the home of a friend of mine at the west end of the two-block core over a hardware store owned by his mother and step-father. On one fun-filled night I had the privilege of staying with my friend so I could hear him being yelled at constantly by his mother. And then when it came time for sleep, we moved to my friend's "bedroom," a huge storage room filled with boxes and other items headed for the hardware store. Nearly lost in all this jumble was his single bed near the front of the room, overlooking the highway. Even at my young supposedly impervious age, I was not one who could sleep on a hard floor. So my friend and I jockeyed around on this single bed, hoping to find some means of comfort. To add to the joy, the windows overlooking the street had no curtains, so we faced a neon sign that blinked on and off all night. I won't say it was the most sleepless night of my youth, but it had to be close to the top in an urban environment—if you could call Belgrade urban.

Belgrade received an economical shot in the arm in the early 1950s when a group of families from Oregon moved in and started up Yellowstone Pine, a logs-to-lumber operation that generated a fair number of jobs. A few years later, a swashbuckling entrepreneur named Lloyd Shelhammer stormed into Belgrade and established The Beaumont, a nightclub/horse track that generated more jobs. Lloyd had a glamorous wife who was a descendant of the fabled Ringling Brothers circus family, and three beautiful daughters whose alleged level of sophistication was an eye-smacker for us gawky long-timers. Royalty had come to Pantherville.

The horse track was important because it gave Belgrade something Bozeman didn't have and, for a change, people could have some sort of activity in town during the long summers. Before Beaumont, summers were dreary for aimless youth who had nothing to fill their day. During the infrequent times I traveled to Belgrade from our farm in the summer, I went hoping to see a fight, but was nearly always disappointed. So I retreated back to the farm where, if I couldn't witness a bloody bout of eye-gouging, vitals-destroying senselessness, at least I could read my father's latest issue of *Time* magazine.

On one occasion when I did go to Belgrade in the summer, a group of us decided that if action could not be found, then perhaps action should be generated. We found a car a fellow female student had parked and vacated a half-block from the school, and after sneaking up and letting the air out of all four of her tires, we fled to a hiding place and waited for her return. When she found all of her tires deflated, she let forth with a long stream of profanity loud enough to be heard over the entire north half of Belgrade. As I look back, I'm ashamed we did it; I slap myself whenever I think of it. Still, to have the rare opportunity to hear that level of outpouring was worth the *pffft* from every tire. Which reminds me of a friend whose brother placed barricades across a busy arterial in Seattle during rush hour redirecting traffic down a dead-end street. From his disguised location, he too heard the volume. But instead of a solo, he got the whole choir.

The school near the infamous tire incident of which I spoke was the Belgrade complex at the north edge of town. A large grade school stood in the middle. Built in 1908, it looked like an aging insane asylum (which at times it was). It wasn't the original school in Belgrade—I saw a photo of that in a book—but it seemed like it must be. When I sat in our room, the old radiators and exposed plumbing hissed and knocked, providing our music for the day. The desks, each with an ink well and joined together in rows on tracks, had innumerable knife-carvings made over the years affording hiero-glyphics for scholars to unravel. The walls and floors of the bathrooms and the hallway leading down to the lunchroom and on to the gym were made of concrete and painted a cold prison gray, reminding me that maybe I really was in a loony-bin. And then one morning I walked into the school to find the sizable main foyer in a mess: the water pipes had leaked, causing the plaster from the entire ceiling to collapse. I wonder now how I survived grade school without therapy.

To the right and east of the grade school was a modest, two-story WPA-era high school, big enough for 130 students when I was there, built entirely of concrete on the outside and topped by a flat roof. It wouldn't have made the first cut in an architectural beauty contest but it did have attractive all-glass double front doors, a nod to art deco, perhaps. One day after lunch, a student came bounding up the steps to the front entrance, stiff-armed one of the usually swingable glass doors to enter the building, and shattered it into a million pieces. I tell you, life was tough on the Belgrade educational frontier.

The interior of the high school was like the outside, fully func-tional and nothing more. Just inside and to the right of the front entrance was the superintendent's office, a modest-sized room staffed by William (Bill) Erickson, a bookish man in looks and manner who carefully cultivated his fingernails. Other than that, I knew little about him; I wasn't exactly in his orbit, ensconced in the building next door as I was, but everyone thought well of him as far as I can remember. The rest of the building was lined with lockers along the hallways both upstairs and down, and all of the rooms were classrooms with a larger room for a study hall. Throw in a few bathrooms and that was the alpha and omega of our basic-basic high school. What is important here is that, as with most small towns, the high school was next to the grade school, so I was near secondary education the entire time I moved up through the grades: at school assemblies, during lunch, even during recess. On one occasion when I was in the first grade, during recess, I wandered away from the traditional play area where I was supposed to be and edged over to the walls of the high school, where a second-story window opened and two boys peered out. They motioned me closer, telling me they had "accidentally dropped a knife"; would I be so kind as to retrieve it for them? As I sauntered directly under the window looking for this mysterious knife, they spat on me. Thus began my filial relationship with students of the high school.

On the west side of the grade school was the gym. The floor was less than regulation size, but otherwise it was a great gym. There were three rows of seating on both sides, plus three rows in the balcony directly above the seats along the floor. The gym never felt cramped, and never was there a time when someone who wanted to see a ball game could not get in. The entrance to the south and stage to the north were far enough away from the floor that a player could storm in for a layup without feeling intimidated by collision. The floor was in great condition, the baskets well-anchored; everywhere on the floor a player could put a natural arc on his shot without hitting something overhead.

Residents had been lucky enough to have this venue since the late 1920s. Before that, in the fall of 1904, basketball began in Belgrade with the building of Waterman's Hall, which had a large room in the second story for basketball and was, as I recently learned, the same dismal storage room where I spent the night with my friend. Little is known about that first year of competition, but in 1906 at least one game was recorded when the Belgrade squad, presumably a town team, defeated Chesnut, a coal-mining hamlet east of Bozeman, which no longer exists. Basketball stayed at Waterman's until the building of the new city hall and auditorium in 1913. That same year is the first mention of a high school team, which edged the town team 21-19. The high school boys earned their first visit to the state tournament in 1916, when they defeated Gallatin County (Bozeman) High School in a challenge game after losing the district championship to Whitehall. At the state tournament, Belgrade was drummed out of competition, losing to Forsyth and Lewistown. In 1927, Belgrade managed another trip to the state tournament only to get cremated this time by eventual state champ Billings 49-8. Disillusioned, Belgrade lost the next morning to Stockett-Sand Coulee 26-11.

Belgrade became the Panthers in 1930. The high school held a contest, each participant offering a suggestion for a mascot. To the winner would go a piece of history: her entry to be the team mascot forever, or at least for some time after she passed into eternity. Two students came up with the name "Panther," and in a coin flip, young Nellie Cline won the contest. Her two sons, Jim and Ken Jenkins honored her by becoming Belgrade's two top basketball stars in the 1950s. In August 1997, when Belgrade High's new 5,000-seat basketball arena was dedicated, Nellie, in her wheelchair and accompanied by her two sons, was given recognition.

Basketball practice at Belgrade in the 1930s was the same as today, always after school, but it was more important in those years that it *was* after school because getting home was no hop in the car for a short ride. Robert (Shorty) Cline (Nellie's brother) told me that after practice, the coach would take him out to the barn where the horse was kept, and Shorty would ride the three miles to his house. Of course, 1930s basketball was primitive beyond rides home. The cramped gyms have been discussed in a previous chapter, but the district tournament was usually held in one of these gyms; most teams were likely to never see a regulation-sized floor in an entire year. Belgrade never got out of the district when Shorty was on the team.

It wasn't just the gym that obstructed a team. Balls were regulation size and bounced well enough, but they were of inferior quality and varied in material or seam indentation from town to town. So a team traveling to a neighboring town had to adjust not just to the gym or the baskets, but to handling the ball itself. This differentiation existed into the late 1940s. Leo (Bubs) Durham, who played for Belgrade in those years, said the balls were still not standardized.

He noted: "Everywhere you went, the home team had a tremendous advantage. They would have the game ball; there was no standard ball. You might have a Wilson ball one weekend, a Spalding ball the next weekend. They each would have different seams. One would have a deeper seam than another. If you were used to a deeper seam, then you would not be used to a fine seam.

Shoes and socks were also inferior, giving the possibility of blisters, a constant headache for players. Shorty Wise, however, who played for Belgrade in the thirties, told me he never had a struggle with blisters. "I kept my socks clean and my shoes tight. A lot of other kids had blisters because they didn't keep socks clean and shoes tight. Or the shoes didn't fit." Shorty also talked about the baskets. "The baskets had solid board backs, steel rings and nets with tough string. The ball would hang up in the net once in a while. Someone who could jump high would whack it and knock it loose."

Playing in primitive gyms with inferior equipment and clothing would impede the pace of a game, but scores were kept low more than anything by rules—or lack thereof. The jump ball after every basket was still in effect during the 1930s, which brought action to a stop, preventing the opportunity to build momentum. The jump-ball rule changed the game in another way: if one team had a center who could tip to a teammate each time, that team would control the contest. It was better than stalling because the team could keep possession and still score baskets. In the thirties there was no over-and-back rule, no ten seconds to move into front court, so a team could park itself all day in the backcourt, the opponent needing a full-court press in hopes of getting the ball back (a tactic not used much in those days). Because of the ponderous pace, it is little wonder that games had typical scores like 25-9 or 17-11. Shorty Wise said when Belgrade played at Wilsall in 1936, the opponents were big farm boys, tough but unskilled, and prone to foul. Belgrade managed to win that game 21-20 without scoring a single field goal.

The fast break started coming in during the late forties, but the average score of a game was still low. Lynn Durham, who was the star for Belgrade during that era said a team scoring 40 points in a game was unusual. Then scoring made a dramatic change upward from 1949 to 1952. In 1949 the average score of Belgrade versus opponents was 35-28; by 1952 the average was 51-37. What accounted for the difference? Lynn and his brother Bubs Durham, who were a year apart in age, said part of it was improvement in the equipment. The standardization of basketballs, better shoes, all this quickened the game, but differences also came in the game itself.

The jump shot opened up scoring, but what may have increased scoring more than anything was not a change in a rule, but how the rule was interpreted. "The scores changed when the dribbling rule changed," Bubs Durham said, but Jim Haugen, former head of the Montana High School Association, said no—the rule had never changed. What Durham was really talking about was the *relaxation* of a rule. Arnie Wise, another player for Belgrade in the early forties, said the coach emphasized passing over dribbling. "The coaches didn't want the guys to dribble hardly at all. No! No! No! Pass it to the other guy. Pass. Pass. Pass." Why? In those years, players could only dribble the ball straight up and down. If they did anything beyond that they would be called for traveling.

Lowell Miller, who played for Gildford in 1950 remembered constant traveling calls. Durham said, "You had to keep your hand on top of the ball at all times. Now you can have your hand on the side of the ball; it makes it easier to change direction and get free of your man. It was tough then to get open. If you palmed the ball in any way, the refs would take it away from you. It was very difficult to get clear for a shot. Even the poorest defender was tough to get away from. About 1951, they would give you more leeway with the ball, kept giving more and more."

The game continued to quicken through the 1950s. Better gyms were coming in, better equipment, a faster game, the jump shot fully integrated. By 1956, the average score of Belgrade versus opponents was 69-48.

THROUGHOUT THE 1930S BELGRADE MAY HAVE HAD ABOVE-AVERAGE teams in the district, but the Panthers never won the district tournament, even when, starting in 1934, they were competing against only Class B teams. They had good coaches: Lou Edwards, who coached Belgrade for many years, and his tall, able assistant Bill Johnstone; the two of them were stars for a town team that was unbeatable. But the high school team could never get past fourth place in the district tournament.

In the late forties the Panthers' fortunes began to change when Bill Munger became the new head coach. He was a good coach, but he had some very good players on his team, mainly the Durham brothers and Casey Keltz. Lynn Durham and Keltz made a strong guard combination. They each also had impressive athletic statistics after leaving high school. Durham is the patriarch of the only three-generational line to play basketball at Montana State. He, his son, and his grandson *and* granddaughter have all been players for the Bobcats. As for Keltz, he went on to coach at Townsend, building his 34 football game victory streak before coaching at Western Montana for 31 years. Lynn Durham often played in the corner and was a great outside shooter, the top scorer for the district his last two years. In his senior year, 1948, he scored 471 points, helped by teammate Pat Goggins, who added 330, with Bubs chipping in 225. These totals together exceeded the seasonal output of many opposing teams.

It easy to compare Belgrade teams of the forties unfavorably with teams of the fifties because in the earlier years, Belgrade never went to the state tournament. But it must be remembered that Belgrade in the 1940s was still competing in Class B. The Panthers won the district tournament in 1946 and 1949, came in second in 1948, moved on to the division tournament each time, but sooner or later ran into the two powerhouses of the Southern Division, Laurel and Hardin (not only powerhouses but a comedic duo? Laurel and Hardy?). In 1948, Belgrade defeated Laurel in the first game, a team considered one of the top Class B teams in the state and, a likely winner of the championship. The victory was a huge deal for the Panthers, but the Belgrade boys couldn't settle back to normal and lost the next two games, including one to Hardin.

In 1949, Lynn Durham and Goggins had graduated, but Keltz and Bubs Durham were back, along with two other very good players, Dick Pittman and Gary Delano. Delano was unique: he was always a threat on offense, and because he had a heart condition, the coach would always have him hang back at his own team's end of the floor. Because of this, Belgrade used a four-man zone defense. The Panthers may have been ready to have four players defend five on the other team, but most opponents understood the danger of leaving Delano alone, so their offense turned to four on four.

Belgrade would win the district in 1949 and go nowhere in the division just as in '46 and '48, but one element was different: Belgrade had a new coach, Mike McCormick. He had been a star for the Bobcats in both football and basketball before entering the high school system and would be another person who would move on to greater horizons after leaving Belgrade. He became assistant coach at Montana State while getting his Ph.D. in education, then moved to Arizona where he eventually became state superintendent of public instruction.

McCormick entered Belgrade in a storm not of his own making. He was Catholic, and several members of the "state church" of Belgrade at the time, the Masonic Lodge, did not want a Catholic to be coach. McCormick overcame that opposition to find he was given a break in 1950: Belgrade was now part of the newly formed Class C. No longer did he have to deal with the Laurels and Hardins of this world. The Panthers had a very good year, and for the first time made it to the state tournament, losing a heartbreaker to eventual champion Nashua by a single point in the semi-finals, and winding up in fourth place. The boys could afford to pat themselves on the back; their overall record had been 24-6. They would do even better in '51, amassing a 24-0 record before losing to Helena Cathedral by a single point in the district championship. Because only one team could advance from the district, the Panthers were done for the year.

The kids loved McCormick[11] who believed in team basketball and a good defense. But he was a strong personality and tended to be autocratic in style. He could also lose his temper. There was a rule at Belgrade for a student walking through the corridor from the school to the gym; he was not to jump up to touch pictures, the lights, or anything. One day Jim Jenkins, who was a freshman on the team, arrived at the locker room to look around and see teammate Dick Pittman come rushing in, heading for the single toilet stall, which had a door on it, to hide. McCormick came down the stairs, walked into the room, looked around and said, "Where is he?" He looked again and saw a pair of tennis shoes inside the toilet stall. He reached up and pulled the entire stall away from the wall, reached in, grabbed Pittman, banged him up against the lockers, and said, "Don't you *ever* let me catch you [touching those lights] again." That is how mad he was, Jenkins said. But he treated everyone the same. Casey Keltz had been the star guard on the team, had according to Jenkins done "a lot of strutting." But he didn't strut around McCormick.

As for Jenkins, he started out in 1950-51 on the JV team as a freshman. Soon McCormick called him in and said, "You are a freshman and aren't worth anything anymore, but I want you to start practicing with the varsity." The very next game, Keltz went down with a sprained ankle; Jenkins went in for him and continued to start for the team the rest of the season, playing with the likes of Keltz (after his ankle healed), Pittman, Delano, and Howard Kennedy.

If Belgrade was continually successful from 1946 on into the 1950s, it was because the school had the exceptional coach, the talent, but also unusually good training in the seventh and eighth grades. The junior high coach in those years was Ralph Goggins, a star on the town team, which could fill up the gym. Goggins would match McCormick in teaching the fundamentals and was nothing if not a disciplinarian. Jenkins said, "You talk about a tough, hard-nosed coach; he got me to play with the junior high when I was in the sixth grade. I wasn't very big but I went and played for him and he would work your butt off. He just kept feeding the system."

He was also a disciplinarian in the classroom. Jenkins said, "You could hear a pin drop in Goggins' classroom. One time a kid was talking when he wasn't supposed to; Goggins looked up, grabbed a book, threw it and hit the boy right across the eyebrow, laid it open with blood coming down. In another incident Goggins grabbed a boy and dragged him down a flight of stairs into the principal's office."

I was too young to have Goggins as a teacher or coach, but oh, how I remember him! At an all-school assembly, a kid was sitting up in the east side balcony with some friends, acting up, making a disturbance. In full view of everyone in the school, Goggins walked up to the balcony, grabbed the boy, jack booted him the length of the balcony, down the stairs, and slammed dunked him into a rear-row folding chair on the main floor. You didn't cross Ralph Goggins.

In the spring of 1951, McCormick was offered a job in Red Lodge, which he accepted, and Belgrade had a new coach, Archie Lucht. Jenkins couldn't stand Lucht. "He had no concept, no offense." One time when the team was falling behind, during halftime Lucht made unseemly remarks to the players and then stormed out. "That incident lost the whole team," according to Jenkins. He claimed Lucht got halves of beef from farmers who wanted their kids to play. The school got rid of him at the end of the year because all the players were threatening to change schools. Jenkins said, "I was thinking seriously about going to Bozeman and told the administration I didn't want to play for him anymore, and he was gone after that."

Still, for all the disharmony, Belgrade had a 20-4 record in 1952. The team had a good nucleus with Jenkins, Bert Gibson, Jim Munger, Loren Lovald, and Gene Tudor. Herb Tonn was growing and would soon take Jenkins' place at center, moving him to forward. Gibson and Munger were the guards and Tudor the other forward. Unfortunately the team lost to Three Forks in the finals of the district tournament and for the last year, only one team could advance to the playoffs for the state tournament.

Lucht was out and in walked Joe Lutz, who was originally from Nashua and graduated from University of Montana. He had come to Belgrade after teaching in Culbertson, but not before he went into the Marines for three years and with that experience would always sport a Marine haircut. The *Bozeman Daily Chronicle* once said "The Marines are coming when Lutz's Panthers hit the deck." If Belgrade had been good up to this point, they would become even better during the Lutz era, for he was a key factor in what arguably became the golden age of Belgrade basketball. Lutz told the players, "I don't care what your dad does, or how many sides of beef he wants to give me, if you can play you are going to play and if you can't you won't."

Lutz was generally affable at public gatherings, was a good neighbor, but at school he was no nonsense. The kids seemed to take to it. Ron Iverson who was younger when Lutz came to town but still knew him well said, "There were two influential people in my life, my dad and Joe Lutz. He was so organized. When he was coach, he had note cards and everything was written and listed on those cards. On his desk he had every card laid out exactly the way he wanted it. He was the most organized person I have ever been around. The organization caused him to be able to communicate so well."

He was also intense. This is what I remember about him at games, and everyone I spoke with heartily agreed. Even, it seemed, when he was congenial away from school, he had a personage one millimeter under his skin that was ready to pounce. And he certainly could do that. After he went from coaching to becoming superintendent at Belgrade, he came one morning to substitute teach for our eighth grade teacher, who had to be away. Lutz was teaching in his friendly, organized way when several kids in the back of the room acted out. Lutz pleasantly told them to line up in front, facing the class. He then proceeded to give each boy a swift kick in the rear.

Lutz could get angry at games. After a football game in Whitehall, Lutz beat up Dean Lavertry in the bus (most who knew Lavertry would say he deserved it). Gene Cook, who was a freshman said, "He must have bruised his hands because he just pounded on him. The other coaches came in and got him off Lavertry. He could really lose his cool."

Jim Jenkins said, "Lutz knew how to handle each individual; that was one of his strengths. Herb Tonn tended to be lazy, and during one game, Lutz came down at halftime, grabbed Tonn off the bench in the locker room, slammed him up against a locker and said, 'Tonn, if you don't start hustling out there, get me a rebound or something like that, you won't walk correctly again.' Tonn would come out mad that second half and he would rebound, run, and all that sort of thing."

Joe Brookshier who played for Belgrade three years, ending in 1955 said, "If I made a mistake out on the floor, I was the last one to the huddle for a timeout because I knew I was going to get it."

In practice, Lutz had the kids work on fundamentals far more than they had experienced under Lucht. He worked on shooting, free throws, out-of-bounds plays, things to do in the last few minutes of a game or quarter, dribbling drills left or right handed, how to attack a set screen, how to attack against both a zone defense and man-to-man. Lutz stressed that a player must feel prepared to play the game and it didn't matter who the opposition was.

In the Lutz system, no team could depend on Belgrade using a certain kind of defense, because he used whichever defense best suited the Panthers against the type of team they were playing. He could use a combination of zones: 2-1-2, 1-3-1, box-and-one against a good player; or man-to-man if he thought the team had the advantage there. If one defense didn't work, he would install another. All things equal, the team would win because it was better coached, which he proved during the years he stayed there.

Lutz didn't mind if members of the team dribbled as long as they could get the ball down the floor. During one game, however, the opponents quickly stole the ball from Belgrade three or four times. Lutz called a time out and said, "Can't I get anyone who can get the ball from one end to the other?" Don Kilwine raised his hand and said, "Give it to me; I'll take it down there." Kilwine was a bruiser of a football player, a running back, but when he carried the football he ran with his head down, and he would do so on the basketball court. The ball was inbounded to Kilwine, who dribbled the ball the length of the floor, the opposing players jumping out of his way, allowing him to slam into the bottom of the stage. He got up, smiled, and said, "Coach, I told you I could get the ball down the floor." Lutz just shook his head. Jenkins said it was the most amazing thing he had ever seen.

In fact Lutz was open to a freestyle game. Joe Brookshier, who was a sophomore guard when Lutz first came to Belgrade in the 1952-53 season, said the team was freelance on offense, didn't have much structure. "He didn't have a specific system like some coaches; he had basic plays but generally it was freelance. That was the way it was through high school, but he had good players so he could get away with it."

This was the point; Lutz could be a great coach but in a small school he had to have luck with talent to go very far. I say this because no Class C team in 1953 was going to defeat the Belfry Bats. The Bats had won the state title the year before, had most of the same players back such as Mily Bakich at center and Tom McDonald, who had the best hook shot Jenkins had ever seen. The Bats had tall, very talented players to be sure, and they also had Bob Rae, who was not only a good coach but a first rate-recruiter. He managed to steal Buck Gaustad from nearby Red Lodge. He would go on to make a name for himself at Butte Public High School.

Still Lutz held his own very well that first year, amassing an 18-4 record through the district tournament, but those four losses all came at the hands of Three Forks. The Panthers went down to the Wolves in the District 8 finals just as they had done the year before, this time by a score of 59-53. However, for the first time since Class C had been established, the second place team could advance to the Southern Division tournament. Belgrade lost the first game in that tournament to Bridger, then reeled off four straight victories—including one finally over Three Forks—to make it back into the state tournament. The Panthers were then eliminated in two games *without* playing Belfry. The Bats easily won the trophy.

The Three Forks Wolves had been a thorn in Belgrade's side, Helena Cathedral a headache also, but Three Forks waned the next year, Cathedral moved up to Class B, and it looked like Belgrade would shake off all defenders in District 8, even to become a force statewide in Class C. *Except* that Belfry was still lurking in the Southern Division with the same cast of characters. In 1954 the Panthers built a 21-1 record, cruised through the district and the first rounds of the division, looking this time like they would avoid Belfry, which was upset by Lodge Grass in the semi-final. Belgrade unfortunately lost to Lodge Grass 50-47 in the final and now faced Belfry in the challenge game. The Bats had had an off night against Lodge Grass, were back to normal and destroyed the Panthers 67-45 in the challenge match. Belfry had no trouble at the state tournament in 1954, winning for the third year in a row.

Lutz still had an enviable track record coming into the 1954-55 season; he had taken Belgrade to state in 1953 and came close to repeating in 1954. And now this year there would be no more Belfry Bats; all their good players were gone, the coach moved to Butte. But Belgrade's top player, Jim Jenkins, was graduating. Senior Joe Brookshier was coming back, a capable guard and natural leader; a couple of good juniors, Joe Gowin and Roger Stradley, were returning. But these three players weren't going to take Belgrade to the next level. Lutz needed something more, and fortunately for him, he got it. Jim Jenkins had a younger brother, Ken, who had been only 5'6" as a freshman, scrawny, barely able to make the varsity as an alternate. But as a sophomore he was 6'2", filled out, and for the next three seasons would arguably be the greatest player to ever don a Panther uniform.

The Jenkins family had always lived near Belgrade. When Ken was growing up, his home was in the country. Now, without ever having been relocated, the house sits across the street from the new high school. His father, Lester Jenkins, had worked in Bozeman at Idaho Pole until he was injured. He went to a back specialist who offered him a job managing his ranch near the Four Corners area west of Bozeman. I remember Lester walking into Jensen's Fountain when I happened to be there, never forgetting his schedule when he began a sentence, "When I got up this morning at quarter-to-three......"

Lester had been an athlete, but his sport of choice was track: the high jump, the broad jump. He had also been a boxer and got Ken into that sport at an early age. There had been a club, about a dozen kids, which met at the Belgrade City Hall upstairs in a large room where a number of activities were held: dances, basketball. But when anyone played basketball there, they had to shoot over two iron support beams that stretched from one wall to the other. The boxers often traveled to Manhattan for events at the American Legion Club, a large room in the back of a bar on Main Street. It was a big gathering place for the valley; dances were held there on weekends, cock fights at times, but there were events for kids, too, "smokers" they called them, and the kids all knew each other. Lester bought his kids boxing gloves and they would go down to the American Legion and match up a little bit now and then.

In time, Jenkins involved himself in baseball. He started out in

Little League, then advanced to Coke League, playing against teams from Three Forks, Spring Hill, Bozeman; the Bozeman Americans were the dominant team. He was selected to be with some all-stars who took on a touring group from Las Vegas in the Legion Park at Bozeman's east end. "I was the starting pitcher, but our team was destroyed. It was a terrible deal." He even played one year of Legion ball or, as he said, maybe part of a year. His teammates Joe Gowin and Bob Rector had talked him into it. Jenkins was also in football for one year in high school but quit. He didn't like it.

His mainstay would be basketball. His brother Jim had been a star for four years, so it was only natural that Ken would take an interest. Jim was three years older than Ken; it seemed that they would play together for at least one year. But Ken hardly played as a freshman. Then the two hoped to play one year together at Western Montana College. It would be "a dream come true." But Ken had a problem with his hernia and was forced to stay out of college for a year. These two brothers, so close, who would both make the Basketball Hall of Fame for Western, would never play together in official competition. The only time they were able to play together in a real game was for a benefit up in Conrad.

But Jenkins loved basketball. He would play for hours at Joe Gowin's farm around a basket nailed to the front of the shop. He spent hours, days at the basketball hoop in the old tennis court across the street from the school. His house was not far away so he could get there easily. He and his friends would play there at night; people would park their cars and shine the lights. There would always be six to eight boys for the games. The surface on the court was horrible (as I knew and like me, Jenkins never saw anyone play tennis there). Often the kids would go there in the winter with shovels and scrape lanes for layups, lanes out for free throws. When Jenkins was in high school, he was able to have a key made, but when that "dissipated," he and friends would during the day in PE, pry open a window and then at night crawl through that window and play basketball by the light of the exit signs.

Jenkins said, "There were two doors exiting, one to the south and one east to the school. Over those two doors large exit signs were lit up and gave enough light to be able to shoot. The balls were always locked up downstairs and we would use plastic cards to pick the locks. The same guys were in on it: the two Gowins [Joe and his cousin Jim], Bob Rector, Allen Shearman, and others. We would have six to eight players there. If anyone caught us, they never said much."

How times would change over the years. Jenkins said, "My friends and I broke into the gym. Later when I became a teacher, kids would break *out* of the gym."

People have compared Jim and Ken in basketball style. When both were inducted into the Hall of Fame at Western, that question was hashed over. Brookshier, who played with both said, "Jim was a better floor person; when he went to Western, he had to move out to point guard. But he was able to get the ball, move the ball, set screens, and make better passes. He could get the ball to the open man. At Belgrade, Ken was not too much for ball handling, but he didn't have to be. If he got the ball down low it was all over."

It was all over because Ken Jenkins could jump. He was 6'2" which might be short for a center even in Class C, but as Gene Cook, who later played for Belgrade said, "He could stand in a bar and jump up on a regular-sized bar counter flatfooted; he had enormous spring in his legs." This helped him against taller players, but 6'4" Allan Hopper from Three Forks claimed Jenkins traveled. Hopper, who went on to play with Jenkins for four years at Western, said to him, "You traveled every time, the only one who could get away with it. There was no way I could guard you because you always took two steps."

But what really set Jenkins apart was his devastating shooting ability. Rector, who was the backup center for Belgrade said, "I could guard him because I had been around him so long, but for a guy less familiar with Jenkins, it was difficult. He was left-handed, which by itself threw a lot of people off. The players would work the ball around the perimeter until they could get it into Jenkins, who had a turnaround jump shot at the free-throw line that was deadly. I can't tell you how many times I saw him plant one in from there. He was also a great shot from the corner and later developed a great hook shot, which also helped him against taller players. In his senior year Jack Feddes covered the inside for Jenkins so he was able to get outside more."

Jenkins had a psychology about his shooting on game night. Brother Jim said, "Ken did not believe in shooting during warm-ups. The only thing he would do was layups and during shoot-a-rounds, he would catch the ball as it came through and pass it to the other players. He felt that if he missed shots during warm-ups, it would put him at a psychological disadvantage during a game. This was not just at Belgrade, but everywhere."

But Jim agreed that Ken was the best shooter he had ever seen. "If they had the three point shot, no telling what his average would have been." As it was, in his senior year, 1957, Jenkins made 831 points for a 27.6 points-per-game average; his average percentage for field goals was 55.3 percent and his average for free throws 79.3 percent. In four years he made 1,641 points, was first-team all-state both his junior and senior years, second-team all-state his sophomore year, and went to the North-South All-Star game after his senior year, the only participant from Class C that season.

For us kids still in the seventh and eighth grades, he was a rock star. During one spring afternoon a group of us were playing workup baseball out behind the high school when Jenkins stepped up and asked if he could take a swing with the bat. Well, uh, yeah! He grabbed the bat and said, "I'm Mickey Manhole" (Mickey Mantle, for those who haven't followed 1950s baseball), took a swing; the bat accidentally slipped out of his hands, went sailing toward the chain-link backstop and bounced off without hitting anyone. It was a little scary but for a few minutes we had KEN JENKINS with us.

Jenkins and Joe Gowin were on the team at the beginning of the 1954-55 season, as was another young guard, Roger Stradley, now a junior, and the other senior guard, Joe Brookshier, who was the team leader. As would happen for the remainder of the time Lutz was coach, Belgrade would play half-court. Lutz practiced some fast-break but almost never used it in a game. Jenkins said the team was too slow for that style of basketball. Mostly the method of play was to pass around the perimeter, to get it into Jenkins if possible. The team went 21-1 through the district tournament, easily beating Three Forks in the final 70-46.

In the divisional tournament at Red Lodge, Belgrade rolled over opponents as usual—Rosebud 80-43 and Bridger 75-58—until the final against Lodge Grass. Lodge Grass had beaten Belgrade the year before in the championship by three points and was back again with its two stars, Bill Jappe and Woody Schenderline. Schenderline was a bull who had been a football star running back, had humiliated the Panthers that fall when the two teams squared off in a playoff game. Jappe was the center and strong as an ox. On one play when Jappe went up for a shot, Brookshier was on his arm and Jappe lifted him right up, didn't slow Jappe down at all.

Years later when Jenkins became a teacher at Columbus in south-central Montana, many people from that vicinity told him the Lodge Grass-Belgrade game in 1955 was one of the best games they had ever seen. Certainly the game was white-hot from start to finish. With just a few seconds to go, Belgrade was leading by two points and had possession with Stradley bringing the ball down the floor. He reached the mid-court line when suddenly Schenderline stole the ball away from him and strode down all alone for an easy layup. All of us who watched were crushed; now the game would go into overtime and we would probably lose. But Brookshier brought the ball down the floor, and with no time left, flung up a prayer from midcourt and it went in. Jenkins caught the ball as it floated through the net. Belgrade was off to state again.

The State Class C tournament was to be held in Conrad for the third time in seven years. People wondered why. The town had few accommodations; in fact many fans stayed in homes, and the gym seating capacity was never enough for all the people who wanted to attend. The officials at MHSA must have gotten the message; it would be the last year the tournament was held there. In the first game, Belgrade was playing well against Wibaux (not the high-powered Wibaux team Belgrade faced the following year). Jenkins already had 17 points at halftime but just as the second half was starting, he sprained his ankle and the team fell apart. The Panthers lost to Wibaux 56-49 and were shot down by Drummond the next afternoon 68-53. Belgrade, which ended the season with a 24-3 record, would have to think about next year. Stanford took the crown, beating out Highwood, a team from its own District 10.

Brookshier was graduating but all the other players were back: Jenkins continually improving at center, Gowin at small forward, and Stradley at guard. Gowin could shoot nearly as well as Jenkins, Stradley was a great driver and ball-handler, and the team had a new addition—really a return addition—Jack Feddes. Feddes had been on the team as a freshman and sophomore, transferred to Manhattan Christian, then transferred back to Belgrade. Feddes would have to wait out a semester before rejoining the team, but he was invaluable. He was nearly as tall as Jenkins, was rugged inside, allowing Jenkins to go out to the perimeter more often. And Feddes, himself could shoot from out as well as near the basket; no one could ignore him, which took the pressure off Jenkins. Ed Droge at the other forward was a person of great ability and intelligence who worked on our farm for four summers and was one of the most conscientious people I have ever met; he would eventually become a physician in McCall, Idaho. He was modest and self-effacing to a fault; it is hard to tell how good of a shooter Droge might have been because he rarely took a shot, was happy to let others get the attention. Six points was a good night for him. But he was tenacious on defense and a good rebounder. The other guard was Allen Shearman, who as a junior was still improving his skills, but good enough to help carry the team.

The only team in District 8 that was any kind of threat to Belgrade was Three Forks with Allan Hopper starring at center; playing in Three Forks, the Panthers eased past the Wolves by one point. At home Belgrade won by seven points. Two non-conference games against Big Timber were noteworthy. At Belgrade, the Panthers lucked out again by one point, but we all figured the Sheepherders would have their own way in Big Timber; after all, they were a strong team in Class B. Big Timber scorched the nets that night but Belgrade scorched even more. The Panthers won 88-80 with Feddes, Gowin, and Jenkins supplying 77 of those points between them.

No team came close Belgrade in the district tournament; Three Forks was upset in the semi-final, which allowed Belgrade to face White Sulphur Springs in the final, another easy target. In the division tournament, Belgrade dismissed Shepherd and Joliet by 21 and 22 points respectively. It was now just a matter of overcoming Three Forks—again—in the finals. The Wolves had always been a tough opponent and this time won 59-57.

It was to be Belgrade's only loss. At state, taking place in Bozeman at the old Romney gym, Belgrade took care of Moore 70-40, followed by that legendary game against Wibaux. And now it was Three Forks one more time in the finals. Belgrade was in control from start to finish. The Panthers had beaten Wibaux and were not going to let up for a minute. They were on an emotional high, and Three Forks wasn't prepared for that. After the night before, it was an anti-climax; the final score was 58-47. Belgrade's record for the year was 29-1; they were finally state champions and another legacy builder for Joe Lutz.

The following year, the 1956-57 season, Gowin and Stradley were gone, Feddes gone, but Jenkins and Rector, who was a strong sixth man on the team, thought the 1957 team was even better than the championship team of 1956. Rector said, "If Belgrade had had Feddes back for one more year, no one could have touched us." Even as it was, almost no one could. As everyone who looked back would say, it was a hybrid of the 1956 and 1958 championship teams, still mostly half-court, but quicker, with two new members in the starting lineup, Roy Sharp and Phil Langston. Sharp was smaller than Feddes but more mobile and very effective in his own way. Droge and Shearman were back, had improved from the previous year, and of course Jenkins was back with a greater arsenal of shots; he perfected a hook shot, something he had not done much in the past.

It looked as if no one in Class C Montana could stop Belgrade, certainly not Wibaux, which was now missing Jim Owens. Belgrade lost to Big Timber in a pre-season tourney final by a whopping score of 76-50. Otherwise, the Panthers again sailed through the regular season plus the district, and divisional tournaments. Their first contest at state would be against a much weaker Wibaux.

BEFORE I GET TO THAT, I SHOULD FIRST TOUCH ON ANOTHER SUBJECT. As good as Belgrade was in basketball during the 1950s, Bozeman/Gallatin County High School was equally as bad. In 1954 it won only two games despite the point output of its only star, Wes Jandt. Jandt, with his cherubic face and general pudginess, looked like someone more at home hacking into computers than scoring baskets. In some years after Jandt left, Bozeman would rise mightily to mediocrity, only to fall back again. It didn't help that early during one season its best player, Doug Raley, broke his hand punching a wall locker after a defeat. Of course he was out for the remainder of the season. It was frustrating because fans knew Bozeman was never going to be any good. Students would come out to the games, if they came at all, laughing and joking, not paying much attention to what was happening out on the court. This was natural; the bad play was boring.

There was a reason for this lousiness. Bozeman never had a system for basketball in those days; if the coach was in charge of one sport, he was either the coach or assistant for all sports. Which meant in reality that the hired-to-be football coach or his assistant was coach over basketball, never the other way around. Basketball was on the low end of the pecking order, a sport to occupy kids during the winter if they weren't on the wrestling or ski teams, which happened to be very strong programs.

Under these conditions, it was only reasonable that fans in Belgrade started clamoring for a game against Bozeman. This was not about to happen. Bozeman was in Class A. No Class C team had ever played against a Class A team, likely not even in a scrimmage behind closed doors. A Class A team would never risk playing such a game when the outcome was in doubt, when a loss would generate indescribable humiliation. It wouldn't be enough to ride the team out of town. A special all-school ceremony must take place with the entire team and coaching staff crucified upon the hallowed rafters of the school gym. Erase the idea. It just wasn't worth it.

Yet, Bozeman was willing to accommodate. A contest could be set up on Belgrade's own court if the folks in Pantherville so chose to agree. It sounded like a deal too good to be true. And it was. The offer was for the Belgrade varsity to play against Bozeman's *junior* varsity. It should be said here that if the Bozeman varsity in 1957 was bad, the junior varsity was below wretched.

For some reason, I thought that JV team was winless for the season; I talked to one of the players who wasn't sure, but it made sense to him because the coach, Bob Barton, was hippopotamusly atrocious. I never had him for a coach but my younger sister and I each had him for a teacher and thought he was worthless. He knew nothing about basketball, and when given the JV chore, picked up a book from somewhere and got the idea into his head that the players should always pass, never dribble. If they dribbled they were benched. So they passed the ball around, often not even trying to score. The process of the game became more important than the outcome; the players functioned his way regardless of what defense the opponent might have. As one player told me, "It became a laughable deal. We didn't like to go to practice because it was the same thing in practice.

He was like a prison warden; you are going to your cell, you are going straight there, and you get nothing off for good behavior."

But at least something for bad behavior. Three of the players had so little regard for the coach and his program, they took off to Idaho for a week, never telling the coach they would be gone and would miss practice. They figured they weren't missing anything; not only were the practices useless, but because Barton didn't like basketball, he often didn't hold practice at all. When the players came back, they were promptly kicked off the team, then brought back later because there were so few other players.

Yet Barton's team was from a much larger town, so it was anyone's guess as to the outcome against Belgrade. The big match was set for January 12, 1957. From the opening whistle, the Panthers jumped off to a jackrabbit start, leaving the hapless Bozeman boys in a daze. The youngsters might as well have stood back and, with a synchronized sweep of their arms, welcomed Belgrade to the basket. By the third quarter, when Panther scores were only seconds apart, the fans' cheering turned to laughter. They were witnessing improvisational comedy of the first order. The final score was 107-20. As Casey Stengel, the famous New York Yankees skipper would have said, "You can look it up!"

BUT BACK TO THE STATE TOURNAMENT. BELGRADE WAS READY TO breeze through three games. To tune up and properly get ready, the Panthers practiced at Montana State. At one of those practices two days before the tournament, Jenkins again sprained his ankle. The other players were good, but Belgrade was largely a one man team offensively. With Jenkins out, the Panthers could not defeat Wibaux. The final score was 61-49. Fortunately Jenkins recovered enough to help squash the next three teams, Joplin 80-48, Ennis 89-73, and Culbertson 65-49. Drummond, from western Montana was the new state champion. Jenkins said, "They had the Fickler brothers and Morse and all came to play with me at Western. They would have been a tough team no matter what." (One of the Fickler brothers, Larry, actually graduated in 1955. His younger brother Ken and Jim Morse were on the championship team.)

Jenkins had a chance to play at Montana State. When Belgrade's season was over, Coach Dobbie Lambert called Lutz and invited him and Jenkins to the next Bobcat game; Jenkins and Lutz could even sit with the 'Cats on the sidelines and then go out to dinner with them afterwards. By this time Jenkins had pretty much made up his mind he wanted to go to Western to be with his brother Jim. But he and Lutz reluctantly decided to accept Lambert's offer. At the game, Jenkins was invited to stand in with the players during each time out. Lambert spent the entire time in each huddle focusing on his star Larry Chanay and ignoring the rest of the players. During halftime, Lutz asked Jenkins, "What do you think?" Jenkins said, "I think I'm ready to go back to Belgrade." Lutz said, "I am too." They stayed the rest of the game but passed on the dinner. Jenkins thought it was one of the worst experiences of his life.

Lutz told Jenkins before the 1957 season was over, "When you're gone, I'm gone." The coach had tried to treat his players equally, but with a player like Jenkins, there was no way he could do this. He had given Jenkins a key to the gym to practice whenever he wanted. But when Jenkins graduated, Lutz moved over to become superintendent at Belgrade for several years before accepting the same position in Bridger, Red Lodge, Columbia Falls, and finally in Havre where he was superintendent until he retired.

With Lutz and Jenkins out of the picture, it was the end of a chapter for Belgrade. But not the end of the 1950s book. For the immediate future, at least, Belgrade's luck would not run out. With a new coach and new players, against all odds, the Panthers managed to keep their dynasty alive.

Archrival – Reprise

B ELGRADE HIRED A NEW COACH, HOWARD VOILES, WHO PASSED away recently. Which is a shame because I never had a chance to visit with him in person. I did have the pleasure of talking to him by phone as he was sitting in his home in Wisconsin. He was a most gracious person with a positive attitude toward everyone, having a great relationship with his wife, children, and grandchildren. He could remember everyone very well, his mind as good as when he was at Belgrade those many years ago.

Voiles had grown up in northeast North Dakota, playing basketball both in high school and at Minot State, which nearly made it to the NAIA National Tournament while he was there. Voiles said there were things he did on the court he himself would not have allowed if he were coach, but he was given great freedom and shot from all over the court.

Voiles entered education because he knew he wanted to be a coach. He said, "I majored in physical education and minored in social studies. I minored in social studies because I had to minor in something and that was the easiest." Like Roger Freih after him, he knew the pay for teachers in Montana was significantly higher than in North Dakota. He had an offer to teach and coach in Leeds, North Dakota, at $2,800 a year but over the border in Brockton, Montana, the pay was $3,300 a year. After graduating from Minot State in 1951, he chose Brockton.

Voiles and his wife Zelda liked Brockton very much, enjoyed living there with their kids, staying there for two years. The Warriors did very well, chalking up a record of 30-10 for the two years Voiles was there, but the team could never get over the hump in tournaments. He and Zelda decided he had better leave Brockton while he was still young; the school wasn't the best. Still, Voiles recalled fond memories at the time Brockton received third place in the 1960 state tournament. He had helped organize the tournament and when the Brockton team arrived, they brought with them large blankets called "star blankets," very large and colorful, one for each of the coaches of the other seven teams.

In the fall of 1953, Voiles and his family moved to a job in Ennis, fifty miles southwest of Belgrade. He remained there four years, taking his team in 1957 to the state tournament. In one game against Belgrade, Ennis lost 89-73. Voiles would say later, "I think we had overall a better team than Belgrade, but they had Jenkins. We couldn't stop him."

When Voiles was offered the coaching job at Belgrade in 1957, he would take over a team without Jenkins. Not only that, the most successful coach Belgrade ever had would be just down the hall in the superintendent's office. Voiles knew Lutz was an intense individual and might be hard to deal with. When he went to see Lutz about the job, one of the first questions he asked was, "Joe, are you through coaching?" Voiles made it very clear because he didn't want Lutz to "monkey around" and get into what he was doing. Lutz answered, "Absolutely, you don't have to worry about me." Voiles said, "We got along very well. Joe did not interfere with me at all. It was great." When Voiles moved to Helena after two years, Lutz had no influence on his decision.

Voiles got off to a good start, taking the football team to the District 8 championship before bowing to Whitehall in a playoff game. When he took over the basketball team, people in town expected a good team but not great. Only two holdovers were left from the previous year's first string. But Voiles had the same Belgrade system going for him, beyond his players and his own coaching skills. He had other coaches, coaches who coached the junior high and junior varsity, who did an excellent job of preparing the kids.

First of all, he had Chuck Anderson coaching the junior varsity. Anderson was very calm, but he was a tremendous teacher and taught fundamentals like no other. I should know; I was on his team. When Voiles received players from Anderson, he didn't have to worry about fundamentals; he could concentrate on systems of offense and defense.

But Voiles had someone else: he had Phil Langston coaching basketball in the seventh and eighth grades. He too was an excellent coach, very positive, and really tried to give everyone a chance if at all possible. I can credit Coach Langston with the most memorable understatement I would ever hear in the twelve years I was in school. There was this kid Harvey who was grossly overweight, so much so that he could not have found his size in a Big and Tall men's clothing store, if indeed he had the courage to enter such an establishment. He could barely lumber up the floor, let alone back down. Langston's brief summarization of Harvey's basketball skills—said with great sincerity—was that "Harvey just doesn't have it."

Langston had a remarkable background. He had originally come from the Harlowton area where he excelled in all the major sports, was a dominant basketball player at Montana State in the early thirties, was 6'2" which was considered tall for that age and way ahead of his time in that he developed a one-handed jump shot. No one else, at least in Montana, had anything like it. But he quit college, got married, and went down to California where he worked for Lockheed for a time. He couldn't take California, came back to Montana, worked on ranches, competed in rodeos, and then started working for the railroad, where his job was to clean the top of the engine. One day at age twenty-six, he slipped and needed to latch onto *something* to keep from falling off the train. His unfortunate choice was the electrical trolley, known as a pantograph, which took power from the wires above, which the conductor had failed to turn off. Langston never knew how many thousands of volts went through him, but the shock threw him off the train. His son Phil Jr. thinks his father's hitting the tracks may have brought his heart back, but he was burned so badly he lost an arm and a leg. Consequently, the elder Phil Langston I knew in class and on the court worked with a metal leg and arm with a hook on the end. He always limped wherever he went.

Langston, in retrospect, thought it was the best thing that ever happened to him. He wasn't really going anywhere in life, was following the rodeos and was a bit of a rounder. Now he was forced to go back to school. He became a teacher, and according to his son, Phil Jr., the impact he had on kids and people was "unreal." I have to agree. Aside from being nice to everyone, he had a close relationship with all members of his family, and his two sons whom I knew, adored him. They also came with him when he moved to Belgrade from Baker in eastern Montana, where he had previously taught. The two brothers would be an indelible part of the team in 1957-58.

They, along with their fellow team members, were in for the Voiles signature conditioning. The kids would be dragging after practice was over. Denny Langston said Voiles really believed in conditioning, far more than Denny had in college. The coach knew if the team was going to win, the players had to be in shape. They had that little gym, but he really worked them. One night Denny said he could hardly move after practice, was exhausted both physically and mentally. Voiles had pushed him until he could go no further but somehow he knew he *could* go further. In that sense, Voiles set the stage for him in life: if you want to win, you have to prepare.

Voiles certainly demanded respect. When he first began teaching in Belgrade, one of his students acted out. Voiles grabbed him, picked him up out of the chair and said, "You will not—behave—that way." Everyone else thought, oh, oh. From then on, Voiles never had any discipline problems. One day when a group of us were riding in a car on Broadway between the high school and the new grade school during lunch hour, Voiles, who happened to be walking across the street, stood out in the middle, daring us to run over him. It was a joke, or maybe not, but we slowed to a stop. Generally all Voiles had to do was look at someone who was misbehaving and the student got the message.

Nevertheless, he was part of the new brand of teachers coming into schools who were not given to physical abuse. And this attitude spilled over into his coaching. Most of the players loved Lutz but there was no getting around that he ruled by respect and to a degree by fear. Voiles, of course, was not one of the boys either, but he was a motivator. Once the players were in shape and learned his system, he gave them free rein. Periodically, Phil Langston asked Voiles what he might do in a certain situation, and the coach would tell him, "Do what you think is right." Players would play hard out of pride of being a great player. For Phil, both Lutz and Voiles were dominant figures who had an impact on the way he himself taught school.

Still, Voiles had specific preparation. Denny Langston said, "His defense had been a 1-2-2 matchup zone that I characterized as revolutionary, way ahead of its time. Against the old zone, I would look for spots to shoot my jump shot. It was quite easy to dissect. You couldn't do that with this zone because there would be one or two guys on you all the time. Because the 1-2-2 had a lot of options, you really had to move the ball around quickly to get someone open. You couldn't dribble against, it and if there were one or two dominant players on the other team, this much more flexible zone would shut them off; one would be on them and the others were in the zone. Today it wouldn't work at all [because of the three-point rule] but it worked then."

The team was much more fluid on offense. Denny added, "We tried to move the fast break whenever we could. If it looked like Belgrade was going to get the rebound, I would just take off. If it looked like I would get the rebound, someone else would take off. We got so many lay-ins that way. One or two would take off. Three people would box the rim; we always had good coverage."

With the system Voiles instituted, the team developed into a machine with equally important moving parts. It began with Roy Sharp at forward. He was the stocky forward in constant motion, with emotional impact that set the tone for the entire team, who would right the ship when all else was falling apart. But if Sharp was chairman of the board, Phil Langston was the court manager who brought the ball down under pressure, acted as point guard, but also worked as a forward, driving the base for a layup or dishing it off after setting a screen.

Sharp's cousin Stan Craver now joined the first string, a player who had been twelfth guy on the team the year before, if the team even had twelve players. In other words, he didn't play at all. But he had been nursed along by Lutz and Anderson, who taught him to shoot and during both his junior and senior years would be the high scorer on the team. Craver was the scoring machine down low, and if he didn't have the outward emotional intensity of Sharp, he was another workhorse who could pile up the points, in fact was top scorer often because he got one more garbage basket, constantly scrapping, never stopping.

Denny Langston was like that too; in a way he was a combination of Sharp, Craver, and his brother Phil. He was a freshman, looking mature beyond his years, a player who would only improve. He began each game on the bench. But only for about the first three minutes. From then on, unless there were unusual circumstances, he was out playing the forward or center position. These four players were approximately the same height, around 6'0". Gene Cook was much shorter at 5'5, generally staying out front, trading off with Phil to bring the ball down. He was a scoring option, and if it was difficult for him to penetrate because of his size, he was all over the place, doing whatever he needed to do or as Denny Langston would say, he "worked his buns off." Stan Carlisle usually started at center but got far less playing time than Denny Langston. Basically Voiles ran with six players.

Everyone was involved in the offense; standard practice in the half-court was to pass, then break away for a screen; pass, break away, screen. "It might look chaotic," Denny said, "but it was pretty simple. It was powerful when you could get five guys who could do it. We had a bunch of scorers and it was hard to check them all. Everyone knew where everyone was. It was never an issue with the 1958 team, who got the rebounds or points."

At the beginning of the season, the team struggled because essentially it was a new team. In a preseason tournament with three Class B teams, Belgrade was blasted in the first game by Harlowton 46-29. This was a tough one for the Langston brothers, particularly Denny, who said he could hardly breathe. It was his first high school game, and he was playing against two cousins, both whom would go on to play college ball. Voiles laughed at him because he couldn't even run. In the second game, Belgrade lost to Big Timber 63-58.

Then the team started to come together. The Panthers reeled off 11 victories in a row before losing to Three Forks 55-53 and Townsend 63-55. The Three Forks loss was the first regular season conference loss in 75 games. During the 11 game winning streak, Belgrade had defeated Three Forks by a mere three points. Three Forks and Townsend, among other schools, had tall, talented players.

But Denny Langston was up to the task of guarding them. He said, "Three Forks had a good team. They had a big guy [Allan Hopper]. Voiles usually put me on him. I don't know why he did that. Whitehall had a guy 6'6" or 6'8' and he would put me on him also. I also guarded 6'4" Bob Hoppe [from Townsend] who was a high jumper. There were some really good athletes then. Hoppe was tough, better than the guy from Whitehall. I would use my butt a lot and get them out of there. I loved to guard the big guys. I would use my elbows a lot; it wasn't quite legal but it worked well. I was strong and that helped. They couldn't push me around and my center of gravity was always lower than theirs so I got a lot of rebounds flat-footed, because they were all over my back and couldn't do anything about it.

"I found out what adrenaline could do, because in a game against

Townsend, after I got mad at [Pete] Carson, I was rebounding over Hoppe. I had never been so angry in my life. Carson had gone underneath Phil on purpose and sprained Phil's ankle. It took him out. I saw it happen and it was very obvious. It took four guys to stop me from hitting Carson."

Belgrade won its last four games of the regular season including a season-finale 69-47 victory over Whitehall. In the district tournament, Belgrade dispatched White Sulphur Springs easily, barely slipped by Townsend 56-54 in the semi-final, but this time had more success against Three Forks in the final, beating the Wolves 50-42. The divisional tourney was far easier than District 8. Belgrade defeated all three opponents by an average of 17 points, including a 75-57 victory over Bridger with center Bruce Zinne, who was tall at 6'7" but not terribly mobile.

The state tournament was an entirely different story. Against Outlook in the opening match, the Panthers struggled for three quarters just to get things moving. Outlook had some veteran players who had played together for many years. Both Langston brothers said Outlook should have won that game. But the Panthers managed to keep the game close the entire way, and with no time on the clock and Belgrade behind by two, Denny Langston, "in a desperation attempt to get a bucket up," was fouled and would be shooting two shots. The freshman made both of them to put the game into overtime. Then Phil Langston took over. Up to that point he had scored only three points, but scored all the rest in the overtime and Belgrade won 55-53.

Against Drummond in the semi-final, Belgrade was against essentially the same taller team that had won the state championship in 1957. The team had a kid by the name of Jim Morse, who was an excellent player, in fact had been all-state for three years. They also had 6'5" Dick Applegate.

Phil Langston said, "It was incredible what Denny did to check him. It was a freshman against a senior. After the first quarter Drummond was up by 15-12. I still remember Morse running by his coach and giving him the high sign. Like this was going to be simple. Then Sharp got the hot hand. They could not stop him, and we ended up winning by four points, 77-73. At breakfast the next morning, all the teams gathered together in the same building and Belgrade sat across from Drummond. They were still in shock. They couldn't believe they had been beaten the night before by a bunch of kids, none whom were all tournament-selections. But you have to play the game to find out who is really going to win."

And finally in the championship, Belgrade was up against another very tough team, this time Troy from the northwestern corner of Montana. The Trojans had a big kid by the name of Don Morrison at 6'3", but the undisputed star was Gale Weidner, who at 6'2" played guard. He would soon be star quarterback for the University of Colorado and after that, for a few years third-string quarterback for the Denver Broncos.

Phil Langston said, "He could really get up in the air, just a great athlete. Troy had the dominant two, but when you get five people playing as well as we did, we couldn't be stopped. Morrison got into foul trouble and may have sprained his ankle. They weren't at full strength. I tried to check Weidner but he would jump over the top of me. I guarded him most of the night and got to know him real well; I guarded a good player. Again, we shouldn't have won, but we did 65-64 and this time I was in shock. I remember Gene Cook throwing the ball up into the rafters as the buzzer sounded."

The Belgrade Panthers were the state champions—once again.

THE 1959 PANTHERS SHOULD HAVE BEEN JUST AS GOOD AS OR BETTER than the champions of 1958. Roy Sharp had graduated, but all four of the other starters were back: Phil Langston, Craver, and Denny Langston, all natural forwards who rotating playing post, and Gene Cook doing his yeoman's job on the perimeter. And now Belgrade had its shooting guard in Larry Moore, a kid who could toss them up from half-court, a shooter par excellence. Belgrade had in essence an all-star team and for Belgrade fans, nothing less than a state championship would do. Voiles, himself said, "I thought the '59 team was better than the '58 team and I have said that many times. Belgrade should have won the state tournament in 1959."

But other dynamics were in play. Carson and Hoppe were back for Townsend, which continued to improve. They were coached by Belgrade alumnus Casey Keltz, who had been the great football coach and had stopped Belgrade earlier in the fall on the gridiron. And now it looked as if he might do the same in basketball. Townsend was considered the team to beat in District 8.

Did the Panthers lose their enthusiasm? It is hard to say. Dennis Langston said the team just didn't have the same chemistry. "In 1958, the team didn't care who scored, but that wasn't the case in 1959. Voiles was still the coach, but you have to have players who buy into it; when you get to this level, chemistry is what makes the difference."

Still, talent carried the team a long way through the season. The team opened again with two lopsided losses in a preseason tourney to Roundup 72-52 and Big Timber 57-41, both Class B teams. But from then on through the rest of the regular season, Belgrade ended 16-1. The Panthers did lose to Townsend 56-47 but also defeated them at home 58-55. This did not look like a team that was weaker, that was going to be sitting on the sidelines in the tournaments. It was just that Belgrade for so many years had dominated District 8; Three Forks had always been the main rival, but had generally been the bridesmaid in recent years. Now Belgrade had a *real* nemesis in Townsend. Life was not going to be the same as it was before. In the district tournament, Belgrade easily beat a substantially weaker Three Forks team 77-62, and Manhattan 72-47. But in the final, lost to Townsend 54-49 and then nearly lost to Rosary in the challenge game 56-51.

And, unlike the year before, Belgrade was not going to have an easy time of it at the divisional tournament in Red Lodge. In the first game the Panthers faced run-and-gun Busby. Phil Langston said, "I remembered Eagle Feathers and TuTu; the Indians were fun to play against because they were going to run with Belgrade and didn't play much defense; it was a shootout, but we really had fun playing them." Voiles remembered Busby's strange strategy in the fourth quarter: "Belgrade was ahead two or three points and Busby was stalling, just wasting their time. Busby stalled half of the fourth quarter." The Panthers ended the game winning by a single point 75-74.

The Panthers were now up against 25-0 Bridger, a much stronger team than the year before, a team many considered the best team in the tournament, even better than Townsend. They had a kid by the name of Schweitzer who was exceptional. Still, Belgrade stayed with Bridger, with the score near the end of the game tied and Belgrade with possession. The play was set up for Craver to shoot down low. Craver had been terrific throughout the game scoring 35 points. But Craver was triple-teamed and threw it back out to Moore, who said he was "out there looking silly because I knew I wouldn't shoot." But Moore had the ball and swished it. The final score was 66-64 Belgrade.

In the final against Townsend, although it was a close game all the way, Belgrade lost 68-63, the third loss in four meetings. The only good thing that can be said about it is that Belgrade didn't have to play Bridger in the challenge match. Their boys finished third and had the privilege of staying home. They would say Belgrade lost to Townsend on purpose.

Belgrade was off to the state tournament for the fifth year in a row. For Townsend, it was a first; many considered the Bulldogs the favorite to win the championship. And there was a good possibility its opponent could be Belgrade—the two meeting again for the 5th time—but it was not to be. Townsend beat Medicine Lake handily in the opener 68-53, then lost to Plains in the semi-final 60-52, a game in which Plains led the entire way. The following morning, the Bulldogs lost to State School 77-68.

Belgrade's experience was worse. The Panthers, as we have seen, lost in overtime to Gildford. Because it lost, Belgrade was relegated to the losers' bracket, playing the next afternoon against State School and George Yelloweyes. And it just so happened that the Panthers would meet Yelloweyes when he had the game of his life. Moore said, "They set up a four-man screen for him; if he wasn't open for one, he would go to the next, and so on; he would either drive or shoot a set shot. He burned the nets." Voiles remembered hearing that Yelloweyes had scored 44 points in one divisional tournament game. "I knew who he was; he was only about 5'6". I remembered saying this, if Belgrade plays State School in the state tournament, we might get beat but Yelloweyes is NOT going to score 44." Voiles' prediction was of course correct. Yelloweyes scored 46. The season had ended with a game that no one who saw it would ever forget. The Panthers would become the nameless victim in a great performance.

Voiles was starting to feel the pressure. He said, "My last year in Belgrade was a tough year. I would be nervous before every game, no matter who the opponent was; I just wasn't feeling good at the end of the season and decided I was going to get out of basketball for a while. Then a job came up in Helena, and because I had been to the state tournament for three years in a row, I was able to get acquainted with some people there in Helena, the coaches and administrators who were running the tournament. I had a pretty good advantage and was offered a job in Helena. I was mostly away from sports, but admit that in the first year, I did miss coaching.

Voiles was off to Helena for the 1959-60 season. Phil Langston, Stan Craver, and Gene Cook were graduating. Phil Langston Sr. was offered a job in Havre, which meant that his younger son Denny, one of the great hopes to keep Belgrade competitive, would also move away. Larry Moore was returning, but otherwise, the prospects for the upcoming season were not promising.

People in those days forgot that Belgrade was still a very small school with only 130 students, exposed to the vagaries of coaches staying on and with the unlikelihood of a continuous supply of better-than-average talent. Belgrade had had an unbelievable run. It probably didn't really sink in to many people in Belgrade (myself included) that other schools in District 8 had similar-sized enrollments and they, too, could acquire a good coach and develop talent. Townsend's best boys were gone. No worry there. The Bulldogs were predicted to be worse than perhaps they had ever been in recent memory. But there was a new set of Bulldogs from Rosary on the horizon, and they would more than take Townsend's place. Fans in Belgrade had to become accustomed to the fact that their Panthers could not always dominate.

JOE LUTZ HIRED A NEW COACH, MATT TELIN, FRESH OUT OF COLLEGE with no previous coaching experience, who was likable and in his own way one of the most talented individuals Belgrade ever had. He was to be in Belgrade only one year and did not leave under a cloud, as some people thought. He had a good relationship with Lutz and with many people in Belgrade who would remain his friends through the years. He could have remained as Belgrade's coach had he chosen—in fact he actually had a contract with the school to come back, and the school board let him out of it. He had a science background and in the spring of his first year was offered a job in that field, a much higher paying job in Idaho that he simply could not refuse. He gravitated from that job to the University of Idaho in Moscow, where in short time he became head registrar, and for a period of time concurrently head of registration *and* admissions. Telin would prove to be a man of great ability.

Because of the avenues opened in his life, Matt Telin would only coach for one year anywhere. It will never be known how good a coach he could have become had he stayed in the profession. As it was, he inherited a team with a single starter, Larry Moore, returning, the one player with much experience even playing varsity. Moore was back, but everyone else in reality was new. Three members who would become starters that year—Ron Iverson, Ken Tonn, and Bruce Huffine—had not been brought up to the varsity the previous year until tournament time, and only then because three reserves had been kicked off for breaking the rules. During all three post season tournaments, the three boys rode the bench. With all these challenges and with the boys coming forward, Telin still finished the regular season with a 13-7 record, defeating Big Timber in the season opener 57-52.

Telin had played all three sports when he was in high school just over the mountain from Gallatin Valley in Twin Bridges. Basketball was his favorite sport, something he took up in the third grade. When he was on the basketball team in high school, the goal was to win the state championship, and his team did achieve that goal in 1952, but in football. The Falcons were hardly bereft in basketball during those years. When Telin was a sophomore, Twin Bridges reached fourth at the state tournament and third at state the following year. Belfry, of course, won state both years with one of its players, Buck Gaustsad, hired as Telin's assistant coach at Belgrade.

Following high school, Telin went to Western Montana on a basketball scholarship and majored in science with a minor in math and PE. He never made the varsity in basketball, but did play three years of football. He was scheduled to graduate after his senior year and had a job teaching seventh and eighth grade in Deer Lodge in the fall of 1958. But the coach called him back and told him he had one more year of eligibility. The school would fund him for graduate work. He had about a quarter to go on his master's when he took the job at Belgrade.

Telin was hired by Belgrade because of listings; two jobs were open for a combination science teacher/coach: one at Belgrade, the other at Dutton. Telin applied for both, but Belgrade responded immediately. Joe Lutz interviewed Telin, followed by a session with members of the school board. To this day Telin, and a lot of people in Belgrade, wonder how he got the job. The answer was simple; no one else could match his credentials in sports *and* science. Telin figured that if he had stayed in Belgrade a year or two longer, he would have ended up retiring in education as a principal or superintendent.

Surprisingly he was hired as coach first, with science as an add-on.

He taught the range of science and math classes for all four grades, but he loved his physics class the most because he was armed with a first-rate text-book. But his chemistry text was terrible, unacceptable. He promptly went to Montana State and acquired the freshman outline series. That is what he used for his chemistry class; the kids had in essence an honors course.

Telin, like Voiles before him, got along well with Joe Lutz. The superintendent never put any pressure on him, never interfered with him in any way. Telin would have to ask Lutz questions about administrative matters: scheduling, money; Lutz would provide the money for basketball. Lutz was very supportive and would end up becoming a lifelong friend.

Telin said, "Once when I was at the University of Idaho, and going south, I stopped for a break in Winnemucca [Nevada]. My wife and I had a chance to go through the casino and I stopped and heard this voice and said to my wife Karen, 'I think Joe Lutz is over there.' Sure enough, I went around the corner and Lutz was playing the slot machines. He had a unique voice and I knew it was Lutz. So we chatted for a while. We exchanged Christmas cards yearly. He later passed on."

When it came time for Telin to size up players on his basketball team, Larry Moore would be a starter; that was a given. Telin knew he had other good juniors and they got playing time, but for a fresh coach it was hard to qualify potential. He decided to have seniors fill out the remainder of his first string. Here too were competent players: Ron Iverson, Ken Tonn, Bob Feddes, Bruce Huffine. Tonn, a forward, had a football knee injury and while he continued to play and start, his time on the court was limited. Junior backup Gary Hellyer would play significant minutes in his place. Huffine was the other guard alongside Moore. Iverson became the center mainly because Telin had taught him the hook shot, which he used effectively. But he was 6'1" and slender, which put him at a disadvantage against opponents. The bruiser rebounder would be the other forward, Bob Feddes, who while not as good his brother Jack was still a plugger who took offensive rebounds from the weak side and threw the ball back up for an easy score. Juniors Rob Otheim and Ken Cook filled in as forwards and Gary Cook and Chuck Wright were backup guards.

The team would improve as the season progressed, but in the eyes of several juniors and at least one senior, Telin made the strategic mistake of relying too much on seniors at the expense of juniors. Telin, himself, acknowledged he made a major mistake at tournament time not bringing up Larry Karinen from the junior varsity, who might have made a contribution at center. The following year would prove how good these juniors would be, but at the beginning of the season, this was potential that no one—players and coaches alike—could have foreseen.

Telin turned the first two weeks of his practice over to his assistant Buck Gaustad who, Iverson said, "ran our hind ends off." The boys were in great condition when Gaustad returned the team to Telin and focused on the junior varsity. From then on Telin ran what amounted to a hybrid of Voiles and Lutz. He believed in good conditioning, fast breaking, but he also relied more on the half-court than Voiles did. Telin said he used a "free forming" offense, not using many set plays but a series of screens, which meant moving and passing the ball. Telin did not like his team to dribble any more than necessary, especially when a player got the ball near the basket. If he ball went to the post, the player would either shoot the ball or pass it back out. The ball was never to go to the floor. Otherwise, Telin reasoned, the opponent would take it away. On defense, the coach used almost exclusively man-to-man.

The Panthers started the season well, defeating Big Timber, Willow Creek, and Townsend. Then at home, Belgrade lost to Clyde Park, a school the Panthers hadn't lost to since, it seemed, the beginning of time. The Panthers bounced back, defeating Three Forks and Twin Bridges, then traveled to play Rosary at the Montana State Field House. It was always a thrill to play on the big stage as a preliminary to a Bobcat game.

It was a disaster. Telin was forced to bench Iverson and Moore for the entire game because they had broken the curfew rules. Telin said, "We had rules at the beginning of the season and the players were to uphold them; at the first offense the player missed a game." Iverson and Moore were forced to sit by the coach and listen to the Rosary fans yell, "Poor Iverson, Poor Moore, Poor Belgrade" repeated ad nauseum.

Rosary took Belgrade through the buzz saw that night 69-32. Telin said, "Belgrade got manhandled pretty badly up there, but they were a good team. We just couldn't handle them. They were so well-coached. You could tell those kids had played together a long time."

Fortunes looked up temporarily for the team. The Panthers got back at Clyde Park in the Blackbirds own gym 58-50, defeated White Sulphur and for the second time in the season, won over Twin Bridges and Telin's old coach by five points. But another upcoming team in the district, Manhattan, defeated Belgrade on the Panthers' home floor. From then on, it was back and forth, a win over Townsend, a loss to Big Timber, close wins over Wilsall and White Sulphur, and another victory over Three Forks.

Belgrade was pounded again at home by Rosary 56-37. Then it was back to topsy-turvy: a win over Gardiner, another loss to Manhattan, and finally a close loss in Whitehall 54-53. Thirteen wins and seven losses; would Belgrade even get into the finals of the district tournament? Would the team get out of the district? If it didn't, it would be the first time since 1952.

In the district tournament at the Field House, Belgrade easily defeated Clyde Park 64-46, but the next night in the semi-final faced Manhattan, a team the Panthers had lost to twice. I watched that game and remember the Belgrade kids being tight as a drum. They were in an unfamiliar position of being in a District 8 semi-final and not necessarily favored to win. Telin agreed the boys were tight. "They couldn't make a basket. Other than Moore, none of them had had tournament experience before. But we were hanging with [Manhattan], had good defense, were making our free shots; that kept us in the game."

Suddenly the play of Iverson created momentum for Belgrade; the Panthers were controlling the game and Manhattan was panicking. But the Tiger coach put in a kid by the name of Ballantyne who proceeded to make three long shots, who got Manhattan back into the contest. With just a few seconds to go, Belgrade was behind by one point, 44-43. The Panthers had three shots before the buzzer went off—three shots, two offensive rebounds, three misses—just couldn't get the ball in the hole. The score remained 44-43.

The Manhattan game broke the boys' hearts. The next morning, an exhausted Belgrade team took on Three Forks, a team it had defeated twice during the season, and lost 60-58.

Belgrade had committed the unthinkable; it was not going to the divisional tournament in Red Lodge. There is no question it was a rebuilding year for Belgrade and Telin was a brand new coach, but for some fans, used to winning for so many years, this was no excuse.

Matt Telin nevertheless had every intention of returning to Belgrade for another season. In the spring after the basketball season, he had been approached for a job as a health physicist for a test reactor in Arco, Idaho. Nothing seemed to have come of it for several weeks, so he renewed his contract and forgot about the interview because he enjoyed teaching so much. Then one day he was in chemistry class, got a call from Idaho that took him out of the room. The personnel manager told Telin there was an opening and would he still be interested? An offer was extended. Telin and his family would live in Idaho Falls for eight years.

The future looked precarious for fans in Belgrade. Again, Larry Moore was the only starter on the team returning. Many knew there was talent among the juniors, but how well could they meld as a team? And now the school was forced to, for the second year in a row, look for a new coach. Had Belgrade lost its edge? Maybe the town referred to as the "Hub of Gallatin Valley" had finally, permanently, run out of gas.

Adversaries at the Helm

T HE 1960-61 SEASON WAS UPON HOLY ROSARY, A SEASON ON PAPER that was not terribly encouraging. The only starters returning were Tom Monforton and Ken Schweitzer; Murphy, Gaffke, and Ward were gone. So was Coach Christensen. The new coach, Jim Owens, was untested, just out of college. But there was reason for optimism: Monforton had been first-team all-state in Helena. Schweitzer had rapidly improved, was now considered as good as Monforton. The fans in Bozeman believed Owens had the smarts to assemble the right supporting cast around them.

Rosary had three boys, still juniors, who were proven backups: George Gallagher and Joe Cahill up front and Jerry Monforton as the new guard. Gallagher, the tallest player on the team at 6'1", had considerable playing time at center the previous two years. Cahill was only 5'10", small for a forward, but fast, athletic, had shown his skills both in basketball and as an end in football (he would become the first Rosary player voted to play in the East-West Shrine game). And of course Jerry Monforton had played alongside his brother, it seemed, all his life. He was nearly as short as Tom, only 5'6"—in fact the brothers were known around town as the Two Midgets. But like his brother, Jerry was extremely quick and a crack shooter in his own right. Terry Corcoran at guard and Dave Noyes, a forward/center were the main players off the bench. (Noyes excelled in football far more than basketball. He also played end and would become the second Rosary player to play in the East-West Shrine game.)

Owens had the right lineup, knew what he wanted and how to

accomplish it. To begin with, he lived and died with fundamentals: shooting, ball handling, defense; he was particularly big on defense. Christensen had stressed defense, but the kids thought Owens was better. At least 50 percent of every practice was on defense in some form. He ran a tight-pressure man-to-man, would tell his players, "Glue yourself to your guy; if he goes to the bathroom, you go with him" (apparently hardly an original maxim). Half-court pressure man-to-man was closest to his heart, but he changed defenses constantly. In his system if Rosary made a shot, the team would put on a full-court press, then fall back to a zone. If Rosary missed the shot, the team would use a half-court man-to-man. After a free-throw, the team would go into a half court zone. His zone could be a 1-3-1 zone or a zone trap. The team members were able to adjust easily from one defense to another.

On offense, Rosary went to a fast break whenever possible. One would rebound and the others were down the floor. If the fast break couldn't materialize, the Bulldogs would go 1-3-1 against a zone. Cahill would station himself at high post near the free-throw line mainly as a passer; Tom Monforton would be out front, Jerry Monforton and Schweitzer at the wings, and Gallagher roving down under. If the opposing team used man-to-man, Owens developed a unique system in which two or three players were on the left side of the lane, Schweitzer out toward the corner on the same side, and Tom Monforton staying out front at the top of the key. Schweitzer would then move underneath to the opposite side, curl around and set a screen for Monforton, opening him for a shot. If he was open, he would take the first shot, which he usually made. If he was blocked, he would flip the ball back over to Schweitzer, who was usually open. This play was used repeatedly and worked 70 percent of the time. If the combined execution was unsuccessful, Owens had no set maneuver, but the ball would likely go to Jerry Monforton, who dropped back from the lane on the opposite side. But the play was designed in essence for a two-on-two game, because Schweitzer and Tom Monforton were the

Frank Spragg

target shooters. (Owens told Cahill years later that he never used that play again with any other team he coached. It worked with Rosary because it was uniquely suited for Schweitzer and Tom Monforton.)

The team quickly gelled, in large part because the players liked Owens. He was a cerebral coach, not a rah-rah guy. He seldom raised his voice either in practice or during games. His mother would say, the only way you could tell Jim was antsy was by watching his feet draw further and further underneath as he sat on the bench. Otherwise he seemed calm. He always encouraged his players, never belittled them. They never ever saw him angry with referees or anyone. They themselves gave him little reason for frustration.

He had driven his boys, prepared them, and now they were about to play their first game away at Helena Cathedral. Tom Monforton did not remember Cathedral being that good, but neither was Rosary in a good position to confront them. On the way over to Helena, the bus threw a rod and was useless. The coach had to arrange for cars to come and take the boys the rest of the way to the gym at Carroll College. They arrived an hour late and when they entered the gym, the place was jammed; people were screaming and hollering; the young visitors went into psychological meltdown. Tom Monforton and Schweitzer were not hitting, so the other players had to try to step up. Considering that Rosary was battling itself as well as Cathedral, the Bulldogs still lost by only five points 51-46.

Rosary quickly put the defeat behind it, cruised to victories over the next four games, but was now scheduled to play Belgrade at the Montana State Field House. Like Christensen before him, Owens was able to arrange opening acts before Bobcat games, always a choice deal because the team would be on that full-sized floor again before a huge crowd. Owens and his crew knew the Panthers were vastly improved over the year before. It should be a closely hard-fought game; fans and players from both schools were looking forward to it.

It was a fiasco for Rosary. Everything went wrong for the Bulldogs and right for Belgrade. The mess was exacerbated or perhaps generated by one play in the first quarter. Marvin Craver from Belgrade went over Tom Monforton's head to block a jump shot on a fast break, absurdly caught his teeth on the top of Monforton's skull, splitting it wide open. Monforton was covering his wound with his hand to stanch the flow of blood, when his brother Jerry ran up and unaware of the wound removed the hand. Blood spurted all over. Whatever chance Rosary might have had at that point was gone. Belgrade won 64-34.

BELGRADE ALSO HAD A NEW COACH, A RELATIVELY YOUNG MAN HIMSELF by the name of Chris Small, the same Chris Small who coached the year before in Power. This small school north of Great Falls had not sent its team to the state tournament that year, but everyone in town at the time would tell you it should have. The Pirates were the only team, they said, that could have challenged Gildford for the state title. After all, Power was the only squad that came even close to defeating the Broncs in post season tournament play. But the Pirates did not win, and not only was their season a disappointment, their coach was leaving for a new position in Belgrade.

I never knew Chris Small. I may have seen him; I may have walked past him. But I wouldn't have known if I did or not because at the time I had no idea what he looked like or that he even existed. When he came to Belgrade, I had transferred to Bozeman for my senior year in high school. So I have to be satisfied with photos of Small. With his glasses, he looks like a no-nonsense accountant. He was anything but.

There are folks in this world who need the companionship of others, no matter the time or place. They deal with people all day, must be "on," and you would think this would drain them but it does not. Because being on is who they are, and when the day is over and all have left, they long for more. Chris Small was one of those people. If you dropped in on him unannounced, hey, perfect! Have a beer. We'll go down in the basement and talk, have a laugh, bring up old times. Small had built a bar down there twice as long as a normal table and there would always be beer. His son Scott said, "There were piles of cans on the bar, almost to the ceiling sometimes." That Small was a people person is beyond all doubt. Terry Keel, who was on his team in Power, said, "When Small made friends, they were friends for life. He knew hundreds of people. At one point Small lived up Gallatin Canyon, renting a place, and I visited him several times when he was up there. I visited him when he lived down in Utah. He was the kind of person his friends, his players came back to visit with time and again through the years." He had been a great parent. His daughter Karen said, "At home he was a great dad, fun to be around. After the season there would be a lot of parents, players, big parties. It was a lot of fun growing up with him; he had people over all the time." She added, "If he looked like an accountant, it was because his eyesight was horrible; that is why he wore glasses. But he was a funny guy, a practical jokester. He had a lot of enthusiasm."

He got along well with kids who had nothing to do with athletics. Karen said, "The kids would call him Chris, not Mr. Small. He would go down the hall and the kids would say, 'Hey Chris! Hey Chris!' The kids just loved him. Some of the kids didn't have any money so they would borrow money from him. They would always pay him back. He chewed tobacco his whole life. A kid would want a pinch of Copenhagen, he would always give them some. He may have given players a chaw of tobacco too. It was a different time. He could be that kind of guy and yet they still respected him. He had no discipline problems in class. None at all. He was a laid back-kind of guy, but no one ever crossed him either. I can never remember him having discipline problems."

Maybe it was because Small was passionate about teaching. That is all Small ever wanted to do (after his first year in college), was to teach and coach. But he did not teach history or civics or some related subject as one might imagine. Instead he taught science and proved to be very capable. It may be hard for people to visualize a fun-loving, outgoing person steeped in science. Aren't scientists supposed to be alone in a lab tinkering, conducting experiments? But Small had a knack for science and loved teaching, so he could make it come alive for the kids. My sister Susie told me Small was one of the best teachers she had in Belgrade. He could describe, for example, in great detail how a television worked, making it interesting, describing the process in a way the kids could understand. Terry Keel said, "He was passionate about teaching science in the classroom. I went to Eastern Montana after I graduated, took a general science course, and it was a breeze because of what Chris had us taught us in high school." Jack Anderson, another player from Power, said, "It was unusual for a coach to teach biology, chemistry, and physics, but Small was a very sharp, very intelligent man."

Where had the science connection come from? His son Scott thinks a lot of it might have had to do with the military. But Chris also liked to repair things. He had grown up on a farm and became proficient as an electrician, at finished carpentry, at car mechanics; he had had to learn to fix the combine and other machines, which contributed to his interest in how things work. He loved various forms of construction. When he started a ski club in Belgrade, he built racks for the buses, racks that are used to this day.

The ski organization was another connection with his students. Karen said, "He would go around and pick everyone up and then he would pick me up. So I wouldn't have to get up so early." He was kind that way, particularly with people who were his favorites.

Larry Moore, his star guard said, "I was in his house more than anyone else. He protected me very well, made sure I wasn't out on Saturday nights raising Cain. I was always at his house; he had me babysit his kids when he and his wife Jackie went out. Or he would say his wife was gone, 'Come on over; I have an extra steak.' He protected me from the elements of everyone else. He had received quite a few phone calls that I was out doing things when in fact I was in his living room."

Later in life, Small became an avid golfer, which is for most people—as it certainly was for Small—a social avocation. He loved golf literally to his dying day; he would die from a heart attack at the most appropriate of all places, the eighteenth hole on the Cottonwood Golf Course west of Bozeman. A tree has been planted there in his honor. This is significant because as much as he loved everything else in life, he loved sports. And he always wanted to be a coach.

Ron Iverson, who never played for Small but knew him well, said he was an excellent coach. "Small knew the game right up there with Lutz. Chris knew everything. He knew offense; he knew defense; he was an awfully good fundamentalist, but most important, he knew how to handle the game in the game." And he knew how to motivate the kids. Gary Cook, who played starting guard for Small, said, "I remember one of the first things that happened when Chris Small came, he lined the players up on the old stage and said, 'You're the best team and I'm the best coach. Together we can win state.' I remember distinctly him saying that."

For vacations Small and his family often would visit his relatives. They would go to California, or up in central Montana where he still had a farm. Part of the farm had come to him as an inheritance. The sports, the mechanics, the farm, his siblings—all these components together help in the understanding of Chris Small. He was born January 15, 1928 on that farm fifteen miles south of Fort Benton near Highwood, the youngest of ten children. His oldest brother was eighteen when Small was born; some of the older siblings left the farm and Small hardly knew them. Herman was the only brother who stayed on the farm and was like a father figure to Small. When Herman died, his sister Bernice and her husband came up from Missouri to manage the farm. But Small would go up and help with the harvest. He enjoyed doing that; his kids thought it was fun being there, and it helped that Small was a wiz with mechanics.

From the time he was young, he was outgoing and athletic. His friend Jack Lepply first knew Small when both were in junior high, and they were close all through high school. "He was a pretty good athlete from the time he started and he got along with everybody." Lepply and Small got to be good friends because they lived a block and a half apart and would often join each other for the seven-block walk to school. When Lepply was a freshman in 1943, Fort Benton elected to have no interscholastic athletics, never traveling to other towns for sports, all the gasoline instead being used for the war effort. But Small was a year behind so he never missed out on football and basketball, which were reinstated when he was a freshman. It is important to note here that Chris was the first in his family to even have time for sports. (His brothers and sisters used a horse and plow and didn't have time for sports even though they were athletic. Nearly all of them went into the military.)

The advent of the steam engine allowed more efficiency on the farm and freed Chris for leisure time. In football, his team won the state championship his senior year. He played end and was invited to play in the first East-West Shrine game. His heroics in basketball measured up to football: he and teammate Greg Stott, forming a great tandem together, helped Fort Benton win its first twenty games when he was a junior before bowing out in the divisional tournament. (When Stott was in college, he was mauled by a grizzly bear in the Bob Marshall Wilderness Area and bled to death.) When he was a senior, Fort Benton won the state championship. He was named overall athlete of the year.

Track was not reinstated until Small was a sophomore, but it was here that he would distinguish himself even more than in football or basketball. He won the state half-mile for Class B three years in a row, also placing second in the mile. His record in the half-mile for Fort Benton stood for many years. When his daughter Karen taught school in Cut Bank, she would go back to Fort Benton, look at the trophy case in the lobby of the high school, and his record was still there. It wasn't until recently that the record was finally broken. When he was both a junior and senior, he and one other track participant nearly won the state title by themselves. (Fort Benton took second both years.)

Because of his track accomplishments, he accepted a scholarship at the University of Montana in Missoula with the intention of majoring in pharmacy. He soon lost interest in pharmacy and found college track competition much stiffer than in high school. He didn't compete in sports after his first year, but came to the realization that he really wanted to teach and coach. While in Missoula, he became good friends with Professor O.I. Jackson (simply called Jackson by friends and family) who was offered a position in the engineering department at Montana State. When he and his family made the move to Bozeman, Small went with them, lived with them for a time, even helped them build their new house.

After graduating from college, Small went into the Air Force and began his service in the Korean War as a courier. He had a pass to travel on any available plane to deliver messages all over Korea, messages to be handed directly by hand to the receiver. One day Small found himself extending papers to General Douglas MacArthur. Following the end of the war in Korea, he was deployed to the Philippines, where he again traveled in planes as a personnel officer dealing with discipline and morale among the soldiers. After Small passed away, his son Scott and others looked through his records and discovered he had received two bronze stars. That he saw action on the front lines surprised his children, because Small talked little about his experiences in the military. He would continue as an Air Force officer for many years in the reserves, attending monthly drills, eventually reaching the rank of captain. At one point he was almost called up to go to Viet Nam.

After Small left the military, he immediately went to student teaching in Whitewater for a year, then on to Huntley Project as a regular teacher, staying there for two more years. It was at Huntley where Small met fellow teacher and future wife Jackie. They would marry and eventually have three children, a boy Scott, and two girls, Karen and Christie. From Huntley Project, Small went to Power, where he taught and coached for an additional two years. He wanted to be in a town that was as close as possible to his farm.

When Small arrived in Power, the Pirates' basketball program had been stuck in the middle of the District 12 pack for years. Keel said, "The school board had fired the current coach. Small was farming for the summer, and when the board found out about him, members went over to his farm, got him off the tractor for an interview, and hired him right there in the field to be the next coach."

Jack Anderson said Small was one of the better coaches to come around. "He didn't line the kids on the stage like he did in Belgrade, but he kept on telling us kids how good we were and that we had lots of potential. Some kids were skeptical at first, but what he said turned out to be true. He was enthusiastic, dedicated, and had the ability to watch teams, found what he could do to take away from teams more talented than Power. He got it across to the kids and could work with a disadvantage very well."

When Power won the state Class C championship in 1973, Anderson believed a large part of it was Small's scouting the opponent, Manhattan Christian, which was near Belgrade, where Small still lived. He told his former player, Buddy Williams, who coached Power, that the only chance the Pirates had of winning was to use the press, know when to use it and know what to expect. Williams followed his advice and Power won the championship.

Small would use this same insight in 1960. When Power played Gildford in the semi-finals of the divisional tournament, to contain Don Miller, Small ordered a box-and-one zone defense, telling his center, Buddy Williams to stay on Miller and stick to him like glue. (Williams was not told to step on Miller's feet as the Gildford players claimed.) In that game both Miller and Cady fouled out and Power nearly won, one of only two teams to come close to defeating Gildford that year. Anderson still thinks Gildford and Power were the best two teams in the state and should have played for the state championship. "You can dream and dream and dream and it isn't going to happen."

Small had made lifelong friends in Power, but Belgrade, with its storied history in basketball, was beckoning. Small had grown attached to Gallatin Valley as a college student, and when an opening for a science teacher/coach in Belgrade popped up, it seemed like a combination that couldn't be refused. Still, Small wanted to cover his bases. Before coming to Belgrade for an interview, he stopped in Three Forks for a haircut; he asked about the players in the district, asked about Belgrade. He didn't tell the barber he was interviewing for the coaching position. When Small arrived in Belgrade, he first talked to the janitors; they would know if there was a good group of kids coming up. This critical element was important to him before he would accept the job. He went not only to the janitors but to others around town who were in the loop.

They knew enough to say that the incoming senior class was promising, but how promising no one could predict for sure. Larry Moore was coming back, the off-guard who had been the star the year before; he alone could keep the team competitive. But who would fill the other positions? Would Gary Cook or Charles (Chuck) Wright compete for point guard? Likely Gary Hellyer, Rob Otheim, or Leon Stiles be the forwards? (Stiles and fellow player Tom Saisbury would mostly end up in reserve status.) Hellyer, even though he did not start the year before, had logged a bag-load of playing time. The real concern was who would be center. No one vying for the post had even been on the varsity the previous year.

Mounted on the hallway of our home is a photo of the 1959 Belgrade junior varsity of which I was a member, all of us in our sophomore year. The ten members of the team stand single-file diagonally to the camera, Chuck Wright in front, Rob Otheim in back. The increase in height from one player to the next appears remarkably consistent; you could lay a long two-by-four on top and it would touch the scalp of each player.

But one young man was missing from the photo; had he been there, he would have stood in the rear, a noticeable jump from the top of Otheim's head to the top of his. He was tall but also bulky, almost blob-like; he didn't look like a basketball player, and officially that year, he wasn't. His name was Larry Karinen, and the most he could do when he was a sophomore was play for one of the intramural teams. The next year as a junior, he would toil for the junior varsity, nearly always out on the floor, but droning nonetheless in obscurity. Many years later at a school reunion, Matt Telin told Karinen he had plans to bring him up to the varsity for the district tournament. But Karinen became ill and was forced to listen to games on the radio. It seemed as if he were destined to never play varsity basketball.

But beneath Larry Karinen's placid countenance was fire. He had worked relentlessly the previous summer refining his skills. He had no ambition to be a star or even a starter; he just wanted to make the team. He would find when he tried out for the team at the beginning of winter, all the summer practice and slog-time on the junior varsity were not in vain. The assistant coach, Buck Gaustad, had stressed fundamentals, had worked with Karinen on his position, had really brought him along. The only other player even considered for center was Tom Verwolf, but he was still an awkward, unseasoned sophomore. The starting position belonged to Karinen if he wanted it, and he hadn't practiced all summer to say no.

He became very effective under the basket, piling up garbage shots from offensive rebounds. Karinen could not jump well so he learned to use his bulk to get opponents out of the way and became the main rebounder. Coach Small taught him a trick on the jump ball: just as the ref threw the ball up, Karinen would throw his hip into the other center and knock him off. Because of that, he got most of the tips. Only Coach Casey Keltz from Townsend caught him doing this, and complained to the ref, who called a foul on Karinen. Otherwise he always got away with it.

Small would find that he had a bevy of skills at every position. Verwolf became more proficient at center and forward and would often start as the season progressed. Rob Otheim and Gary Hellyer were the forwards but over time, Hellyer often played out front on offense, bringing the ball down the floor, becoming something of a point guard. But he was a good rebounder and particularly adept at rifling the ball down the floor, usually to Moore for an easy layup. Marvin Craver, one of the few juniors on the team, was another forward and toward the end of the season often started in place of Otheim. Karinen said, "Craver was clumsy, would kind of stumble around on his feet; he wasn't as good as his brother Stan, but he was aggressive and would stay in there and fight for the ball. Because of his unique style, it was hard to guard him."

At the guard position, Small had Gary Cook usually starting, who was much in the mold of his brother Gene. Like Gene, he wasn't the star but he was a speedster on the fast break, effective on defense, and a good shooter. Chuck Wright would come off the bench and accumulate a wealth of playing time. In the divisional championship against Rosary, Wright came in after a minute and a half and played the rest of the game. He was more of a true point-guard than Cook, a good ball handler and very effective stealing the ball. He could keep up with Tom Monforton. And of course Small had Larry Moore. Of the stable of Panther headliners from 1948-1961, Moore would be the last. He had played off-guard in previous years but in the Small system would find himself more often than not as a small forward. He could shoot from anywhere, had won several games on last-second shots, and would have a season scoring average of 21.8 ppg. He was the man opponents had to stop if they had any aspirations of winning.

Small had been a disciple of John Wooden before Wooden became famous (he didn't enter the national consciousness until 1963) and followed Wooden's principle of harsh conditioning. Like Wooden, he went to the fast break and sometimes used The Wizard's patented full-court zone trap, but mostly Small liked man-to-man. He thought the zone was a lazy man's defense, for people who couldn't play defense. On offense he thought he could destroy the zone because his players could shoot from outside, getting them open with rapid passing around the perimeter (a departure from his policy in Power).

Because of the fast break, the Panthers didn't have to set up often, but when they did they used screens, often they were double screens to get someone open. The players were numbered (not their jersey numbers) one though five, with the plays numbered accordingly. For example Small would call out "35!" That meant the three-man (the off-forward) would set a screen for the five-man (the center). Because he had Moore, Small used another trick assiduously. When the other team brought the ball down the floor, Belgrade would go to a 2-2 defense, four players on defense with Moore nowhere to be seen. He was still down at Belgrade's end melding in with the crowd. This confused the opponents; they looked to the coach for guidance. Should they leave a player with Moore or take advantage of the five-on-four overload at their end of the court? They left Moore alone at their peril. Karinen would get the rebound, flip it over to Hellyer who bullet-passed to Moore for an easy bucket. Even if the opponents left someone with Moore, he would be the point man for a quick fast break, with the option of dumping it off to a teammate for the score.

With his operation, Small guided his troops to 13 victories in a row, including that notorious thrashing of Rosary at the Field House. Before that game he had told his players to relax, and they did. They shot well and were helped by opponents who mismanaged everything. Now it was time for Rosary to come back to Belgrade. With Belgrade's 13-0 record, the other coaches were conversing on ways to halt the Panthers, and foremost among them was Jim Owens, who was at least as innovative as Small. The one tactic he had to refine was how to stop Moore, and his best tool was Tom Monforton. With Rosary, Moore could never get away with the "loner" trick. Monforton would stay with Moore and was quick enough to coop him up. He would pick up Moore at the other end of the floor and stick to him like a rash. He had to; Moore could drain the ball from half court or make hook shots from beyond the key.

In the Belgrade game, however, Owens decided to put Cahill on

Moore. Cahill said, "I was quick enough to keep up with him and he scored only 10 points. He just gave up in that game." Meanwhile, Cahill scored 15, but no one else on the Rosary team scored much of anything—except for one player: Schweitzer went into his own outer space, bombing from everywhere, tanking the nets for 40 points. Tom Monforton, while not scoring much, was credited with 15 assists. Rosary won 67-55, and Monforton remembered the Belgrade fans after the game remaining in their seats, just sitting in shock. Their team wasn't invincible after all.

Rosary won its last seven games ending the regular season with a 17-2 record, 13-1 for conference play. But two of those seven victories were not easy. The Bulldogs beat Townsend 51-47 and Manhattan 45-43. In that game, the Tigers were leading by seven points with five minutes to play when Schweitzer went into bomb mode again and Rosary pulled out the victory.

Belgrade rebounded from the Rosary loss and won its last six games, ending the season 19-1, 15-1 in conference play. But like Rosary, two victories would be difficult. The Panthers came away with a razor-thin victory over Whitehall 63-61, a would-be participant, as we shall see, in the state tournament. The other win was over Townsend 59-55, a team the Panthers had defeated earlier in the season by the same margin; if any squad could be the spoiler in the district tournament, it might be the Bulldogs from Townsend. Small could get steamed at another coach, especially Casey Keltz from Townsend. Chuck Wright was sitting next to Small in the fourth quarter when it was starting to really get nasty between the two coaches. Wright recalled Small telling him and Gary Cook, "When Keltz comes my way, you guys grab each arm or I will bust him."

In another game against perennial bottom-dweller Willow Creek, however, the Panthers could do no wrong. Again Small told Wright, who was sitting next to him, "I'm sending you in and if you don't shoot, I'm pulling you out." Wright was a good shooter but reluctant to take shots. On this night, however, he did as he was told. On

Willow Creek's standard-sized floor, he banged in five shots in a row "ten to fifteen feet beyond the arc." The final was 100-37, a spectacular win in a rising-like-the-phoenix regular season.

Down to the End – Part 2

THE DISTRICT TOURNAMENT BEGAN WEDNESDAY, FEBRUARY 8, AS always at the Montana State Field House. Of course, the Field House was an adjustment for players who had never competed there before. Which gave Rosary and Belgrade an additional advantage—as if they would need it. The format would again be the same, 16 games crammed into four days, possibly a 17th on Monday evening if a challenge match was necessary. There was little doubt in District 8 that Belgrade and Rosary would be in the finals, but others could possibly upend one or both of them, teams like Townsend, Manhattan or even Wilsall. The Longhorns competed against Rosary and Belgrade once each during the regular season and were beaten badly both times, but otherwise had a winning record. Townsend fared well against Rosary at home but lost by 22 in Rosary's own gym. Manhattan, on the other hand, stood tough against Rosary but was pummeled in both games against Belgrade, losing one by 32 points. Even if there were no upsets, a title match between Rosary and Belgrade was reason enough for excitement; even local experts could not predict the winner. Everyone looked forward to the tournament with anticipation.

Wednesday night was the grind: four games in five hours. Rosary and Belgrade were given byes and did not play. Clyde Park won over Willow Creek, Three Forks over Gardiner, and the two most interesting matchups: Manhattan barely winning over White Sulphur Springs 52-48, but Wilsall manhandling Townsend 57-41. Because of their records during the season, Manhattan and Wilsall were given a free pass until the semi-finals on Friday evening.

On Thursday night, Belgrade and Rosary easily advanced, Rosary putting away once mighty Three Forks 50-30 and Belgrade over Clyde Park 65-49, a rugged match that saw 51 fouls. The winners would advance to the semi-finals on Friday night, Rosary against Manhattan and Belgrade against Wilsall. With the way Wilsall dispatched Townsend on Wednesday night, the Longhorns were looking to be a spoiler.

Instead, they were spoiled and thrown into the compost heap. Larry Moore put on a one-man show for Belgrade scoring 31 points, by far the most points by any one player in the tournament thus far, and the Panthers took advantage of subzero shooting by Wilsall in the second quarter to put away the game for good. The final was a laugher 62-44. Meanwhile Rosary continued to struggle against Manhattan, falling behind by seven points at the end of the first half. The Bulldogs managed to catch up 40-40 by the end of the third quarter and then dominated the fourth quarter, winning 58-49. The stage was set for the showdown between Rosary and Belgrade.

Neither game between the two teams during the season had been close; would this championship be another blowout? Owens had a two-part strategy: wrap up Moore and slow the game *way* down. Small surprisingly had no distinct strategy, feeling confident enough in his players that they should keep on doing what brought them here. He did realize that if Moore got into trouble, he would use him as a decoy playing forward, opening up scoring opportunities for the other players. At the end of the first quarter, Belgrade led 14-11, would extend that lead to 18-11, but Rosary fought back, establishing a halftime lead 25-22. From then on to the end of the game, with the scoring nearly even, Rosary won 48-44. The difference was free throws. Rosary made 12 of 19 attempts, while Belgrade could manage a pathetic 6 out of 20. In the closing minutes, the Panthers were forced to foul Rosary players who made their shots when they needed them. It had to be discouraging for the Belgrade boys, knowing that if they had canned but five more of their free-throw attempts, they would have gone out the winner.

Rosary earned the right to advance to the divisional tournament being held for the first time in Livingston. But Belgrade was relegated to playing a challenge match against Manhattan, because it had not met the Tigers during the tournament. It should be another easy game for Belgrade, if the season's history was any indication and it looked that way for two and a half quarters. Belgrade was leading 42-31 in the middle of the third quarter, when suddenly Manhattan rallied and by the end of the quarter, was trailing only 56-50. In the fourth quarter, led by Martin Douma who scored 10 points, Manhattan lit up the Field House and with two minutes left to go moved ahead 66-61. Every player from Belgrade would say Manhattan should have won that game. All the Tigers had to do was stall, but they did not. They instead went into shooting and missing while Belgrade maintained the press. Wright stole the ball twice, on one occasion feeding it to Cook for a score on a fast break. Belgrade grabbed the rebounds and in the end won 72-67. The Panthers would join Rosary in Livingston.

The divisional tournament had been held in Red Lodge for eight years in a row, but now, beginning on Thursday, March 2, it would be in a new venue at the old Livingston Civic Center down by the Yellowstone River. It was a small facility seating only a thousand fans, and Livingston wasn't as fun as Red Lodge. It had always been a rail-road town, a mean place, some thought. When players from other towns went to dances after the games, they were tested by youth from Livingston itching for a fight with anyone willing to grapple with them. When Joe Cahill walked into a dance, a Livingston punk gave him a shove, but he continued to walk and escaped a battle.

Because Livingston was larger, a Class A town, it had a state tournament feel, but Livingston also created a psychological advantage for Rosary and Belgrade; it was much closer for fans. Livingston was just over Bozeman Pass and twenty-six miles from Bozeman. Many fans would be on hand and could go home after every game. But the two District 8 teams lacked an advantage in another way: all teams were back to a more traditional gym. The floor was regulation size, but the fans were once again up close.

Rosary Coach Owens reported to the newspapers that he would use the same lineup he had all season, Tom and Jerry Monforton at guards, Cahill and Schweitzer at forwards, and Gallagher at center. Belgrade coach Small would start with a slight change in his lineup: Marvin Craver would start in place of Tom Verwolf at forward. Larry Moore would be the other forward, Larry Karinen at center, and Gary Cook and Gary Hellyer at guards. Verwolf and Wright would be the first players off the bench.

Belgrade, slated to play in the second game of the afternoon against the Belfry Bats, found itself in a hole in the first quarter, falling behind 16-4. Then Coach Small had his boys go into a full-court press, and the Belgrade players were able to steal the ball almost at will, leading at the end of the half 36-29. The amazing aspect of this game was the scoring duel between Moore of Belgrade and Don Lewis of Belfry. Moore had 13 field goals and 10-for-10 at the free throw line for 36 points. Lewis connected on 12-for-12 at the charity stripe, along with 9 field goals for 30 points. The final score was a Belgrade victory 82-68.

Meanwhile Rosary was scheduled to play at 9:15 p.m. on Thursday evening; its first opponent to be Colstrip, a team it had faced in the first round of the divisional tournament the year before. Rosary had little trouble then and would not now. Colstrip did have 6'4" Maynard Bills who controlled the back boards and scored 22 points. Schweitzer from Rosary got into foul trouble early and had to sit more than a quarter. Under these conditions, Colstrip kept up with Rosary for a time, keeping the game tied 13-13 ending the first quarter. But in the second quarter, the Bulldogs took charge and by halftime the score was 36-21. The Colts rallied in the third quarter, closing the gap to 47-40, but Rosary controlled the fourth quarter, pulling away for a 61-50 victory. If Schweitzer had a subpar performance, his co-star Tom Monforton put on a show both in his floor game and shooting getting 25 points.

Belgrade would not have it so easy against Rosebud in the opening game of the semi-finals. Rosebud was above its game most of the evening, playing against a team that was having something of a letdown after a brilliant game the night before. Moore was the poster boy for bad play, scoring only 7 points. Rosebud had identical twin brothers at guard, John and Jim Polich, who, according to Belgrade players, were a special headache. "You couldn't tell them apart," Wright said, "one of them got into foul trouble, and nearly fouled out. During halftime, I swear they switched jerseys, because the brother who had zero fouls started fouling." Wright had to admit, however, that Rosebud was a good team. Belgrade managed to win in a close match 62-58.

Rosary had an even worse time of it in the semi-final against Bridger. Bridger was a larger team than Rosary, and as Jerry Monforton said, "they were very athletic, in fact may have been the best team Rosary played all year." Tom Monforton didn't agree with his brother's assessment, but he couldn't do anything right, he said, and fouled out. No one else could shoot with any accuracy, so Owens had his team stall the last six minutes of the fourth quarter with the game tied at the end of regulation. Both Jerry and Tom Monforton said the only thing that saved the Bulldogs was defense. Essentially it was a tie game all the way through, Rosary leading 13-12 at the end of the first quarter, tied 25-25 at the half, 37-37 at the end of the third quarter, and 45-45 and end of regulation. In the overtime period, Rosary took possession and again stalled for nearly the entire three-minute period; finally one of the Bridger players fouled Schweitzer with ten seconds to go and he made the shot. That was it, an ugly game with Rosary winning 46-45.

Which meant that on Saturday, March 4, Rosary and Belgrade would be meeting once again for the championship. It seemed each could not get rid of the other. Belgrade jumped off to a 16-9 lead at the end of the first quarter, then Rosary settled down and narrowed the lead to 27-25 by halftime. Rosary never led in the ballgame, but often kept the game tied between quarters. Belgrade led 39-37 at the end of the third quarter, and for much of the fourth quarter but Rosary tied the game at 50-50 and from then on it was a virtual tie until the end of the game.

The score was 55-55 with less than thirty seconds to go, with Rosary in possession, going for the last shot. The shot was taken but too soon. Belgrade got the long rebound, Moore took possession of the ball and *he* shot too soon, throwing up the ball from half court. Karinen said Moore had plenty of time; he could have driven all the way to the basket but he didn't. But Karinen was still running down the floor after Moore took the shot, grabbed the rebound, threw it up, missed, got his own rebound and this time made it with only two seconds to go. Rosary still had time to get a shot off, however; Monforton tried to throw it in from the sidelines but the much bigger and taller Karinen was guarding him. Karinen said, "He tried a trick by pointing at my feet. I knew right away he was trying to trick me. He never did get the ball out and ran out of time." Round four had passed between the two rivals and this time it was victory Belgrade 57-55. There would be no challenge game; Bridger had won the consolation and could not play Rosary a second time. For the second time in three years Bridger came within an eyelash of going to the state tournament. Now if their players traveled to Helena, they would go as spectators.

FOR THE FIFTH YEAR IN A ROW, THE STATE TOURNAMENT WOULD BE held in Helena, beginning on Thursday, March 16. This tournament will always be associated with mascot trivia; it had two sets of Panthers (Belgrade and Boulder), two sets of Cardinals (Dutton and Froid), and two sets of Bulldogs (Rosary and Moore); only the Whitehall Trojans and Plevna Cougars would escape duplication.

The *Bozeman Daily Chronicle* made much of the fact that since Class C had been established, District 8 had always been strongly represented. In 1961, Rosary would be the only team returning from the state tournament in 1960. For the past seven years, some team, mostly from Belgrade, had represented District 8. In 1956, as we remember, Belgrade played Three Forks for the championship.

The *Chronicle* also emphasized the similarities between Rosary and Belgrade, both teams that had a tireless running game and preferred a tight man-to-man defense. The paper did not mention that both teams were adept at the half-court game, and as already stated, Owens could slow the game way down as he did in the district championship. The *Chronicle* also said that both teams had a balanced offense although there was no question each had designated scorers: for Belgrade it would be Larry Moore, and for Rosary, Ken Schweitzer and Tom Monforton. The *Chronicle* pointed out that Belgrade had the edge on the bench with three players regularly getting significant playing time. Rosary, on the other hand, could boast maybe one or two off the bench with meaningful minutes of play. Tom Monforton said Rosary was essentially a five-player team. Of the two teams, Rosary easily had the best floor manager in Tom Monforton, Belgrade had the more consistently good scorer in Larry Moore; Belgrade also had the edge in the center position with Larry Karinen, who was taller and heftier than George Gallagher and who could score more often on a regular basis. All put together, however, it amounted to two teams coming up even.

THERE WAS LITTLE INDICATION HOW EACH WOULD STAND UP TO THE other six teams in Helena. The only connection to any of the other teams was the home-and-home series between Belgrade and Whitehall. Over the years, these two schools regularly faced each other in football and basketball. In this latest cage series, Belgrade defeated Whitehall at home 58-52 halfway through the regular season; in the next-to-last game at Whitehall, Belgrade managed a narrow victory 63-61.

If Belgrade often had Whitehall on its crosshairs, it was because the town was sixty miles to the west, closer to Belgrade or Rosary than some of the teams in District 8, such as White Sulphur Springs, Gardiner, or even Townsend. But in those days, before the freeway was built, Whitehall residents could not make a speedy trip west or east; Butte was only thirty-six miles to the west, but because motorists had to take the narrow and treacherous drive over Pipestone Pass on the Continental Divide to get there, a visit to the Mining City took an hour. Heading east to Bozeman wasn't much easier. Part of the route was along the windy Jefferson River gorge, and once escaping that, there was a series of towns in Gallatin Valley to slow down for along the way. Arriving in Bozeman generally took an hour and a half.

If the major east-west routes out of Whitehall were laborious, the town itself sits at the north end of the broad Jefferson River Valley extending twenty-five miles south to Twin Bridges and far beyond along the river's principle tributaries. The Jefferson Valley had always been suited for ranching, but farmers also tried growing sugar beets and potatoes, mostly for seed. The folks in the immediate vicinity of Whitehall took to gardening because Whitehall at one time was a major food source for Butte. In 1960 there were also a considerable number of dairy farms in the northern part of the valley. Today, along with the demise of the sugar beet industry, there is nary a dairy cow to be found.

If agriculture has been important in the area, Whitehall itself was another child of the railroad, a siding established here in September 1890. The railroad had always been important providing jobs for many years. In 1890 a gold mine was also established, but that industry was always hit and miss, never a stable source of employment.

The appearance of Whitehall in the 1961 Class C tournament would be its third, having participated both in 1950 and 1955. The 1955 team went nowhere, losing two games and out, but the 1950 team had better luck before becoming an unfortunate party to one of the most bizarre stories in the history of Montana basketball.

Whitehall had put together a good team in 1949, which made it to the Class B state tournament, an achievement to be proud of, even if that is where its fortunes ended. Getting to the state Class B tournament before 1950 was very difficult, because nearly 170 schools battled for eight seats in the tournament. In 1950, however, Whitehall would find itself, along with over 100 other teams, in the newly organized Class C for all the smallest schools. Now assigned to this lower level, the players at Whitehall had every right to believe they could win the state championship. And the team did very well: during the regular season, the Trojans claimed nineteen victories, losing only three—to Belgrade, Class B Dillon, and as should have been expected, to the Western Montana College junior varsity. The team breezed through three victories in the District 16 tournament in Butte, becoming champions there, then defeated Stevensville in a playoff game (which was the system in 1950), giving the Trojans the honor of being in the first state Class C tournament to be held in the Romney Gym at Montana State. At state, Whitehall continued on its victory path, destroying Centerville 61-35 and a not-too-close win over Poplar 38-29 in the semi-final.

Which landed Whitehall in the State championship against Nashua.

The Nashua players, traveling from northeastern Montana, had a reputation for being tough, quick, a formidable adversary for any team at the state tournament. Someone from Whitehall, probably the assistant coach, had traveled all the way to Nashua and managed to get the Porcupines on film. Coach Hiney Lund had seen the film and convinced his players that if Whitehall were to win the state championship, they would have to meet and defeat Nashua. The players got hold of the film and studied it every day leading up to the tournament.

There were certain misconceptions about Nashua. Many thought the town was in the Fort Peck Indian reservation, the team filled with Indian players, when in fact the town sits just outside the western border of the reservation, with no Indians on the 1950 team at all. And if the folks in Whitehall had worries about Nashua, the Porcupines saw themselves as a Cinderella team predicted to take a back seat in the tournament to other participants such as Belgrade and Whitehall.

Nashua had been undefeated thus far against all Class C competition (it lost a lone game to Class B Wolf Point), but for four straight tournament games prior to meeting Whitehall, it endured difficult challenges. The six-point margin over Frazer in the district championship looked comfortable enough, but the game was tied with a minute to go before a Nashua player drove in twice for what amounted to two three-point plays. The playoff game against Medicine Lake went through two overtimes and three minutes of scoreless sudden death until, with ten seconds to go, a Porcupine player was fouled and made the free-throw, giving Nashua the one-point victory.

There was little letup at the state tournament. Nashua defeated Charlo by eleven, but made eight points in the last forty seconds. Then in the semi-final Nashua faced powerhouse Belgrade, which was favored to crush everyone. But Nashua clamped a zone on the normally high-scoring Panthers and won again by one point 31-30.

The Porcupines were now up against Whitehall for the championship trophy. Conventional wisdom would say that Whitehall should dominate; the Trojans had the easier path, were more rested. On the other hand overcoming multiple struggles surely strengthened Nashua. The game was dramatic from start to finish. With two minutes and forty seconds to go, Nashua opened up a seven-point lead only to see it evaporate again. With thirty seconds to go, Nashua hung on 40-39 and for the remaining time elected to stall with guard Mike Tahista putting on a one-man dribbling show along the perimeter. This strategy might have worked, but with just seconds to go, Tahista accidentally backed over the center line, giving Whitehall possession.

Coach Lund called a time-out telling his boys to get the ball to Gene Lutey who was only a sophomore but already one of the best players on the team. The ball was indeed thrown to Lutey, who was facing away from the basket at the free throw-line, but had accidentally been knocked down (no foul called) and caught the ball in a kneeling position. Still on his knees, Lutey wheeled around, cut loose, and the ball went in just as the buzzer sounded.

TIME FOR CELEBRATION!! But for whom? Did the basket count? The Whitehall fans said not only was the ball in the air, but through the basket before the horn went off. "Everyone in the crowd knew that," said Norman Clark from Whitehall who was in the audience that night. According to Clark, one referee agreed that the basket counted but the other referee said it did not, and the first ref "caved in."

Wayne Waarvik from Nashua—no surprise—saw the situation differently. Three people—the scorekeeper along with the referees—were in on the decision, with the scorekeeper having the final say. Their verdict claimed that Lutey's shot was still in its upward path when the horn sounded. Had it been on a downward path, Whitehall would have won. The referees and scorekeeper discussed the matter for three or four minutes with everyone in the stands in rapt silence, still in their seats. It was only after the announcement was made that Nashua fans came screaming and dancing out onto the floor. The 1950 tournament is still a bone of contention for those Whitehall folks who are still living.

In the previous season, this largely same Whitehall team experienced drama of a different stripe but no less compelling. The boys were playing in a polio-benefit game against Deer Lodge at home. Unlike regular school games, everyone had to pay to get into this game, and apparently fans were not only willing but anxious to pay. No doubt a big part of the draw was a game against a very good opponent. But whatever the motive, in a gym that was meant to seat 500 people, 1,800 showed their faces; it was packed, standing-room only no matter where you were. People were squished on floor-side seating, on the stage from front to back, on the balconies on both sides. The problem arose in the balconies; so many people were jammed in that the walls on both sides of the gym started falling outwards. If they continued on that course, the ceiling girded with railroad rails, would collapse to the floor. Parts of the walls could also cave inwards. It took cables, turnbuckles, and painstaking hours of work to bring these poor walls back to their original position.

In the fall of 1960, the Whitehall football team walked away with the Western Division Championship. The school hoped to trump that in the spring by winning the state basketball championship as well. The team was coached by William (Bill) Ball, a religious man, who according one player, Jim Bennetts, "was a motivator type, non-swearer, a church going guy, who had a fairly large family, a really nice gentleman who cared about the players and everything." He was fortunate to have a core of eight strong players who could be rotated in and out, giving him the advantage over teams with lesser depth. He was further helped in that the scoring was evenly distributed among his starters. Skip Stout at high post may have dumped in the most baskets overall, but 6'4" David Payne at low post and guards Joe Fouts and Gary Moore alternated as leading scorers. Jim Bennetts, Gene Baker, Dwight Capp and Wayne Allen saw frequent action. Ball generally used a 1-3-1 offense if forced to a half-court, but tried to use the fast break whenever possible. In defense, Ball generally used man-to-man although he could revert to zone, especially the box and one when the situation called for it.

Of the eight schools in the state tournament, Whitehall with 140 students had easily the highest enrollment, should have been the powerhouse in Helena, the bullyboy. In fact the Trojans snuck into the tournament. They placed third in the district tournament but were able to advance without a challenge match. The Western Division had only three districts (the Southern, Northern, and Eastern divisions each had four); in order to place eight teams in the Western Division tournament, two out of the three districts sent three teams on a rotating basis. In 1961 it was District 15's turn to send three teams. Some thought they remembered Whitehall winning a challenge match, but this could not have happened. Twin Bridges won the District 15 championship, and yet Whitehall and Boulder came to Helena from District 15.

At the divisional tournament—in, of all places, Whitehall—the Trojans again began by losing, this time to a very strong Corvallis team (the Blue Devils would win the state championship in 1962 before moving up to Class B). But the Trojans trudged through the losers' bracket winning four games, including a rematch with Corvallis and the challenge match against the Superior Bobcats, another team that had been expected to make a strong showing at state. It would be Whitehall and cross-county rival Boulder representing the Western Division in Helena.

If Belgrade or one of the other teams in District 8 regularly scheduled contests with Whitehall, they almost never in my memory competed against Boulder, also from District 15 and only thirty miles from Whitehall on the way to Helena. Why this happened, no one could say; it was no farther away from Gallatin Valley than, say, Twin Bridges or Sheridan. For some reason the Panthers never had District 8 on the radar screen. Boulder was the closest team in the tournament to Helena; for fans and players alike, going to games was a short day trip. Boulder was a natural rival for Whitehall since both were not only in the same district but in Jefferson County. Though Whitehall represented a larger population, Boulder was (and is) the county seat.

Boulder sits along the Boulder River, which flows south into the Jefferson River near Whitehall. It is assumed by many that the town was named after the many boulders that can be seen in the area. *Names on the Face of Montana* says that Boulder was named "for the massive stones strewn about the valley." Wikipedia says Boulder was named for "the many large boulders in the vicinity." But Dr. Philip Pallister, resident of Boulder since 1947 (and at age ninety-three still possessing an encyclopedic memory) says this is not true. It was really named after Bowlder, the man who did the original survey. After that, according to the doctor, the name was corrupted with a spelling change. The survey was named Boulder Valley, and the town was incorporated under the spelling Boulder.

What can't be disputed is that Boulder was founded as a stage-coach station in the 1860s, although again there is some disagreement as to what route it served. Wikipedia says it was a point between Fort Benton and Virginia City; Pallister says it was a link between Helena and Yellowstone Park. Judging where the town is located, likely both are true. Dr. Pallister says that the original station was on his ranch just outside of town.

Boulder became the county seat of Jefferson County when it was formed on February 2, 1865. The county was one of the smallest of the original counties in Montana Territory, and county government would always be part of the local economy. Agriculture and mining played a part of the economy also, but over time, the largest employer would be institutions. At first it was a home for the deaf and blind. Then quietly, in a downtown duplex, twelve children were housed who were considered mentally disabled. Eventually, the mentally disabled unit moved next to the facility for the deaf and blind, and kept adding residents, until the deaf and blind folks were unhappy with the arrangement and moved to Great Falls. The institution for the mentally disabled continued to grow until, by 1961, along with county government, it had become the main economic foundation for Boulder.

Boulder was a much smaller school than Whitehall with a more typical (for Class C) enrollment of ninety students. The school had made one previous appearance at the state Class C tournament but did not place. The Panthers had not even won the district tournament until 1951 under then-coach Maynard Olsen. Olsen became superintendent of the Boulder School District and was responsible for hiring the present coach, Don Kieckbush.

Kieckbush had graduated from Montana State and Boulder was his first job. He had already been at the school for four years by 1961 and would remain there for ten years. Dr. Pallister's son Jeff, who was on the team, said Kieckbush was a "fundamentals kind of a guy, a no-nonsense person, who didn't take any guff from anyone. We

Frank Spragg

worked hard for him." Kieckbush himself said that nearly all of his coaching was on fundamentals. "We didn't have any plays, any patterns; we worked with kids individually; the kids had fundamentals." According to Greg Pallister, another son of the doctor and also on the team, Kieckbush was an unusually good player coach. He was on the tall side—about 6'2"—and, when scrimmaging with his players, none of the kids, not even 6'5" Larry McCauley, could stop him from scoring. There is good reason to believe that if Kieckbush had been one of the players, no other team in the state tournament could have kept Boulder from winning.

With the potential it had, the team might have won anyway. The Panthers established several school records, including most wins in one season (22) and most points in one season (1,529—the team once scored 30 points in one quarter). McCauley set records in nearly every individual scoring department, finishing his career with 1,104 points. Jeff Pallister at guard was a very good ball-handler, his brother Greg a good shooter. Other players on the team that played significantly were Keith Buckles, Bruce Saarinen, John Heide, and Mark Graesser. One of the best players on the team was Marvin Timmer, who personified a power forward, a rugged rebounder, one of the best in District 15. He was one of the most consistent players on the team.

And this was the problem with Boulder; the team for different reasons was not consistent. The best player of all, according to Kieckbush, was a kid by the name of Larry Hamlin, a burly point-guard. "Far and away the best player I had," Kieckbush said, "if we had him we would have won state pretty handily." Hamlin had started for Kieckbush when he was a freshman, but his home life was so dysfunctional that by his junior year, you never knew what you were going to get on any given night depending on what was going on at home. Finally one day, Hamlin got into a row with his father, quit school, and joined the military. With Hamlin gone, the team often did not play well together. Still it built an impressive record during the season, with 17 wins against 4 losses. Unfortunately three of the losses were to Whitehall, one by a humiliating score of 67-48. Kieckbush's dilemma was which Boulder team he coached would show up on any given night. In the district tournament Boulder didn't have to face Whitehall, easily defeated Harrison, slipped by Sheridan 51-50, and then lost to Twin Bridges in the championship 47-42.

Because of the present system, Boulder automatically advanced to the divisional tournament in Whitehall and then something magical happened: the team came together as it never had before. The Panthers were matched against three of possibly the best teams in Class C in Montana: the speedy Plains Horsemen in the opening match; the Corvallis Blue Devils in the semi-final; and the Superior Bobcats in the final. They defeated them all. None of the victories were decisive, but they weren't down to the wire either. Boulder defeated Plains 49-43, Corvallis 54-43, and Superior 45-39. Jefferson County High School was in the driver's seat to take the state championship.

AT 7:30 P.M. ON THURSDAY EVENING, BOULDER WAS SCHEDULED TO play its first game against the Dutton Cardinals, which had taken second in the Northern Division, losing to Moore. Like Boulder, Dutton had been to the state tournament once before, in 1953, and like Boulder did not place. Dutton and Boulder had similar records coming into the tournament, Boulder at 22-5, Dutton 20-5.

Dutton High School, with only sixty-one students was one of the smaller schools at the state tournament. Situated thirty-two miles north of Great Falls, Dutton was part of District 12, the area surrounding Great Falls. The town's origins were typical of those east of the Rocky Mountains, born from the expansion of the Homestead Act and the advance of the railroad. The name Dutton came from a Great Northern freight and passenger agent who was stationed in Helena in 1905. The post office was established in 1909, the year of the expansion of the Homestead Act. According to *Names on the Face of Montana*, the land began as wheat country when "cowboy-turned-homesteader, 'Sinker Bill' Frixel made final proof of his homestead in

September 1909. His nickname had come from his days as a cook for roundup crews who described his biscuits as 'sinkers.' Dutton now stands on what was his property." The book goes on to say, "George Sollid had the idea of getting people to locate in this area, even though the land was free and open in all directions. Sollid set up shop near the old Frixel ranch and began locating homesteaders sent to him by his brother at Conrad. According to the *Dutton Jubilee Booklet*, newcomers were told: 'Just go down to the depot and sit around looking like a sucker. It won't be long before George will show up.'"

Except for the flat bottomland along the Teton River, which flows five miles north of town, the land around Dutton can be described as rolling, gentle enough that in 1961 most of the land was used almost exclusively for growing wheat and barley. The Teton Ridges, a series of east-west divides trailing away from the Rocky Mountains, were the exception: they were too steep for farming and hence left to growing cattle. Dutton had been a very stable community: Judy Herber, who graduated from the high school, said eight out of twelve of the students in her graduating class had one or more parents who attended Dutton High.

The Cardinals were coached by William (Bill) Conners, who was in his third year coaching at Dutton and would stay for another eleven years. The players considered Conners an outstanding coach; he would take the Cardinals to the state tournament again in 1962. Influenced by the type of players he had on his team—none were over 6'0" tall—Conners emphasized an up-tempo, run-and-gun style of offense. "We were all in shape," said Charles Proff, who played center-forward on the team. Norman Bailey, who was manager of the Boulder team, said, "The Dutton players were runners and shooters; you couldn't stop them." Proff said, "The team did play defense (as if he were not convinced); we played a 2-1-2 zone, but sometimes we picked up a player and went [man-to-man] with him." The starters on the team were Larry Thorne and Jack Gallagher at guards, Dick Trebesch and Jack Becker at forwards, and Charles Proff at center.

Proff should be considered a special part of history because it was on his family's land where the Lewis and Clark party shot the Blackfeet Indian (one of only two fatalities from the entire expedition).

Dutton had some competition in District 12, mostly from Belt, but when it came to the district tournament, the Cardinals had little trouble winning the championship. At the divisional tournament, Dutton faced Big Sandy, a team like Corvallis that had potential to be in the state championship, having the Klimas brothers, among others who were tall and talented. But the Pioneers could not match up with the smaller, quicker Dutton boys, who defeated them decisively.

It only remained for Dutton to get past Moore to take the Northern Division championship. Moore was a very good team, undefeated in 25 games. Dutton lost but the game was close, an outcome that could have gone either way. Proff said, "Moore got away with murder, especially Yeager underneath. The refs couldn't see what was going on." But it didn't matter, because both Moore and Dutton were headed for state.

The Moore Bulldogs were scheduled to play Rosary at 2:00 p.m., the first game on Thursday afternoon. I had traveled by Moore several times through the years, but because it is situated off the highway, I have never been into the town itself. On my last trip through the area in 2011, I wanted to see Moore up close, but had to hustle to Denton for an interview, and couldn't take time to approach the city limits. Moore, a dry-land farming community fifteen miles west of Lewistown, sits on a sweep of land gently rolling, but like the Hi-Line, moderately sized mountain ranges can be seen in the distance, notably the Judith Mountains to the northeast, the Big Snowys to the southeast, and the Big Belts to the west.

Moore was named for a "Mr. Moore from Philadelphia who rendered financial help to Richard A. Harlow when he was building the 'Jawbone' railroad from Harlowton to Lewistown. Later Lady Catherine Harlow Moore of Wateringbury, England, visited this part of Montana, indicating a relationship between the Harlows and the

Moores that may have been personal as well as financial. The Moore brothers operated a large ranch near here in 1884 and may have been part of the same family. The post office here was opened in 1904."

In 1961, the team was coached by Irving Holzinger, who was from the area, who had begun coaching in Moore in 1949 and would coach there until 1962. All the players liked him; he was an "x&o guy, a student of the game." He was willing to play up-tempo or slowdown, depending on the players he was working with. Holzinger had brought the team to the state tournament in 1956, but that team made little headway. In 1959 and 1960, Moore advanced to the divisional tournament only to be defeated by Gildford in the opening game each time. But the Bulldogs had continually improved through those years until, by 1961, it was one of the most dangerous teams in the tournament. It had been undefeated for a 25-0 record, easily the best team in District 9, winning the championship of that district with little trouble. St. Leo's had been a rival in the past, but by 1961 the Catholic school had lost its best players to graduation so in a real sense, Moore High School stood alone. The other schools in the district—isolated schools such as Grass Range, Winnett, Buffalo, Judith Gap, Roy, and Winifred—were never going to be much competition. In 1960, the stars for Moore had been center Fred Yeager and forward Ron Tilzey. Now in 1961, Tilzey switched to guard, working alongside Gary Nessan. The forwards were Gerald Tyndall and Milton (Butch) Nelson. Tyndall, Nelson, and Nessan had not been starters on the 1960 team but had been part of the junior class that easily defeated the senior class in an intramural contest. In 1961, Yeager and Tilzey were again the stars; Yeager at 6'2" was particularly difficult, slender in stature, but who had matched up well against Don Miller when Moore played Gildford the year before. He was quick and could shoot from long range.

If the Bulldogs had cruised through the district, they would not fare so easily in the divisional set in Great Falls. Tilzey thought the first game against Centerville was the most difficult the team had experienced all year. "We didn't beat them by very much, three points or something like that," Tilzey said. "We were having trouble adjusting to the divisional tournament, weren't used to playing that early in the day. Maybe it wasn't Centerville, maybe it was Moore not playing as well." Moore had an easier time against Stanford in the semi-final, but in the championship against Dutton, Moore was struggling, leading by only a single point with a few seconds to go. Then Nessan drove in for a layup, was fouled, and made both shots. Moore was the new Northern Division champion.

THE SECOND GAME ON THURSDAY, AT 3:30 P.M. MATCHED WHITEHALL against Froid which represented District 2 in the Eastern Division. Froid, with 73 students, was small, like most schools in the area, was one of a string of small towns leading up to Plentywood in the north-eastern corner of Montana. Like Dutton, like so many other towns in the state, Froid was born from the combination of the expansion of the Homestead Act and the arrival of the railroad. No one knows for sure where the name came from, but the theory is that it was selected from an old map of Nebraska. *Froid* is a French word meaning *cold*, which is certainly appropriate for this part of Montana. The people who originally came were from Scandinavia: Norwegians, Swedes, Danes; they came in large groups. One valley in the area is known as Dane Valley.

The Froid post office opened in 1910; by 1961, the town numbered 500 people. There had been some coal mining, but when electricity came to the rural areas near Froid in 1949,[12] the coal mines shut down. Beginning in the 1950s, land was leased out for drilling oil, but unlike Williston, thirty-five miles to the east, oil production (so far) has never amounted to much.

What carried Froid through the years was farming and ranching. At first settlers wanted to farm all of the land; the soil everywhere looked promising. To the north and northwest, the land leading into the Fort Peck Indian Reservation was ideal for farming. But when the soil was plowed to the south and east, it became increasingly less suitable, culminating in the dune-like Sand Hills. When drought and wind hit this sand section in the 1930s, there was no way to prevent it from blowing away. Fences were built, but sand covered them, making them invisible. All this area was then turned into ranchland and has been useful for grazing.

People came hoping to homestead but found complication three miles west on the opposite side of Muddy Creek. This land belonged to the Fort Peck Indian Reservation; in order for Indians to be able to sell the land to homesteaders, they had to receive a "patent" on the land—to be able to gain deed to the land—before it could be sold. At first patents were easy to obtain, but with much of the land sold under-value, the government stepped in and the process slowed to a trickle. Much of the land then and now has been leased, avoiding the loopholes of trying to sell the land.

This would be the Cardinals' first appearance at the state tournament; prior to 1961 the school had never even made it out of the district. The boys would find coming to Helena an otherworldly experience; for some players, it was the farthest away from home they had ever been. The altitude took some getting used to; Froid sits at 2,000 feet, and to suddenly come to Helena at 4,000-plus feet was an adjustment; it was hard to keep from wearing out. The boys had also never dealt with glass backboards before. Glass had more give, more spring, and so if there was a bank shot of any kind, it was a challenge to reduce the force. On the way to Helena, the team stayed overnight in Lewistown and was able to practice on glass backboards at the Civic Center, but that would be their sum total of preparation.

This in no way took away from Froid having a competitive team. The Cardinals were coached by Adrian Megrund, who was in his sixth year coaching at Froid. He had good teams in the past, but misfortune—sickness, injuries—kept the team from going far in tournament play. Now Megrund had the talent he surely thought would succeed. It was a short team—Jim Waller and Floyd Johnson at 5'11" were the tallest players on the starting five. Thus Froid did not have a true center; Waller and Johnson played closer to the basket, with 5'8" J.B. McNeil, 5'5" Mickey Reiter, and 5'9" Jerry Waller around the perimeter. But the team had attributes that helped overcome the height differential. McNeil was an exceptionally good point guard, could jump with the six-footers, often staying close to the basket on defense. The team also had plenty of depth: Stan Sundheim, his cousin Larry Sundheim, Jim Rued, and Stan Krohmer made capable substitutes for the starters, and Megrund was not stingy about making substitutions.

Megrund did something else to overcome height problems. He would often have one of his guards jump center under the theory that even if the other team's center controlled the tip, the ball more often than not landed in the hands of one of his taller players positioned around the circle. The Cardinals could fast break if the ball was stolen in a full-court press, but mostly the team played control ball, setting up for good shots; rarely was a shot taken beyond the perimeter. The strength of the team was defense, almost exclusively man-to-man although the zone could be used in a full-court press.

His system worked well enough that Froid compiled a 16-4 record entering the state tournament. Two losses during the season were to Savage and Brockton. But one loss went to Lignite, North Dakota, a school that no longer exists. Lignite had beaten Froid by one point, then went on to participate in the North Dakota Class B state tournament (North Dakota had only two classes at the time). In the district championship, Froid and Culbertson met, with Culbertson winning decisively. But several players on the Cardinal team were out with illness. Froid was able to defeat Brockton in the challenge game and advanced to the divisional tournament in Wolf Point, this time with better luck. The Cardinals met Culbertson again in the championship, this time with all players healthy, and won in overtime. The loss took something out of Culbertson, because the team folded before Plevna in the challenge match.

Belgrade was scheduled to play at 9:00 p.m. on Thursday against Plevna, one of the more remote towns in Montana, seventy-seven miles east of Miles City on the way to the North Dakota border. With only forty students, Plevna was the smallest school in the tournament. That did not stop the Cougars from winning the District 4 title. And when Plevna placed third in the Eastern Division tournament, it was able to move on to state by winning a challenge match.

Plevna may have had one of the more unusual histories of any school arriving in Helena. Nearly all the people in the Plevna area were of "German-Russian" descent; in other words their ancestors had been Germans living in Ukraine (which was part of Russia at that time). When the czars of the late nineteenth century decided to amalgamate these people into the Russian system and revoke many of the privileges they had once enjoyed, such as having their own schools, they emigrated en masse to America. The center of this immigration had been in eastern South Dakota, with follow-up settlers fanning in all directions, Plevna being on the western periphery. In eastern Montana, Plevna was one of the few communities consisting almost exclusively of German-Russians; the other towns nearby, for example, Ismay and Baker, had none. These Germans had been very cautious in their immigration, preferring to migrate in packs, forming one community rather than spreading out salt-and-pepper like as their fellow Scandinavians did.

Coming in large groups as they did, forming separate communities, implied a religious order, but the German-Russians were not of one religion. They might be Catholic, Lutheran, Baptist, Congregational; because of these differences, some Germans in a particular settlement would separate themselves from others, but not in Plevna. The people here were largely Baptist and Congregational, with no religious contention among them; they were by and large a homogeneous lot, and through the years largely got along.

The settlers had homesteaded a half-section per person, but this area generally wasn't farmable. The land is so cut up with geological formations, river gorges and coulees, that those in agriculture were necessarily dependent on ranching. These days a rancher has to have at least six or seven sections of land to make a go of it near Plevna. Some people found money to be made in resources aside from ranching. The Himsl family, for example, owned a bank that went under during the Great Depression, the depositors losing all their money. But somehow the family retained a half-section of land north of town, struck oil on it, and by the 1970s paid back all the depositors at 6 percent interest using oil proceeds. Gas and oil remained a cottage industry in the area for some years.

This would be Plevna's first trip to a state Class C tournament, but not the first trip to a state tournament. In 1934 the Cougars earned the trip only to lose to Poplar in the first game 20-14. One of the star players on that team, Avitus (Vedie) Himsl, also excelled in baseball, briefly managing the Chicago Cubs and continuing with that organization for the rest of his working life. After 1934, Plevna was not terribly successful in basketball, had tied for first in the conference standings in 1954 only to lose out in the District 4 tournament. There were bright spots along the way; in 1957 the school built a brand-new gym with a standard-sized playing floor, which was a major boost for the team. Through those years Harold (Harry) Ehret was the coach, considered "brilliant" by team members, but he left after 1960. Everyone had high hopes for Plevna that year, but star guard Jerry Schumaker sprained his ankle, Ray Allerdings got the mumps and the team never came together.

In 1961 Plevna acquired a new coach, Brendan Murphy who was a tougher coach than Ehret had been, had instituted strict rules that apparently worked, because he developed a winning team. Through the regular season, Plevna had four losses, ending second to the undisputed strongest team, Terry. Everyone expected Terry to represent District 4 in the state tournament; it had better shooters than Plevna, but when it came to district tourney time, Terry did a swoon. In the championship against Terry, Plevna jumped ahead immediately and coasted to a 65-59 victory.

At the Eastern Divisional tournament in Wolf Point, Plevna got the "jitters" and lost to Medicine Lake by one point. Then the Cougars worked their way through the loser's bracket only to meet Terry again in the consolation match. This time Plevna trailed for most of the game but rallied in the fourth quarter to win. In the challenge match, Plevna stomped Culbertson by 20 points to earn a shot at the state title.

One interesting aspect of this Plevna team is that it included two sets of brothers: Ray and Milbert Allerdings, who were a year apart in age and rotated starting at forward; and Jim and Don Hogue, who were the two guards. But the two top scorers were 5'11" Mike Klos at forward and 6'1" Doug Kern, both big and strong. Kern's father was the Lutheran minister in town.

As the Rosary players walked out onto the floor at 2:00 p.m. on Thursday, March 16, they knew their game against the other Bulldogs from Moore would be a trial because of Moore's impeccable record. The boys from central Montana had not slipped in through the back door from their district and division, as some of the teams had done, had not struggled and won a challenge match. Moore had won both tournaments, although team members felt lucky to put down Dutton in the division championship.

It seemed unlikely each of the two teams would know anything of the other before the tournament; Rosary didn't even have the St. Leo's connection as it had the year before, didn't have the Lewistown Catholic team on its schedule. And it was true that Moore knew almost nothing about Rosary beforehand, but Rosary knew Moore, a team it had never seen, as much as an opponent possibly could. Jim Owens believed a big part of coaching was scouting the other team and carried his philosophy forward, calling on a network of people: Bobcat players who became coaches or teachers, relatives, or people in general he knew who could be called on to attend a game and give a scouting report. Owens knew in particular about Fred Yeager, how he was "Mr. Everything," that not only was he Moore's star center but was a good ball-handler and usually brought the ball down the floor. Owens had two weeks to prepare for the state tournament and took his team up to Montana State to play against the Bobcat scout team, players of skill who were just starting out in the Bobcat system. Owens instructed the scout team to "play as Moore would play." One 6'5" future center for the 'Cats, Jim Noning, who was also a good ball-handler, was asked to bring the ball down and maneuver "as Yeager would." Owens put Cahill and others against Noning for practice. Owens took his team to the college three or four times to get them prepared.

Still, for all that, Cahill said Yeager was the toughest player he had ever encountered. He was rail-thin, but so quick. He kept banging in long outside jump shots. Rosary was not shooting particularly well, and yet Moore led by only four points at the end of the first period, three points at the end of the second. In the third period, Moore heated up and led by eight points at the bell. Aiding them was Rosary's leading scorer, Ken Schweitzer, who was in foul trouble. Owens had to take him out for a time.

But if Schweitzer was in foul trouble, so were the two stars for Moore, Yeager and Tilzey. Owens also made a change in guarding Yeager, putting little Tom Monforton on him in place of Cahill. Monforton against Yeager might have seemed like a mismatch, but Monforton harassed Yeager the entire way up the floor, throwing his game off. Then in the fourth quarter, Schweitzer came back in and lit up the scoreboards with three straight long set shots, the last one knotting the game at 44-44. When time-out was called, Schweitzer was late coming to the huddle. Owens instructed the other players to *not* throw the ball to Schweitzer. The coach's thinking was that sooner, rather than later, Schweitzer's hot streak would end and he would be throwing boulders. But Schweitzer had done his job; he had fired up the team, and Jerry Monforton started having a hot streak.

At the same time, Moore was running cold. Then Tilzey fouled out, followed by Yeager midway through the quarter. Moore didn't have it anymore, and Rosary squeaked a 60-58 victory.

Its next opponent would be Whitehall, which, in the second game of the afternoon, had struggled to a victory over Froid 50-46 in overtime. In this contest, Whitehall had superior height, but Froid was still leading by six points with only a few minutes to go. Whitehall was forced to foul but the Cardinals couldn't make their free throws and Whitehall caught up, putting the game into overtime. In the first night game, Boulder, which had been brilliant in the division tournament, fell apart. Dutton had no problem with the Panthers, gradually widening its lead throughout the game, winning 62-46.

The second game of the evening was Belgrade against Plevna; neither team had any way of knowing the strengths or weaknesses of its opponent. Belgrade had some reason to feel confident, since Plevna was a survivor of a challenge game. But Plevna shot with uncanny accuracy during the first period and led 23-12. Then Belgrade made ten straight points to open the second period, bringing it one point behind. Ten seconds later, Belgrade grabbed the lead when Moore netted a lay-in. From then on to the end of the half, the lead seesawed back and forth with Plevna regaining the lead 35-34 at intermission.

Belgrade, however, had begun a press in the second quarter and Plevna had trouble with that. Although the Cougars managed to stay afloat for the first half, with only three seconds into the third quarter Moore sank a tip-in putting Belgrade ahead to stay. By the end of the period Belgrade was up by 11 points and extended the lead throughout the fourth quarter winning 78-60. Larry Moore made 28 points for Belgrade; Karinen added 19. Several players from Belgrade didn't think Plevna was that good; Darrell Losing, who was student manager for Plevna, said, "They put a press on us and we couldn't handle that." He thought the higher elevation might have contributed to Belgrade's advantage, but also Belgrade was more seasoned and experienced, throwing in three subs who didn't slow the game down at all. Over the course of a running game, a tiny school like Plevna had no answer.

The losers' bracket on Friday afternoon saw two anti-climactic games: Moore over Froid 70-51, and Boulder defeating Plevna 56-47. Hopefully the two semi-final games in the evening would provide more excitement. The first game between Rosary and Whitehall did, to a point. Whitehall definitely had a height advantage with 6'4" David Payne at center and 6'2" Dwight Capp at forward. But Whitehall threw a zone at Rosary and the Bulldogs killed it with outside shooting. Both Tom Monforton and Schweitzer were hitting from out, getting 13 field goals between them. Whitehall opened up a small three-point lead at the end of the first quarter, but Rosary came back to lead by 6 points at halftime and 11 points at the end of the third period. The final score was Rosary on top 55-46. The game was uneventful enough that players on both sides remembered little about it.

In the second game, Belgrade had an advantage over Dutton before the players even walked on the floor. Coach Small had been in the same district with Dutton the year before and knew all their players, what they could do and could not. It was a scouting coup, with no one leaving the Belgrade city limits. With their knowledge, Larry Moore said, "We turned the crank on them." From beginning to end, the game was never in doubt after the first quarter. Belgrade won 75-58.

The next morning, Moore defeated Dutton again after another close game. Whitehall defeated cross-district rival Boulder. In the consolation match, Whitehall upset Moore. One Moore player, Gary Nessan, said, "Moore should have won. Because it was the last game, the coach just let us go. We did a lot of things we usually wouldn't have done. There was coaching but it wasn't concentrated." Whitehall led nearly the entire game and won 67-62.

And now, *once again,* the two teams in the championship were facing a very familiar nemesis. The Rosary and Belgrade boys could play each other in their sleep. Each team could do little more than what got them there. Belgrade had to concentrate on Tom Monforton and Ken Schweitzer. Rosary had to stop Larry Moore. This was imperative. The Bulldogs could do that: Moore had been held to 12 points in the District championship. In the division championship he scored 19, but it was still below his average, nothing like some nights, when he could ring up more than 30 points. As for Rosary, Schweitzer also only scored 12 points in the district match and 19 in the division final. Tom Monforton was the man to key on for Belgrade; if the Panthers could disrupt his play, they were off to a great night. The wild cards for Rosary were Joe Cahill and Jerry Monforton. Both were capable of putting up big numbers if necessary. For Belgrade, the person who had to raise his game was Larry Karinen. If Moore was stopped, Karinen would have to be the go-to guy. In this game, it all came down to "who was hot and who was not; who was ready and who was unsteady."

A part of the game, of course, were the fans; the gym would be jam-packed with people, standing-room only; for which team were most of them rooting? The Belgrade fans would all be there, but Karinen thought the majority of the people were rooting for Rosary. The Bulldogs got the loudest support, and why not? Helena was a Catholic town and not only was Rosary Catholic, but the Cinderella of the tournament. Belgrade had practically been an institution at state in previous years; Rosary had never won and now this parochial school had a better-than-even chance of taking the crown.

When a team walks out on the floor for the beginning of something as big as this, no one can know what the confidence level will be; a tiny turn of events can unnerve a player, unnerve a team, or perhaps not. The mental state will not be revealed until the ball is put into play, and on this night Belgrade was falling behind early. Moore said, "I was trying to do too much; they had me double-teamed and when one player tries to do too much, the other players stand around waiting to see what will happen." Belgrade got out of sync. "Owens was no dummy; he took out the guards' (Cook and Hellyer) play and took out mine, so Karinen and Otheim had to carry the load more. I couldn't blame it on them." Rosary still led only 16-13 at the end of the first period. But in the second period, the Panthers really started to break down, and Schweitzer was canning them from afar. Karinen said, "Schweitzer was shooting from way out and no one was out there really guarding him. I had to stay back for the rebound. I did charge out there a few times to get him to shoot quickly. Otheim nicknamed him 'Swisher'." At halftime, Rosary led 38-26.

Because Rosary managed to immobilize Moore, it was left to Karinen and the rest of the Belgrade gang to try to bring the team back. Karinen worked furiously to rebound and score, firing up the rest of the team. By the end of the third period, Rosary was leading by only four, 55-51. Both teams were playing well now, bringing the fans continually to their feet. Early in the fourth quarter, Rosary went up 62-56. Then Karinen made a layup and Wright capitalized on a three-point play and suddenly, with 5:03 left, it was a one-point game 62-61. The fans were going crazy. This was building to be one of the best championship games ever.

But Belgrade's rally came at a cost. Hellyer fouled out in the third quarter. He was followed by Cook early in the fourth. Then Karinen fouled out. Gallagher from Rosary fouled out not long after but it didn't matter much now. Belgrade's heart was taken out. In desperation, the Panthers started fouling Rosary and from then on to the end of the game, it was for the most part an anticlimactic free-throw parade. The final score was 75-68.

Rosary had twelve more free-throw attempts than Belgrade, but like other games between the two teams, the Bulldogs made a much higher percentage of their free throws. Cahill, who was at the line more than anyone, made 11 of 13 attempts, Schweitzer made 6 of 7. Because of his charity line success, Cahill was high scorer on both teams with 21 points with Schweitzer close behind at 20. The Panthers only made 12 for 27 of their charity tosses; if their free-throw percentage had been as high as Rosary's, the game would have gone into overtime; the Panthers had more field goals, 28 to 23. Karinen was particularly poor in his free throws; he said, "I was so tired, I couldn't hit my shots. I missed 10 or 11 shots; I just couldn't score." (He was actually 0 for 8). Still, Karinen was high-point man with 16 points. Moore and Wright each made 11. Tom Monforton had another fine night adding 15 points for Rosary. At the very end, confusion reigned on the floor when an official blew his whistle with one second remaining. Fans stormed out on the floor congratulating teams before the refs could regain order and have the last second played out.

It was the first Rosary title, according to the newspapers "in more than 40 years" (probably referring to the date when the elementary school was established). Fans, friends, and families were delirious. They were all there to accompany the team home the next day. The *Chronicle* said, "Over 100 carloads of well-wishers were on hand when the Bulldogs en-route home from the Helena meet, stopped at the Beaumont yesterday." It seemed only fitting that the Rosary club stop for their press conference at the Beaumont, which happened to be at the west edge of Belgrade. The Belgrade squad, along with Coach Chris Small, was part of the welcoming committee. It was a fine gesture. The players from both teams had gotten to know each other well. Some had played each other in junior high.

Team members and Coach Jim Owens were interviewed by radio personalities. When Belgrade closed the gap to one point mid-way through the fourth quarter, the players in effect remained confident, although that confidence was beginning to fray around the edges. Owens said, "The Bulldogs were able to play the way we had planned. We were able to play our kind of game." Owens got an especially loud ovation from all on hand. And he should have; less than a year before, he had been a college student.

At the Beaumont, the players and coach loaded onto a flatbed truck and rode the ten miles to Bozeman "and a noisy welcome from the business district." The caravan, escorted by members of the sheriff's office, had extended out to more than a mile in length along Highway 10. From downtown, the team unloaded at the high school, where another crowd had gathered. There would be more speeches followed by more ovations.

Celebrations of one sort or another followed throughout the week. Now it remained to be seen how Rosary could perform in the coming year. The team had three promising juniors returning, along with one of the best young coaches in Montana. However, like Gildford in '61, Rosary would take a swan dive in '62. In each case the coach would move on to another job. Which leads us to the fate of both schools. As we shall see, they each took a different path to a similar end.

Aftermath

I'M TRYING TO THINK OF A METAPHOR THAT REPRESENTS THE HISTORY of Holy Rosary High School beginning in the late 1950s. It could be traveling to a fancy aquatic park and climbing a tall ladder next to the pool before whizzing down a long slide into the water. Or it could be an inverted boat floating in that water, of scrambling up one side, crawling on top triumphantly for a time before falling off the other side. Either way the end result is drowning. Neither metaphor, however, is sufficient. While the fortunes of Rosary appeared to be rising, this was a mask for continued general decline; in fact, the very effort for betterment exacerbated that decline. But when the downward path fully kicked in, there were still triumphs along the way.

ALL THROUGH THE 1950S, AS BOZEMAN GREW, THE CATHOLIC POPUlation grew with it. Rosary's increase in enrollment began in the lower grades, gradually working its way to the high school. The poor old school building was bulging, ready to explode. Temporary measures were taken, dividing the auditorium with a folding door, using half of it for a classroom. But it was hardly enough.

Not only was the building too small, it had been built in 1919 with an addition in 1938; it had long needed upgrading. After much deliberation, the parishioners, led by Father Mackin, decided to build a new high school, the project to be Mackin's most ambitious undertaking. In 1958 twenty acres were purchased at the western edge of Bozeman, and in March of 1959, plans were announced to build the high school, most likely to include a new gym. The project commenced, as plans, contracts, finances, and diocesan approval were sought.

It seemed only fitting that a Butte firm, Norman Hamill and Associates, would be selected as architects for the new high school. After all, Hamill was a fine architect and had been a member of the first Rosary High School graduating class in 1924. His vision called for a two-story masonry building with a full basement, allowing for the eventual capacity of 225 students. Rosary currently had 80 students; if Hamill's forecast appeared excessive, he and others knew the school had a 30 percent growth rate over the previous two years.

The cost of the new building was expected to exceed a half-million dollars, no small amount, particularly when there would be no property tax money available, no money from the state, no federal dollars; it would all come from the pockets of the parishioners. A fundraising campaign for $200,000 was established to permit construction to begin as soon as possible. On Palm Sunday, March 22, 1959, after a 2:00 p.m. ceremony with speakers, two hundred men from the parish fanned out, each visiting three families, explaining the entire plan in detail. In less than six hours they had collected the necessary pledges for the new school, to be collected over a twenty month period. On August 26, 1961, Father Mackin led the ground-breaking ceremony to begin building the new high school. It would not be completed in time for the great basketball teams of 1960 and '61, but everyone was thrilled; their longtime dream would become a reality.

The new school was completed in 1962, fully functional, in a way ushering in the 1960s, a decade that brought joy for students at the high school. There had been sadness of course: President Kennedy, the first Catholic president, had been shot. Everyone knelt and prayed for the slim chance of his recovery. When later one of the students gave a speech remembering JFK, Sister Mary Michael, who was still the school principal, cried quietly at the back of the room. But the students rose up, engaging themselves in all manner of extracurricular activities, receiving awards in speech, band, orchestra, and choir;

under the direction of Mary Fuller, the high school vocalists received superior and excellent ratings at Montana music festivals.

The basketball team fared less well in the mid-sixties. The team should have won a state championship, but the discipline, the monitoring, the generally running a tight ship, which had been a hallmark of Rosary just a few years before, was no longer there. Players went out and partied and otherwise made themselves unready to properly play a game. Even so, the teams were good, winning more than losing; in one game, Rosary narrowly lost to eventual state champion Manhattan. The players had the potential but they weren't serious about winning.

That began to change in 1966, when Rosary once again became the strait-laced school of the 1950s. This creed-bound regimen just happened to coincide with the greatest assemblage of raw talent to grace a small school, maybe *any* school, in the history of Montana. In 1966 the freshman team went 18-0 along with a varsity that lost four games. The varsity was good enough that the brilliant freshmen coming up were still largely left off the team. The varsity advanced to the divisional where it would be eliminated.

In 1967, Rosary lost three games with a team that included Scott Koelzer and Dave Ulrich, who were both 6'8". It was unheard of that a Class C team could have not one but two players who were not only that tall but also talented. There were two other sophomores on the team, both 6'4". The team also had competent senior players who, though shorter, were exceptionally quick. Even so, Rosary did not make it to state. Koelzer came down with pneumonia and spent a week in the hospital, a blow to the team, which bogged down and lost out once again in the divisional.

In 1968, the team was unbelievably laden with skyscraper players. The papers said there was one team in the West taller than Rosary and it was UCLA. The players were 6'8", 6'8", 6'6", 6'5", 6'4", 6'4", along with two 6'0" guards and a 5'10" guard. This out of a school with a hundred students, roughly half of them boys. Rosary went undefeated that year until the semi-final at state against Seeley Swan, also undefeated, also blessed with tall players, although nothing like the Rosary lineup. With ninety seconds to go and Rosary leading by 3 points, Koelzer fouled out. Still all Rosary had to do was sit on the ball. But a teammate "who thought he was a player" cast up a 25 foot jump shot and missed. Seeley Swan fielded the rebound and scored. Of all things, there was a replay! The same Rosary player put up another missed jump shot; Seeley came down and scored, winning the ballgame 61-60. In the consolation game on Saturday night, with Rosary matched against another Catholic school, Sacred Heart from Miles City, the coach decided to play exclusively seniors for much of the game, and the Bulldogs lost that game 59-58. The team lost two games, two games by one point each, two games it should have won.

How could a team so rich with height and talent not run away with the championship? The answer was the coach. The kids loved him and his wife, played their hearts out for him, but he did not teach the kids fundamentals or much of anything. The next year, with equally good talent, with one more year of maturity, no team should have come within 20 points of Rosary; in fact no team did come close from the beginning of the season through the district tournament. But the coach made poor decisions. He ran the kids to death getting them prepared for the divisional tournament, pushed them four hours a day. When the kids arrived at the tournament, they were exhausted. They won the first game handily, but in the semi-final, with fatigue setting in, Rosary barely won on a last-second shot. In the championship, the depleted Rosary players lost to Park City 80-55. Fortunately with a two-day rest, Rosary easily won the challenge game on Monday night and advanced to state.

After the tournament, some believe the Montana State coach Roger Kraft (who heavily recruited Koelzer) had a chat with the Rosary coach, advising him to lay off the hard practices. Before state, the Bulldogs hardly practiced at all and breezed through the tournament beating (of all teams) Hingham in the championship by over 20 points. Center Scott Koelzer said that if Jim Owens had been coach, the team's success would have been much greater.

After 1969 and throughout the 1970s, until the school closed down, Rosary never again had teams that were competitive. But there were problems far more serious than basketball. The students had always been taught by the priests and nuns who, along with the students' parents, had inspired the kids to love God above all things and their neighbors as themselves. Most students were gratified to be taught by an ecclesiastical cadre, which excelled not only in spiritual matters, but intellectual as well. Now with fewer women choosing a life in the convent, with a large percentage of those who remained sensing a need to serve the inner city, the ranks of sister instructors diminished rapidly, the Order unable to provide their replacements. It became necessary to hire more lay teachers on a much higher payroll to take their place. That trend alone caused educational costs to accelerate. Also if the parishioners had raised 40 percent of the school building costs from their own bank accounts, there was still the 60 percent balance obtained in a long-term loan to pay off. It was becoming prohibitively expensive to run a school.

It was decided to close the lower grades so resources could be centered on the junior and senior-high levels. In 1966 Father Charles McCarthy, who replaced Father Mackin as Holy Rosary High School superintendent, soon announced that grades one through six of the grade school would be closed. Meetings had been held with officials of Bozeman Public Schools to make transfer of students in grades one through six as easy as possible. After the grade school closed, the seventh and eighth grades were moved to the high school, with the old school building used for educational and charitable programs. Religious training for children in grades one through six now took place after school once a week, and it became the responsibility of parents to make sure their children arrived for classes on time.

Even with the closure of the elementary school, costs continued to mount, with every penny continuing to come from of the parishioners. Numerous fundraising events took place at both the church and the school: bazaars, silent and oral auctions, dinner dances, monthly and sometimes weekly bake sales. Some of the women spent afternoons, days making items to donate to the bazaar. They would volunteer to chair the event and would spend more time making arrangements and soliciting donations from the community. One year there was an international bazaar, with each booth depicting a different country and the people working in each booth dressed in the costume of that country.

Auctions, preceded by a banquet, were held for the sale of art from the community, works purchased beforehand by parishioners or business groups. Dinner-dances were done on a volunteer basis, much of the food prepared by ladies of the parish (all which required countless additional heartfelt hours). There would be some sort of entertainment, usually performed by members of the school choir or other groups. After the dinner, the floor would be cleared, the band would arrive, and the dancing would begin.

These events sound festive, everyone having a good time, but there had to be angst before, during, and after every event, the parishioners wondering if they would ever overcome the dark financial picture. "Working, studying, playing, and praying together" was the motto of the people of Holy Rosary in an effort to keep the school open. In spite of their attempts to raise enough money, expenses continued to escalate until in 1976, the bishop of the Helena Diocese announced that the school would close. Father Mavsar, head priest at Rosary, faced one of the most difficult challenges of his life in the months prior to the decision to close Rosary High School. Bishop Elden Curtiss announced the decision to close Holy Rosary at a special parish meeting on May 22, 1976.

In his statement he said, "Although I strongly favor Catholic school education, I can see no other alternative. Costs of maintaining the school's physical plant has escalated along with salaries of teachers and the salaries of all levels of employees. The debt carried on the school drains parish resources to such an extent that other needs cannot be adequately met. To allow the school to continue under the present pressure would only prolong the agony. I know that letting go of familiar structures will be painful, but it will be necessary for the real healing, and it is by pulling together that we may move toward the kind of healing needed to achieve, unity in this parish, and become the kind of Christian community which Our Lord Himself desires."

The bishop asked the people to concentrate on a religious education program, especially good family programs. Bishop Curtiss concluded by asking everyone in the parish to make a new beginning.

The Holy Rosary High School property was sold to Gallatin County to be used as the Law and Justice Center. The money from the sale of the school and land was enough to retire the church debt and install badly needed upgrades to the remaining facilities.

In 1979 Father Samuel Beausoleil became pastor, more than a simple replacement, because now there would be only one priest to serve the parish. Along with his appointment, Father Beausoleil inherited the task of overseeing the renovation of the church and another painful decision: the demolition of the old Rosary School. This dismantlement was undertaken in July of 1980. Prohibitive operating costs, along with a shortage of religious and lay teachers, forced the parish to demolish the sixty-five year-old building.

But one symbol of the old school would remain; at least that was the intention. For more than half a century, a large granite cross had stood over the entrance to the school. As demolition began, the cross was taken down and set aside for incorporation into future parish development. The cross then disappeared. Demolition workers had set the 200-plus pound cross on the lawn of the convent and by the next morning it was gone. The cross had great historical significance for the parish; "We hope and pray for its speedy return," Reverend Beausoleil said. The general contractor for the building demolition also appealed for the cross to be returned, as it was part of the company's contract to preserve the cross.

But luck had found the church. David F. DeLap, down from

Alaska and visiting his father in Bozeman, had seen the story in the newspapers and spotted the cross along a street. It was actually lying in a gutter by the Sigma Alpha Epsilon fraternity barn on Harrison Street. DeLap called the parish and stayed with the cross until the demolition crew arrived to retrieve it.

The cornerstone of the old building had been removed and put into a secure location. Later a gathering of distinguished Holy Rosary graduates, church elders, and parishioners met to witness the final opening of the school's red granite cornerstone. This was the final chapter, the final paragraph really, in the story of the old Holy Rosary School built in 1915.

THE GILDFORD ROAD TO DEMISE WAS ENTIRELY DIFFERENT. THE bugaboo here had always been enrollment, although the numbers generally held steady during the 1960s. By 1970, however, the locals saw the future and it did not look good. Taxes continued to climb, more school requirements were in place, and with CRP contracts on the horizon, people were going to move away; how many no one knew, but the population trend would likely steepen downward. The state at this time began providing financial incentives for consolidation. If the Gildford people had struggled mightily in the 1950s to keep the school independent, now the hand writing was on the wall. After much discussion, the least painful path for Gildford would be to join up with another school.

The Gildford folks had always had a good relationship with their neighbors to the east in Kremlin. The two towns were like-minded when it came to the accreditation controversy; Kremlin had graciously lent Gildford its gym after the fire, and now Kremlin was in the same crisis as Gildford for the same reason. The two towns began talking; the principals of the two schools came to an agreement and called the townspeople together to explain the situation. On January 9, 1971, an election was held in both towns on whether the two schools should combine. The vote in Kremlin was 63 for and 5 against; in Gildford,

93 for and 4 against. It had been a tough decision but it was *their* decision. Nearly everyone felt good about it—As good as they could feel about losing identity.

The new school district would be called K-G with the new mascot a clever KouGars. The high school would remain in Gildford because that town had the newer school and gym. Kremlin would host the elementary. A few—very few—disgruntled folks in Kremlin sent their kids to school in Havre, twenty miles away. This was offset by Havre families sending their kids to K-G. Essentially the consolidation doubled the size of the new school.

It had been a good marriage. Kids from both towns became close, became used to the additional ten-mile drive when it was necessary. The parents and community members banded around their new school and its teams. When the boys' or girls' basketball teams played at home, fans from both towns filled the gym. People from Gildford and Kremlin served in equal numbers as trustees. Residents from both towns supported levies by an 80 percent majority.

This joining together in Montana had been nearly unprecedented. Other schools had closed around the state, "unwilling to put aside home town differences and sports rivalries for the common good." The move spawned other consolidations: on the Hi-Line alone, Hingham hooked up with Rudyard to form Blue Sky, and Inverness linked with Joplin to create J-I. Other schools did not formally consolidate but co-oped for classes and facilities as well as extracurricular activities. Today this is common, almost universal among very small schools, but Gildford and Kremlin were at the forefront of this transformation.

If Gildford and Kremlin had successfully joined forces to become K-G, the sports programs from this new district sputtered throughout the '70s, '80s, even into the early 1990s, never amounting to much. Then everything changed dramatically from 1994-2003. During this ten-year period, K-G won the state girls' basketball championship (1994), two boys' state basketball championships (1998, 1999), two state football championships (1998, 1999), four state cross country titles (1996, 1997, 1998, and 1999) and five state track titles (1999, 2000, 2001, 2002, and 2003). One boy, Justin Antonich, was on seven state championship teams in three different sports.

What accounted for the change? A part of it was superior talent, of course; good coaching always helped, but also a foundation had been built. In 1986, Jim Stuart started a Saturday basketball program in Gildford for elementary kids. It had begun quietly at first, mainly for his two sons, but soon 20-30 kids from both towns flocked to the activity. Stuart was a Gildford native, had been a big fan of Don Miller and the 1960 team, how they worked together all those years to become a cohesive unit and now, in the late '80s he thought he could he could duplicate these same skills and attitudes once again. He had taught school in Conrad for a time, running a little kids' program there, and when he returned to Gildford to take over the family farm, he decided he could run a similar program, only more comprehensive, for K-G.

This was not cutesy, dink-around basketball. Stuart's son Jake did not remember the program being fun at all. "It was hard-core fundamentals, learning how to play basketball—the right way. We dribbled through chairs, practiced defensive slides, rebounding drills and multiple ball-handling drills. The Saturday program achieved enough notoriety that an article was written about it in the *Great Falls Tribune*. Some of the oldest kids in the program were a group of girls, led by standout Courtney Dees. In 1994, these girls, three of whom were nieces of Don Miller, won the state Class C championship. They had been considered underdogs, but their attitude and competitiveness carried them through. Dees was tournament MVP.

These girls and the boys later had Charles (Charlie) Robinson for their coach, the perfect man for the system. Jake Stuart remembered Robinson being a "college-level" coach. He didn't have to teach fundamentals; the kids already were bed-rocked in fundamentals, so he concentrated on more advanced aspects of the game. Stuart said, "He just steered us in the right direction. He was an x&o guy, big into the mental aspect of the game. On offense he was a guru on knowing the opponents' defense. He was a counterpuncher, understood the game well enough to know what defense the other team was using and come up with an offense to counter it." Otherwise, Robinson had his kids generally running on offense, and on defense they would full-court press—always.

Still for all that, up to 1998, the boys had never yet been to the state tournament. In that year, the boys won the district championship, defeated Valier for the right to be in the championship of the divisional tourney, and when Valier won the consolation match, the K-G boys whooped it up. They would not have to play a challenge match! No matter what, they were going to the state tournament! Unfortunately they did not mentally prepare themselves for the upcoming title match with Power. At the end of the first quarter, Power led 25-5. The Pirates coasted to a 20 point victory. Lesson learned.

In the first game of the state tournament, K-G lined up against Valley Christian, a much larger school from Missoula, a school scheduled to move up to Class B the following year. The superintendent of Valley Christian, staying at the same motel as K-G, was overheard beforehand telling Robinson how unfair it was that a tiny school like K-G was forced into the pit with the much larger Valley Christian. K-G defeated Valley Christian by 20 points. In the semi-final, K-G was down by 17 against Northern Cheyenne in the third quarter, distressing papa Jim Stuart enough that he exited the gym. He was not around when the KouGars fought back to win in overtime.

In the championship, K-G faced Bridger, the undefeated, number-one-ranked team in the state, a team that had crushed second ranked Power by 10 points in the semi-final. The K-G boys had watched them and figured just relax; they had absolutely nothing to lose against this team with two players, Spencer Hay at 6'7", and Josh Henigman 6'5". (Stuart was K-G's tallest player at 6'3".) K-G played much looser than Bridger, winning the championship 60-54.

"If we had played them ten times, they would have won the other nine," Stuart said, "but every time they would try to gain momentum, we would take it away from them." A huge example was just before the first half. With five seconds to go, Hay from Bridger jammed a monster dunk. Everyone was in shock. The KouGars had never even seen a dunk. The Bridger fans went crazy. But with no time left K-G point guard Aaron Stuart lobbed one from half court and it went in, a three-point shot, completely deflating the Bridger crowd.

In 1999, Chester and K-G were ranked 1-2 in the state, Chester having a center, Casey Fitzsimmons who went on to play pro football with the Detroit Lions for eight years. During the regular season, Chester defeated the KouGars by 15 in Chester, by 10 in Gildford, but in the divisional tournament, K-G won in overtime (the two teams were not in the same district at the time), and in the state championship, K-G defeated Chester by 13. "It was a perfect example of playing against Charlie Robinson," Stuart said, "Give Charlie the credit; you don't want to play against him too many times; he will figure you out." Stuart added, "It was a weird game. I was really into a rhythm, scoring seven threes. No one on the team seemed nervous. We had been to the state tournament before, Chester had not and the Coyotes played just a little tight. You could tell they were trying just a little bit too hard."

One of the most vocal fans for K-G was Jake Stuart's grandmother, Irene (Shorty) Stuart, a character with a big laugh and an equal-sized opinion, whom I had the privilege of meeting in person. Jake Stuart said, "Every referee within a hundred-mile radius of Gildford knew my grandmother by name. She yelled loud and clear, never missed a game during my entire high school career and was my biggest fan."

Jake Stuart did not think K-G's success in football, cross county, and track stemmed directly from the Saturday basketball program, but basketball was the "beating heart of the Hi-Line; the pride factor wasn't as great with other sports." But when the kids became success-ful in one sport, they became competitive in general, "in shop class, in the classroom, in all sports." When I walked down the halls of the school, I had seen past trophies in drama and other activities.

When Stuart was a senior, K-G had 48 students, 18 from his own class. All through the grades, he had been in this abnormally large class, almost absurdly abnormal by K-G standards. Five years before when the K-G Lady KouGars won the state championship, the school had 30 students. By 2000, the school would be down to that number again.

As early as 1993, local people had dour predictions for the district and the area. Margaret Sprague, who lived in the first house built in Gildford (her father built the house in 1905, before the town was established), said that if people did not start moving in, in ten years there would no longer be a Gildford. Other predictions were not as extreme, but over the years, other developments— tighter state budgets, people starting to home school their kids—were in play, which forced people to think once again about consolidation.

In 1979 Hingham and Rudyard had combined to form a new district called Blue Sky. By 2000, it was starting to make sense for Blue Sky and K-G to combine. But if the consolidation of Gildford and Kremlin had gone smoothly, this one would not. Talks between the districts began in 2003; then K-G pulled out.

The folks in the K-G district knew Blue Sky was a larger district, would have more say in how things were run. They also saw that if the new school were in Rudyard, there would be less incentive for parents in Havre to send their children to a school twelve miles farther away. Having kids from Havre meant a larger ANB and hence more money coming in for each student; every Havre student bolstered the enrollment statistics.

But a number of people in K-G understood their district could not survive with present trends. After "two years of often heated discussion," on June 22, 2004, the citizens of Blue Sky and K-G voted to approve consolidation to form a new district called North Star. The approval had been decisive in Blue Sky, 126-10 with a 55 percent voter turnout. In K-G the approval was much lower: the vote in the high school district was 123-100, the vote in the elementary district 112-95 with a 66 percent voter turnout. K-G Superintendant John Ballard said, "I had no idea which way it was going myself. I assumed [the vote] was going to be close and it was." Some people, especially younger people, were pleased. Gildford parent Lori Federspiel said, "Everything I can see going together with them is going to be positive." Still, had there not been a compromise, it is likely the voters from K-G would have turned consolidation down. It was agreed upon that an elementary school would remain in Gildford and basketball games would be played in the Gildford gym. In actuality, games are played in both Rudyard and Gildford. Which can make it confusing for other teams in the district. For example, when Chester (now CJI) plays against North Star, the game could be in Gildford. The people in Chester wonder why they have to travel an additional twelve miles when they are going right through Rudyard. The district doesn't always try to accommodate for opponents' travel.

The financial pressure on the present district remains with trying to maintain two buildings, and this will increase with diminishing state revenues. Incentive money for consolidation will have dried up and if enrollment continues to decline, even less state money will be forthcoming. If the district is forced to close a facility, it will most likely be the building in Gildford. Formal education in that tiny town will have limped to an end.

Of course there will be high school students from Gildford, as surely there are Catholic high school students in Bozeman. But none of them will likely ever play basketball under the names Gildford and Holy Rosary. But you can never say never. There could be a wild change in the economy. And one day we will look at our smart phones or whatever the next best device we have before us, and find that one has defeated the other for the state Class C championship.

Notes

1. Tall Erector Set-like structures that house the mechanism for raising or lowering men and equipment into the mines.

2. It was called the Equalization Fund because counties rich in resources, which were able to raise money in excess of the permitted budget, turned over this revenue to the state for districts poor in revenue.

3. • The school building had been painted on the outside "a pleasing cream color".

   • The grounds had been further improved with a new playground planned.

   • A new concrete curbing for parking, the inside of the building thoroughly cleaned, the gymnasium improved with the construction of bleachers and re-surfacing of the floor.

   • The school plant converted to a cleaner and more efficient gas heating.

   • An "excellent" science laboratory equipped with many new features.

   • The library improved with two new sets of encyclopedias and 47 new volumes of books and the addition of 42 magazines in the periodical section.

   • The instructional program widened to include additional courses in journalism, drawing, and chemistry.

   • New high school texts in English I, II, and IV; civics, economics, sociology, journalism, American history, general science, chemistry, bookkeeping, typing, and drawing. Additional new work books have been purchased for many of these subjects.

   • Additional teaching aids such as the Winslow science chart in full color and art supplies.

4. Section 75-107, 'Power and Duties of the State Board of Education – under Section 4 states as follows: to prescribe standards of promotion to the high school department of all public schools of the state, and to accredit such high schools as maintain the standards of work prescribed by the board on all matters of promotion and accrediting. The board shall act upon recommendation given to it by the state superintendent of public instruction'".

5. More often than not, the opposing team would graciously pare down to four players also.

6. Bridger had a 25-0 record before being upset by Belgrade in the semi-final of the Southern Division Tournament and then was penned into 3rd place when Belgrade lost the championship and there would be no challenge game.

7. Class A teams usually didn't bring their JV teams with them; it was too costly for far away games.

8. At 5'10", Murphy was not the right person to block shots. But he still had the habit of jumping up to block a shot while the opposing player would fake a shot and then drive around him. Christensen told him to instead force the opposing player to the sideline or the baseline, but Murphy kept jumping. Finally, over the course of the season, Christensen broke him of his habit.

9. In Bozeman, Murphy also lived with a relative because it seemed more acceptable. In Billings Murphy soon lived with old friend Paul Weber because the Christensen's had scarce extra room in their tight living quarters.

10. The three players each held the ball long enough that it set in motion the eventual passing of the five second rule; a player could no longer stand holding the ball more than five seconds.

11. My sister Sheila said McCormick was very kind to her when she was in the elementary, teaching her how to play volleyball.

12. The towns, including Froid, had electricity long before that. The rural areas charged up lights and other essentials in the home by a battery system or possibly gas powered generators.

Acknowledgements

THIS BOOK WAS CONCEIVED FROM PERSONAL OBSERVATIONS. I WAS there. I witnessed it. But only a tiny sliver of it. The rest comes from everythings and everyones. These everyones, nearly all complete strangers, just jumped out and helped in so many different ways.

I deliberated on how best to sort out acknowledgments in an orderly manner. I decided to list upfront everyone and their contribution large or small and give special recognition later. These people include librarians and others whose names I do not know. Each person's piece to the puzzle was critical even if it were one piece and not 13 pieces or 25. Without that one piece there would have been another awkward hole in the story. I feel confident if the narrative had been centered in another locality or expertise; each "lesser light" for this book would have stepped up and contributed as those who were central to events. I am deeply grateful to everyone who took part.

The list includes:

- Jim Haugen – The structure and history of Montana basketball tournaments.
- Don Miller, Gene Cady, Chris Pappas, Ron Nelson, Lawrence Flatness, Ken Whitaker, Noel Preeshl, and Luella Welsh – The Gildford team.
- Hugh Neill, Don Miller, Gene Cady, Lawrence Flatness, Chris Pappas, Paul Preeshl – Coach Hugh Neill
- Betty Freih Steinwand, Dale Freih, Gene Cady, Don Miller, Lawrence Flatness, Chris Pappas, Ron Nelson – Coach Roger Freih.
- Joann McCloskey Edens, Jim McCloskey, Angelo McCloskey, Chris Pappas, Ken Whitaker, Gene Cady, Ron Nelson, Don Miller, Marilyn Miller – Coach Tom McCloskey.

- Don Miller, Lowell Miller, Chris Pappas – Farming practices in the Hi-Line area.
- Dale Kleincaster, Don Miller, Lowell Miller – Details on the newest combines.
- Mary Lois Hybner and Jerry Hybner – Early settlement along the Hi-Line.
- John Campbell, Bonnie Hanson, Shane Arlene Hanson, Lloyd Curfman, Irene (Shorty) Stuart, Esther Reece, Lynn Fried Hayden, Carla Nelson Clevenger, Jack Fried, Gene Cady, Don Miller, Chris Pappas - The town of Gildford in the 1950s up to 1960.
- Ted Hauser – The Gildford Mercantile
- Lloyd Curfman, Sharon Ous, Noel Preeshl, Don Miller, Lynn Fried Hayden, Gene Cady, Chris Pappas - The Gildford fire.
- Lloyd Curfman, Irene (Shorty) Stuart, Marilyn Wolery, Paul Preeshl, Lawrence Flatness, Don Miller, John Campbell, Bob Rathbun, Bill Rathbun, Marcella Kocar, Bob Chvilicek, Rachel Hanson, Sonja Templeton, Joyce Spicher- The accreditation problem along the Hi-Line.
- Claudette Morton, Ed Argenbright, and Dolores Colburg – Montana government and the role of the Superintendent of Public Instruction.
- Tom Monforton, Joe Cahill, Jerry Monforton, Dick Ward, Frank Seitz, Joel Dubois, Terry Corcoran, George Gallagher, Neal Christensen – The Holy Rosary team.
- Neal Christensen – his own background leading up to the Rosary coaching position, his decision to move to Billings Central.
- Neal Christensen, Shirley Nash, Bitsy Murphy DeGideo – on Mike Murphy.
- Tom Diamond and Rise Diamond– The history of Holy Rosary parish and school.
- Tom Diamond, Neal Christensen, Sister Mary Michael

Costello, Shirley Nash, Bitsy Murphy DeGideo, Joe Cahill, Tom Monforton, Dick Ward, Frank Seitz, Joel Dubois, George Gallagher, Terry Corcoran – The Holy Rosary school, Priests, Sisters, and coaches.

- Neal Christenson, Tom Diamond, Shirley Nash and others – Father Paul C. Mackin at Rosary.
- Father Joseph Harrington – Father Paul Mackin at Carroll College.
- Lois Marie Owens, Mary Jane Indreland, Wayne Marcus, Dale Fasching, Marlene Agnew, Frank Owens, - Jim Owens and the town of Wibaux.
- Gordon Haugen and Tom Sawyer – Montana State College basketball from 1959 through 1961.
- Ron Iverson, Alfred (Shorty) Wise, Shorty Cline, Arnie Wise, Jim Jenkins, Ken Jenkins - Belgrade basketball up to the early 1940s.
- Ward Leon Stiles, Norm Amundsen, and Ron Iverson – The town of Belgrade and its history.
- Casey Keltz, Lynn Durham, Leo (Bubs) Durham, Jim Jenkins - Belgrade basketball in the late 1940s and early 1950s.
- Leo (Bubs) Durham and Jim Haugen – Changes in basketball rules in the 1930s to the early 1950s.
- Ed Droge, Ken Jenkins, Joe Brookshier, Jim Jenkins, Gene Cook, Bob Rector, - Belgrade basketball under Coach Joe Lutz.
- Howard Voiles – his life before Belgrade.
- Howard Voiles, Gene Cook, Dennis Langston, Phil Langston, - Belgrade basketball under Coach Howard Voiles.
- Matt Telin – his life before Belgrade.
- Matt Telin, Ron Iverson, Robert Otheim, - The 1960 Belgrade team.
- Karen Small, Scott Small, Christie Strock, Jack Lepply, - The life of Chris Small.

- Gary Cook, Robert Otheim, Larry Karinen, Larry Moore, Charles Wright, Ron Iverson, Marvin Craver, Gary Hellyer - The 1961 Belgrade team.
- Joe McDonald – The 1959 State Industrial School team.
- Ward Fenton – The 1960 State Industrial School team.
- Charlie Matthews – The 1959 Simms team.
- Robert Nordstrom and Norman Bruce – The 1960 Chester team.
- Jack Anderson and Terry Keel – The 1959 and 1960 Power teams.
- Russ Brazill – The 1959 Superior team and town of Superior.
- Ernest Bighorn – The 1960 Brockton team and town and school of Brocton.
- Bill Engler and Tom Richards – 1960 Corvallis team and town of Corvallis.
- Gary Nessan and Ron Tilzey – The Moore teams leading up to 1961.
- Bailey Eagen – The Colstrip team and town of Colstrip.
- Dick Pollington – The Kremlin teams leading up to 1961.
- Larry Matteson – The 1960 Darby team and town of Darby.
- Darrell Losing – The 1961 Plevna team and Plevna history and area.
- Dick Kountz, Jim Bennetts and Gary Moore – The 1961 Whitehall team and town of Whitehall.
- Bill Kroll – The Bridger teams of the late 1950s.
- Dick Lohof, Tom Kress – The 1960 Joliet team.
- Virgil Bates – The 1960 Manhattan team.
- Bob Swann – the Box Elder team leading up to 1960.
- J.R. Alex – The Hingham team leading up to 1960.
- Charles Klimas – The Big Sandy teams of the late '50s and early '60s.
- Lyle Woosley – The 1960 Wilsall team and Wilsall gym.
- Roy Millegan - Whitehall history and area.

- Charles Proff – The 1961 Dutton team and Dutton town and area.
- Judy Herber – Dutton town and area.
- Floyd Johnson and Stan Sundheim – The 1961 Froid team, town and area.
- Phil Pallister – Boulder history, town and area.
- Norman Bailey, Jeff Pallister, Greg Pallister, and Don Keickbusch – The 1961 Boulder team.
- Norman Clark, Wayne Waarvik, and Carl Martin – The 1950 State Class C championship.
- Bob Hoppe – The 1959 Townsend team.
- Craig Bryant – The 1957 Bozeman JV team.
- Pat Miller, Debby Boyd, Marty Swandel- the Wilsall gym.
- Patty Hebner, Bob Moore, Wally Brownell – The Manhattan gym.
- Tom Kress – The Reed Point and Fromberg gyms.
- Leroy Miller and Norm Amundsen – The Willow Creek gym
- Roger Quaring – The Broadus gym
- Matt Telin – The Harrison gym.
- Dick Gibson – Mining headframes in Butte.
- Pat Kearney – The city of Butte
- Scott Koelzer – Holy Rosary basketball in the late 1960s.
- Jake Stuart – K-G basketball through the 1990s.
- Kathy Preeshl – The merging of K-G and Blue Sky to form the North Star district.

I am also indebted to the everythings: the newspapers, magazine articles, documents, handbooks, yearbooks, court records, even one CD and one video. The Montana Historical Society research members were so kind and patient whenever I entered the library, or when giving help online or over the phone. The same could be said for staff in the library at Montana State University. I want to thank the librarians at high schools in Belgrade and Bozeman, for giving me access to yearbooks, and to librarians in Helena who provided access to old school newspaper articles. The Montana High School Association staff, with introduction by Jim Haugen, was generous for giving me access to their archives. I give special appreciation to Emily Mayer from Havre who spent weeks providing me articles from the Havre Daily News. I was astonished when Larry Moore and Eugene "Toby" Nistler handed over all their newspaper clippings not expecting them to be returned. Don Miller mailed his tournament programs and other personal documents trusting a complete stranger. Joe Cahill, Larry Karinen and others sent information through the mail. For history on northern Montana, I give recognition to the National Geographic Magazine and Distinctly Montana Magazine, special editions from the Havre Daily News, and the book, "Grit, Guts, and Gusto." I want to thank my sister Susie for lending me the book "Helena, an Illustrated History" for background information on the city of Helena. Much would be wanting if I didn't have access to old editions of the Liberty County Times. I am appreciative of the Franciscan Sisters of the Eucharist who provided me a history of their convent/mansion in the Columbia Gorge. An invaluable history on CD of the Holy Rosary parish was sent to me by Tom Diamond, who led a team of contributors compiling a history on the parish. I appreciate a phone conversation with a staff member of the Governor's Mansion giving me the details of its inception. Bitsy Murphy DeGideo provided photos of the old Holy Rosary high school. And finally I thank Tom Monforton and Don Miller for giving me a video of the 1960 State championship game. I tried to find a similar video of the 1961 State championship game but came up empty.

If this book contains my observations from years past, I was also lucky to be given present day tours, without which this book would be sadly lacking. Don Miller gave me a tour of Gildford, the school, his farm buildings, and an amazing look at the old Rudyard gym (now used as a "commons" and place to watch theatre productions) with its pipe fence. Don showed me the huge rock in his son's front yard and tipped me off about his brother Lowell's calf stall which was the original Gildford gym. I happened to be visiting with Lowell when without warning, he invited me to see his farm implements. This tour was invaluable in introducing culture along the Hi-Line. I want to thank Mary Lois and Jerry Hybner for accepting me into their home for an interview and asking me to stay for lunch! One other tour in a completely different side of Montana was provided by Wibaux residents Bob and Marlene Blome. They took under their wing a complete stranger who had spoken with them once over the phone.

I want to thank my sister and brother-in-law, Susie and Keith Wolcott for putting me up at their home while I researched at the Montana Historical Society research wing and the archives of the Montana High School Association. I also want to thank my wife Judith, daughter Terryn Spragg, sisters Susie Wolcott and Sheila Conrads, cousin Carolyn Manley, Tom Diamond, Don Miller, Gene Cady, Chris Pappas, Joe Cahill, Tom Monforton, Neal Haugen, Neal Christensen, Ron Iverson, Frank Seitz, and Ron Nelson for reading the entire manuscript, for giving me encouragement and suggestions, and others who read part of the manuscript, all who corrected misspellings of proper nouns and misinformation. I appreciate the labor Jonathon Josten went through editing this book. He made me realize I needed to slim the manuscript down to a more manageable length. I want to thank Donald (Doc) Christensen for his expertise in changing a photograph to a very real like likeness work of art. I want to very much thank Patricia Marshall and Cecelia Hagen at Luminare Press for leading me through the maze of getting a bunch of words into a format for the public to read.

And finally I thank my wife Judith for suggesting in the beginning I become a writer and gave full love and encouragement for this book.

Made in the USA
Middletown, DE
10 May 2015